OUT OF THE SHADOW
The Story of Charles Edison

OUT OF THE SHADOW
The Story of Charles Edison

A Biography by John D. Venable

CHARLES EDISON FUND • *East Orange, New Jersey*

*If not available in your favorite bookstore, a copy of this volume may be or-
dered by sending a check or money order in the amount of $8.95 to the Charles
Edison Fund, 101 South Harrison Street, East Orange, New Jersey 07018.*

Contents

Preface

Out of the Shadow: The Story of Charles Edison is quasi-auto-biographical in that much of its material was compiled by him or under his supervision during his lifetime. Other portions are the expressions of the author, who for more than a quarter century was intimately involved with his daily activities as a public officeholder and businessman, and even in his social activities, but this latter to a lesser extent.

Shortly after the end of his three-year term as Democratic governor of New Jersey in January 1944, Edison began compiling his memoirs. He did this sporadically and in a variety of ways over the next quarter century, but they were incomplete at his passing on July 31, 1969, three days shy of his eightieth birthday.

One of the ways in which he produced this recounting was to arrange with Professor Dayton D. McKean,* then of Dartmouth College, to assist in reducing to manuscript form the story of his election and his three years as governor. They were stormy years, made so by almost incessant warfare with Frank Hague, at the time the undisputed boss of the Democratic party in New Jersey and a silent but potent power within elements of the state's Republican organization. McKean was admirably qualified for this assignment. Even prior to Edison's election in November 1940, McKean, a political scientist, was one of the strategists assisting Edison's campaign.

Formerly a member of the lower house of New Jersey's legislature, McKean possessed abundant knowledge of both practical and theoretical politics, neatly blended with idealism. At the outset of his

---

*Dr. McKean died November 5, 1977.

vii

relationship with Edison, McKean was referred to within the Edison camp merely as "Exie" or Mr. X," inasmuch as his real name was anathema to Frank Hague. Among McKean's published books at that time were *The Boss: The Hague Machine in Action* and *Pressures on the Legislature of New Jersey*.

McKean served as New Jersey's deputy finance commissioner during much of Edison's term as governor, a position that kept him in intimate touch with all facets of the governorship.

The Edison-McKean manuscript ran about 300 standard typewritten pages, triple-spaced, or approximately 50,000 words. The manuscript was reviewed and emended by Edison personally. Many of its pages bear his inserted corrections and initialed approvals.

In this book, any alterations or deletions from the Edison-McKean manuscript were made either for transitional purposes or brevity. Every effort was made to avoid distortions or out-of-context statements.

Another important segment of the book's first-person accounts was recorded on tape by Edison in cooperation with Columbia University's Oral History Project, directed by Allan Nevins, noted historian and biographer. These memoirs were taped in several segments in 1953 and ran about 50,000 words in all. The copyright to these particular tapes runs to the trustees of Columbia University in the city of New York. Those portions quoted herein are done with the consent of and with grateful appreciation to Columbia University.

Transcribed, these dictated comments were reviewed and approved personally by Edison. They have been altered for this book only for brevity, clarity (to bridge the gap between oral and written accounts) and for improved transition.

Another 100-plus typewritten pages were compiled by the author during Edison's lifetime. Edison edited and approved them as first-person accounts. This segment deals primarily with the period from 1932, with the election of Franklin D. Roosevelt as president, to Edison's election as governor in 1940. During that period, he held important posts within the National Recovery Administration, assisted in devising the Federal Housing Act, and served successively as assistant secretary, acting secretary, and secretary of the navy.

Other portions of the book were drawn from exhaustive researching of Edison's voluminous files; interviews by the author with Edison's close friends, business associates, and members of the Edison family; and from the author's day-to-day contacts with Edison over many years.

Acknowledgments

Scores of persons, many of them friends and past or present associates of mine, helped to make possible this chronicling of Charles Edison and his times. I am particularly indebted to fellow trustees of the Charles Edison Fund—President Paul J. Christiansen, Vice-president Roger M. Dolan, Mrs. Nancy Miller Arnn, James E. Howe, Edward G. Orbann, Miss Alice F. Stevenson, and Melvin J. Weig—and to the fund's staff, headed by Secretary-Treasurer David O. Schantz.

The following also gave unstintingly of their time, talents and knowledge:

Mrs. William Lloyd Bassett	Miss Mary E. Merritt
John Bebout	Stuart A. Miller
James I. Bowers	Aaron P. Mitchell
William N. Cassella, Jr.	Admiral Ben Moreell
Mr. and Mrs. John C. F. Coakley	Mrs. Margaret Miller Newman
Mr. and Mrs. Sidney R. Davis	William R. Rawson
John Deissler	Leo Rosenblum
Mr. and Mrs. Theodore M. Edison	Mrs. Paul R. Scheerer
Donald S. Elrod	Paul R. Scheerer, Jr.
Raymond H. Giesecke	C. Thomas Schettino
Sidney Goldmann	Mrs. John Eyre Sloane
Robert C. Halgrim	George E. Stringfellow
Thomas McKay, Jr.	Ms. Leah Yates

Dr. and Mrs. Clarence J. Zimmerman

Out of the Shadow

1

Birth, Boyhood and Bringing-Up

IN A LARGE BED, ornately fashioned in wood, in the second-floor master bedroom of Thomas and Mina Miller Edison's gabled mansion, Charles Edison was born on August 3, 1890. Called Glenmont, the Edison home, with its twenty-three rooms and thirteen surrounding acres, dominated a prominence within rustic Llewellyn Park, a private haven for wealthy families in West Orange, New Jersey. Also born in the same bed were sister Madeleine, two years his senior, and brother Theodore, eight years younger than Charles.

"I was born at home because at the time hospitals were not very good," Charles related years later. "The Orange Memorial Hospital then was really just a made-over house. A hospital was not considered a place to go except as a last resort when one was ready to die."*

The elegance of the Edison home was such as to cause Miss Lucy Bogue to comment that Charles was "born with a golden spoon." Boguey—as she was affectionately called by the Edison children—came to the Edisons as a music teacher when the children were young and lived at Glenmont until her death not long after the passing of Mrs. Edison in 1947 at the age of eight-two. In her later years, Boguey was the companion and confidante of Mrs. Edison and the factotum over the household. She virtually became a member of the family.

Unusual circumstances contributed to the elegance that was Glenmont's. In 1886, Thomas Edison purchased the home intact, including furnishings, from a New York City department store as a wedding present for his bride.

Charles explained these unusual circumstances in his taped memoirs:

---

*From memoirs taped in 1953 by Charles Edison in coooperation with Columbia University's Oral History Project.

1

Glenmont had come into being through a man named Henry C. Pedder, who, I think, was treasurer, but in any event associated with Arnold Constable and Company in New York. Mr. Pedder had built the house in a rather careful way. He was a man of considerable taste and refinement, and had spared no pains in getting the finest materials and having the house built as a really fine home.

Mr. Pedder had spent a lot of time and effort in bringing the planting and landscaping into a harmonious whole, but—unfortunately for him, at least—it was discovered that he had built the home with money he had filched from Arnold Constable.

The Arnold Constable firm had him put in jail.

In order to retrieve at least a portion of the stolen funds, Arnold Constable offered the entire estate, furnishings and all, for sale.

Not only was Glenmont acquired by Thomas Edison at a bargain price—much below the $200,000 that Pedder reputedly invested in the property—but the home had the additional virtue of being only about a quarter of a mile from his new research laboratory, then under construction.

The word *chutzpah* probably had not migrated from the Yiddish into the American idiom at the time, but Pedder certainly had his fair share of this dubious quality. On more than one occasion he wrote Mr. and Mrs. Edison from his prison cell to suggest ideas for further improving Glenmont.

Over the years, Glenmont became filled with treasured items of the Edison and Miller families, but even many of today's furnishings date back to Pedder's brief ownership. Glenmont stands as a monument to the memory of Thomas Edison. It is a public museum, as is his nearby laboratory. Both are owned and operated as the Edison National Historic Site by the National Park Service.

Llewellyn Park's 800 acres of hills and dales, brooks and brambles, and giant trees served as a playground for the young lads whose families lived in the park's fine homes.

Charles recalled some of his boyhood experiences in his taped memoirs in these words:

> It never seemed to me that there was anything peculiar about living in a big home. There were lots of other big houses around, and it just seemed to be the natural course. I've been asked since many times, "Didn't you feel rather royal living up there in Llewellyn Park in this glorious isolation? Didn't you feel sort of snooty?" It never occurred to me that that wasn't just a perfectly natural way to be, and it never entered my mind that there was any difference between living there and [living] any

other place—small houses, big houses, or whatnot. It just happened that you lived there, that was all.

I had numerous friends that I played around with. One of them was Henry Colgate, of the Colgate soap family. He had a playhouse on their place, which was directly opposite Glenmont. The leader of our gang was Newton Foster, who lived in another large house up the road a ways. Then there were Jerome Franks, whose father was Andrew Carnegie's confidential financial man, and Lloyd Fulton, of the family that owned the H. D. Fulton Iron Works Company, Incorporated. We used to shoot rats in his barn because Lloyd always had the latest things in firearms.

One interesting thing was that there was an old horsecar in the yard of the laboratory by the pattern shop. It had been stuck in there years before, and it was all going to pieces and didn't seem to be much good. As a little boy I used to go down to the laboratory and play around down there, and that horsecar always intrigued me.

One day I asked Father if I could have that horsecar and build a railroad up on the Glenmont grounds. We had a meadow section over by the greenhouse where I wanted to build this railway. He let me have the car. So our gang got together and we got some ties out of the laboratory. Father gave me some lengths of rail, and we started to build this railroad. Father had the old horsecar hauled up the hill into the Park and put in the meadow. We learned quite a little about railroad building such as you couldn't just nail tracks to the ties—you had to use spikes. It was really quite an educational project. We finally got this car on some rails. I guess it was, oh, about five or six hundred feet of rail. We built it so that it would go down a slight grade. In that way, we could push the car off the top and then ride it down hill.

Around the turn of the century, youngsters had their neighborhood "gangs" even if they lived in an exclusive place such as Llewellyn Park. Charles further recalled:

There was a rival gang in the Park at that time. It was headed by a fellow by the name of Park Gillespie. He would gallop around in his pony cart, usually with three or four fellows with him.

On occasions, when my friends and I had stopped work on building the railroad to go home for lunch, Park and his gang would rip up all the work we had done. A feud developed between the two gangs, resulting in a series of stone-throwing fights.

I remember one fight particularly. I don't know how old we were, but we weren't very old. Henry Colgate had a suit of armor. He had a breastplate and a backplate and a helmet and a shield, all made out of metal. It looked very imposing. The rest of us had slingshots and stones. I guess we were just like a latter-day Gashouse Gang, and so was Park Gillespie's gang. We had this knock-down fight one time. One of

Gillespie's boys got a whip out of the pony cart and challenged our leader, Newton Foster. Newton sent me to the barn to get a whip. I rushed back with a long lithe whip, because the coachman wouldn't let me have one of their good wooden whips with a long lash. Newton and this other boy started walking toward each other. There was sort of an armed truce established while these two slugged it out. This fellow caught Newton right around the face, and he carried a scar all the rest of his life. Newton hauled off and wrapped his whip around the other fellow's neck, and he also carried a scar for life.

In the meantime, I'd gotten hit in the head with a stone. Blood was running down into my eyes. We really had a fine fight.

After that we decided to declare a truce; so the two gangs were amalgamated. We couldn't lick each other, so we decided to marry each other—which is the political way of solving difficulties. We continued trying to build our railroad. Well, it was never too successful or a paying operation, although we used to charge for rides. Eventually, we turned to other things, and the car remained over in the meadow there for a long time.

Finally, Mother was at me to either get the car away or do something with it. One Fourth of July we thought it would be wonderful to burn the old car because it was a terrrible eyesore. Father didn't know we were planning to burn it. After the burning we told Father about it and he was really quite upset. He said, ''Don't you know what that car was?''

I said, ''No.'' Mother said she didn't either, adding that it was a terrible old thing, all falling apart and in bad repair.

Then Father explained why he was upset: ''That was the car I used on my railway in Menlo Park. That was the passenger car that the first electric locomotive pulled.'' I always felt very bad about it and so did Mother, but there was nothing we could do about it. The thing had been burned and was gone.

Later on in life I was down in Menlo Park when Henry Ford was moving the old laboratory and the other buildings to his Deerfield Village Museum in Michigan, and I spotted the trucks of this first locomotive—the old wheels, and so on—and I had them dug out of the ground and taken to West Orange. So I feel I repaid to the best of my ability the destruction of that first car. At least, we salvaged the trucks of the first electric locomotive.

Charles' mother, Mina Miller Edison, nineteen years his father's junior, was a middle child of the Miller family of six sons and five daughters. Several of her sisters and brothers were frequent guests at the Edison home. One sister, Mary (later to become Mrs. William Wallace Nichols), was an early adherent of the fashion named for and popularized by

Amelia Bloomer, the American feminist who died in 1894. In his recollections of the turn of the century, Charles said:

> The horrors of bloomers were widely discussed at the time. None of the ladies in our family would wear them when they rode bicycles because that was the height of impropriety. Nevertheless, one courageous aunt of mine decided she was going to wear them to ride her bicycle. That was my Aunt Mary Miller.
>
> She did, and that almost created a scandal in the family. She persisted, nevertheless.

Bicycles were the rage of the day, not just because automobiles had not become widespread, but because they had evolved into machines roughly equivalent to today's. Two-wheelers with a giant front wheel and a small rear wheel had become outmoded, Charles recalled, adding:

> There were bicycles built for two—tandems—and bicycles were the great thing in those days. Automobiles were few and far between. I had a bicycle, and I used to ride down to school when I was old enough. It was a couple of miles down from the house. It was tough pushing it back up the hills, but it didn't seem like much in those days.
>
> We played bicycle polo out on the back lawn with croquet mallets and croquet balls.
>
> I remember how Mother used to scold me because of the number of spokes we'd knock out of each other's bicycles all the time. They were always being repaired. Nevertheless, Mother was quite in sympathy with what we were doing.

Charles remembered seeing, as a very young child, men and boys riding around on bicycles with the overly large front wheel. But they soon gave way to the more traditional two-wheeler. He said:

> This much I remember about the introduction of the two-wheeled bicycle as we now know it. They were a real rage. People talked about what type and make of bicycle you would get in just the way they talked about autos in the early days. People took violent sides.
>
> The old Columbia was a very popular brand. That's what we had. There were no coaster brakes at that time; you just got on the thing and had to keep on pedaling.
>
> One of the great advances in bicycle design was the introduction of the coaster brake. It was dinner table discussion. There were tours organized. People would go on three-day camping trips on bicycles. It was a tremendous rage.

Bicycles may have been his first love, but an interest in automobiles soon took command. Into his eightieth and final year, Charles was still in love with automobiles and automobile travel. He never flew in an airplane. His aversion to flying was variously ascribed by Charles, depending upon mood and circumstances, to guarding against unexpected drops in air pressure to protect against further loss of hearing; to honor a commitment made to his wife Carolyn, also a non-flyer; and to just plain being scared. Since cowardice was foreign to his nature, the author suspects one of the other motivations.

The earliest connection Charles had with an automobile was about 1898. He recalled it in these words:

The Columbia people who had built those bicycles had created an automobile run by storage batteries. I remember it was the year my brother was born. We were down at Deal Beach, New Jersey. At that time Deal Beach only had three houses in it. We had one, and Robert Lincoln—Abraham Lincoln's son—had another. There was a third house, but I don't know who lived in it. We had this Columbia electric. I could steer this thing and was allowed to run it while I was sitting in somebody's lap. I couldn't reach any of the pedals, of course. The reason we'd gotten this was because Father had started work on developing a different kind of battery and had become impressed with the possibilities of the electric automobile as a means of transportation. There were practically no gasoline cars then. Gasoline motors were not particularly well developed or well known.

The steam car came next. The electric was the first real development in this country of any large-scale automobile building. Perhaps what they'd make in a year then would be what Detroit would make in an hour now, but nevertheless it was on a fairly large scale. They had these electric automobiles running around New York. The hansom cabs were converted to electric hansoms, and they had electric closed cabs. There were quite a lot of them then. The batteries were a problem. They were extremely heavy. They didn't last long, and they wouldn't run the car far. The utility companies were very much interested in exploiting and developing this type of transportation because recharging of batteries furnished them such a splendid off-peak load. They could charge them at night when the load was light or at any other time when the load was light, so it gave them a nice load factor. They were promoting these electric automobiles assiduously.

We started getting samples of automobiles made by this or that person so that Father could experiment with the batteries in them. The second car that we got, as I remember, after this old Mark III Columbia, was a Baker. It was a little phaeton. It was like a little box on a frame, with a

6

small electric motor and batteries in it. Then we had another one that was called a Woods electric. I liked that one better because it went at least three miles an hour faster than the Baker or the old Mark III. The Mark III was a lumbering thing. I think it would only go about ten or twelve miles an hour, which wasn't bad in those days. We finally got a Studebaker. I think it went this way—the Mark III, the Baker, the Woods, and then finally the Studebaker electric.

Coincidentally, the other day [April 1953] the president of the Studebaker company came to see me here in the Waldorf. I was photographed in what he claimed was that very same Studebaker—the one that we had had.

Much of my life in my early days revolved around that Studebaker, because I had to run it. For all practical purposes, Father never drove a car. We were in the Baker one time—I used to take him out for a ride—and the Baker had a handle with which you steered by moving it back and forth in front of you. I remember we went down to Westfield, New Jersey. I had him in the car. We were just out for a Sunday ride. We got near Westfield, and an insect—a bee, or something like it—hit me in the eye and I couldn't see. I had to stop, and I was really quite blinded. Of course, there were no windshields in those days. I said, ''Why don't you drive, Father?'' He said he'd try it. He got in and we went on a little bit. I was holding my eye. When I looked out of the other eye we were headed for the gutter. All of a sudden he yanked the thing over the other way, and we headed for the other gutter and finally climbed up the side of the embankment and got stuck. From that day on he never would touch another automobile.

The car was wrecked enough that we couldn't drive it home. The front axle was bent, and the wheels were knocked out of line.

I had to walk into Westfield and find a telephone, which was a scarce item in those days, to call home to have them hitch up the horse and carriage and drive out the several miles to Westfield. We had to wait there about three hours to be picked up in the horse and carriage. Then we had to make arrangements to get the car home. There were no garages or any place you could take an automobile. Nobody knew how to fix an automobile. Bicycle shops were the nearest thing to garages in those days. But bicycle mechanics didn't know much about automobiles.

The roads, of course, were just wide enough for two carriages to pass. New Jersey used to boast of the finest roads in the country in those days. New Jersey and Massachusetts were vying with each other as to which had the finest roads. A fine road was a macadam one as opposed to a dirt road. The great bulk of the roads were dirt roads.

I remember when scrapers were first introduced, and what a great advance that was. Up to that time the people in the county poorhouse or the convicts had to work their taxes out or work out their hard-labor

7

sentences by fixing the gutters and throwing stuff up into the center of the roads and leaving it there. It wouldn't be rolled, or anything else. They'd just depend on the horses and carriages to tamp it down. That was the average road, but New Jersey had built macadam roads, which were made with blue stone from the top of the Orange mountains or the Watchung mountains. New Jersey had quite a system of macadam roads. Despite their being macadamized, they were very dusty; so if you went more than five miles an hour you'd kick up a cloud of dust that would stay there for fifteen or twenty minutes unless the wind blew it away.

Then, gradually, there came the sprinkling of roads with an oily mixture. The cars used to be all stuck up with this stuff. You couldn't get it off. It used to drive everybody crazy. Finally, the first concrete road in the country was built on a short stretch up near our cement plant between New Village and Phillipsburg, New Jersey. The road is still there—a concrete road. It was built as a demonstration piece with Edison cement made in our plant right near there.

During the three-hour wait near Westfield for the horse and buggy to come to pick us up, Father took a nap. He just lay down alongside the road near the car and went to sleep.

We used these cars for testing batteries and for pleasure. Father enjoyed motoring probably as much as anything he ever did in the way of relaxation. He also enjoyed movies when they were silent. He was deaf and, when the talking movies came in, they ruined the movies for him because he couldn't hear them. His real relaxation was motoring.

The next car we got was a White steamer. I'd been at him for a long time to get a car other than an electric, because the White steam car was considered to be a wonderful thing for that period. You could go long distances, and you could go fast. Some of them would get up to thirty-five or forty miles an hour. I was full of the idea that we ought to have a steam car. One day he said, "Well, I'll get a steam car if you'll go down to the agency and spend three weeks there learning how to take them apart and fix them. You must take charge."

Instead of buying just one, he bought two. Motoring became his great relaxation from then on.

I spent three weeks down in this agency in East Orange, and I learned nearly everything about the cars. Everything on an old steam car was hot; so if you went to fix anything, it was always red hot. Making repairs was quite a trick. The apparatus was very complicated. Anyway, we took these short trips around.

A favorite of his in those days was to start out on a Sunday morning, we'll say. We'd leave in two cars, neither with windshields. Everybody would be in their dusters, veils, and goggles. We'd charge down through Westfield, and then get all the way down to near Somerville. By lunch time we would have reached a brook near Somerville, a branch of the

Raritan River, as I remember it, and we'd have a picnic lunch at this brook. Then it would take us the rest of the day to get back home from Somerville, through Morristown. Although we would have traveled only one hundred miles, that was a day's trip, and a really good day's trip, too.

On a day like that you'd have at least five or six punctures. I'd have to fix the tires. You'd carry anywhere up to five or six spare tubes. They were tires you had to pry off the wheels. It wasn't just taking a wheel off and putting another wheel on. They were even more difficult than clincher tires. You'd have to have tire irons. You'd stick it under the tire and pry this thing off, and then you'd have to pry it back on. Usually when you pried it back on you'd pinch the innertube, and then it would blow out again.

You had little hand pumps to pump them up. It was a backbreaking job. Remember, I was only fifteen years old when we got these White steamers, and I had full charge of both of them. We didn't have a chauffeur. I was the mechanic. I was everything, and whenever anybody wanted to go anywhere, I had to take them. Usually every part of me was burned because you had to get under these things, and everything was hot, and oil dripped all over you. My arms were all burned, but nevertheless I loved it.

Later, the White steamers caused so much trouble and broke down so frequently that they were dubbed "Discord" and "Disaster."

Automobiles held a strong fascination for young Charles. At the age of twelve he was driving the family Studebaker to and from Carteret School. Motor vehicle laws were virtually nonexistent around the turn of the century; so no one cared too much about a driver's age or other qualifications.

In addition to the several electrics the Edisons owned—after all, Thomas was creating and manufacturing batteries to make them run— the family had a succession of the new-fangled gasoline automobiles bearing now-obscure names like Grant, Simplex, and Morris.

Charles even constructed his own auto, a handmade model, using a marine engine and a belt drive.

Life at Glenmont frequently was a mixture of the wishes of Mina and those of Thomas. As one half of a world-acclaimed couple, in combination with her own background of family erudition, she enjoyed the company and charisma of prominent guests—kings and queens, scientists, philosophers, presidents, and others. If it suited Thomas' mood at the time—if he wasn't overtired from working too long and too hard on some research campaign—he might well join the group and enjoy it immensely.

9

But let us hear what could happen in the words of his daughter Madeleine:

Mother had planned a gala evening, with several important guests. They had gathered when Father returned home, somewhat tardily, from his laboratory down the hill.

He begged off from dinner, blaming a headache, and retired to his bedroom and bed, where he began to scan a number of scientific books.

I crept into his room to inquire about his health, which suddenly had improved immeasurably.

"What's the matter?" he inquired.

I replied, "I'm too young to be downstairs with the grown-ups and old enough to wish I were." I was about fourteen at the time. With me were my brother, Charles, a couple of years younger than I, and also a cousin, Margaret Miller, about a year older than I.

She was staying with us and formed part of the family circle.

The three of us—me, cousin Margaret and Charles—admitted to missing the party going on downstairs, and Father replied:

"I'll tell you what we'll do. We'll have a party of our own."

So he pulled the bell cord for the butler and ordered champagne, and each of us had a few sips as we sat there on Father's bed.

That was certainly my first drink, and I think it was the first for the others, too.

During the years of their growing up, the Fourth of July was a big family day for the Edison children and their mother and father—almost as big as Christmas. This is attested to by each of the three, who, even years later, recalled Independence Days as particularly festive ones at Glenmont. Charles recalled:

Father worked so hard and long at the laboratory that he didn't have a great deal of time for me or the other children, but in any of our ventures or adventures he would look in on us. He was always sympathetic and kept egging us on to do more.

His big day was the Fourth of July. He always insisted that we go barefoot during the summertime. I don't know just why. On the Fourth of July, he insisted we all get up early.

He did, too, and he spent the entire day with us. He enjoyed coming down, having a very early breakfast, and going out under the porte cochere, which was a rather spacious place with a gravel road going through it. The first thing we'd set off were those little torpedoes. He enjoyed tossing them at our bare feet so that they would go off near our feet, making us jump. It was just a prank. There wasn't anything sadistic about it. He got a kick out of seeing us jump around, and, of course, we did it to him. Then we had Chinese firecrackers. All morning we would

10

sit around on the porch and under the porte cochere, shooting off firecrackers, little pinwheels, and torpedoes.

Then, as the years went by, the firecrackers got bigger and bigger until they got so dangerous that they were finally taboo in most places.

I've always felt that the Fourth of July's becoming safe and sane somehow marked the beginning of the modern idea that security must come first in all things. I've always rather regretted that we have gotten so safe and sane on the Fourth that the whole idea of the thing has gone overboard and there isn't this annual general individualized celebration of our independence and what the country stands for. We now have sort of a community venture which has fireworks in an organized way, but the children aren't brought up to have any knowledge of what the whole thing's about. They don't care much except to go and see some community venture in fireworks, which is never very thrilling. But in the early days, my father certainly made it very interesting for us kids.

In the afternoon he might take a nap, but then he would come down again and start working over the fireworks and the setting up of them on the front lawn, a very large lawn. Then Mother would have some guests in for the evening fireworks. He made me take charge of the fireworks as his assistant. He taught me the dangers of them; so we never had any real accidents, although once or twice the rockets went awry and started shooting toward the house and the guests. Nothing very serious ever happened.

Afterwards, Mother would always have a lot of watermelons and ice cream for the assembled guests. It was really Father's big day with the children, not that he didn't have other days and didn't play around with us. But the Fourth was sort of dedicated to the children.

As soon as younger brother Theodore was old enough, he took charge of organizing the extensive fireworks displays. Here are some of his recollections:

I set up special displays and would see that they went off properly—that is, usually properly.

Once I almost set the house, the family, and all our guests on fire. A pinwheel flew off its axle and landed among some extra fireworks on the ground. It ignited them. Skyrockets and Roman candles and other things were shooting off in every direction, but I managed to separate them and put the fire out before any real damage was done.

Father had nicknames for all the children. Some of these names were rather interesting. For instance, he called my sister, Madeleine, "the budding Buddha." Charles was either "toughie" or "the professor." As for me, I was just plain Ted.

Father liked to go on automobile rides in the evening or on Sundays, but he wouldn't drive. Driving was left up to Charles and, a few years later, to me. On the few occasions Father attempted to drive an automobile, the results were almost disastrous. I remember one day he arrived at the laboratory scarred and shaken. His car was found overturned in a ravine in Llewellyn Park.

Thomas' penchant for exploding torpedoes near the children's feet wasn't limited to Charles and Theodore.

"Father sometimes threw them dangerously close to my feet," Madeleine recalled, "but it was all done in fun. He just liked to see us jump and hear us scream."

Madeleine, Charles, and Theodore were very close during their formative years and into early adulthood. Madeleine recalled those days in these words:

All in all, we had an awfully good time together in our middle and late teens. We would do a lot of things together like going to New York City on an outing and ending up at the Plaza for luncheon.

We'd do many silly things, such as ordering everything on the menu beginning with, shall we say, the letter C.

I also remember a story about Charles when he and another young man were taking a trip.

They went to Pennsylvania Station heavily loaded with suitcases. But before they got themselves a porter, they bought armloads of magazines. As they walked toward the train with the porter struggling behind them with the suitcases, first one and then the other would drop one of the magazines as though it were an accident. The porter would stop, put down the suitcases, pick up the magazines, pick up the suitcases, and continue. This was done until, by the time they reached the train, the porter was not only carrying the suitcases but was carrying all the magazines. They thought it was a big joke. I will say in fairness to Charles and his friend, that porter got one very, very nice tip for the trouble to which he was put.

Because of Thomas' fame—so great that it sometimes bordered on idolatry—life for the Edisons resembled living in a goldfish bowl. His every move, even his moods, were diligently, if not always accurately, reported by the press.

In his taped memoirs, Charles reconstructed the following goldfish-bowl episode:

The year 1911 was a big one for me because I became of age. That I'd been looking forward to for a long time, because I had promised not to smoke until I was twenty-one. That, to me, was the principal reason for becoming twenty-one, so that I could smoke.

There'd been a great deal of excitement in the family because for the first time in a number of years Father had agreed to go to Europe. My mother and sister and young brother went to Europe ahead of Mr. Edison and me. He didn't feel that he could be away all the time. I, of course, was tied up in college until the middle of June. So they had gone on over. He had arranged for them to have a Daimler automobile with a driver to tour England, Belgium, and Holland, then to meet us in Boulogne.

Father stipulated that we were not to go to any of the big cities because he wanted a complete rest. He was fed up. Of course, he was always attracting publicity—not because he sought it. In fact, he usually tried to avoid it. It was because the things he did just made news. I'd lived, up to that time, in an atmosphere of always having a lot of publicity, most of which was unwelcome; so I quite shared his feelings.

We went on the *Mauretania*. I remember that I was to become of age on board ship; so that fixes the date at somewhere around August 1 that we left, because my birthday's on August 3. We landed in Liverpool.

Even though on the way over the sea was rather calm, most of the passengers were seasick. It didn't seem to faze either Father or me. I remember he took a great deal of interest in inspecting the entire ship. He ate very little—he always did eat very little—which upset the steward and the captain. They would get up a lot of special things for him, and then he couldn't eat them—not because he was seasick, however, but just because they were off his diet. He just didn't care for a lot of fancy dishes and a lot of wines and things.

I remember one time I was in my steamer chair and I noticed my father and two other men folding paper into little darts. They were throwing them against the wind as the ship was sailing along. I said, "Well, that's nice to see those three men relaxing. I wonder who they are?" So I went up to them, and it appears they were talking about aerodynamics and having quite a conversation. These papers they were folding apparently were to prove something about how wings would act. One of them turned out to be Peter Cooper Hewitt, the American scientist; and the other one, of all persons, turned out to be Henry James, the British author. I stayed around and listened to them talk. It finally turned into very light banter; it wasn't anything very heavy.

They talked about another thing, which was skin friction along the side of the ship. For three or four feet alongside the ship there was this white water, and they were discussing various ways of cutting down skin friction on a ship. All in all, their talk was largely inconsequential. They were relaxing by laughing and talking together.

When we landed in Liverpool, we were met by Sir George Croydon Marks, who was a member of Parliament. We motored from Liverpool to London that day. The roads were narrow, and there were high hedges on each side of the road; so it was sort of like going through a green trough most of the way. You could see very little of the countryside. We arrived in Coventry for luncheon, and I think I had the worst meal that I've ever had in my life. We finally got to London and spent the night. I think it was the Carlton Hotel that we stopped in.

Sir Marks said there was to be a very historic event in Parliament that night and asked if we would like to go down and see the vote taken on abolishing the veto power of the House of Lords. Father thought he'd like to see it. I did, too; so we went. As we entered this wonderful stone hall, a lot of grim-faced but fine-looking men, all in silk hats and evening clothes, came out. The House of Lords had just adjourned. I got a feeling of great respect for these fine-looking gentlemen. The atmosphere of this great stone hall made a great impression on me. Then we went to the balcony of the House of Commons. There the people seemed to be of an entirely different breed. They had their feet up on the desks. Young as I was, I couldn't help making the comparison between the sort of rowdy atmosphere of the House of Commons and the very fine dignified appearance of the Lords as they filed out.

The debate was going on. David Lloyd George, I think it was, had the floor. There were one or two others that we heard. We got there shortly before the actual vote, and we saw the vote taken that abolished the veto power over the House of Commons by the House of Lords.

After that I went out and saw the town, which seemed rather quiet and dull to me. I didn't see very much of London. The next morning we left early for Folkston. We got on the channel steamer. I'd been promised that my sea legs and ability to take the ocean would be tested then, because I'd been so disappointed that it had been so calm on the ocean and I couldn't test whether I'd be seasick or not. My father had never been seasick; so he was kidding me all the time that I'd be sick. We got to Folkston and looked out over the channel; and, so help me, it was glassy smooth—not even a roll in the thing. We shot across in this rather nice little ship with hardly any vibration. I was disappointed in that. We landed in Boulogne, and there the family met us in the Daimler.

From Boulogne we went south down along the coast of Normandy, avoiding all the big cities. We went to Saint-Malo and went out to see Mont-Saint-Michel. I remember one inn, the Conqueror William Inn. That was a place Father was greatly taken with. It was right in the center of this town. It didn't look like anything; but when you went in, it opened up into a big courtyard and was very lovely.

Then we went on down through the château country and back up the valley of the Loire, staying in small towns. He was enjoying the absence of any fanfare or publicity or entertainment. He kept saying that he would not even go to Paris. Finally we did go to Paris, but he went immediately to his room because he was afraid that he'd get trapped into some kind of

14

a dinner, or something or other, which he was trying to avoid.

One day a man by the name of Valentine called me up and said he had to have an interview with my father. I said, "Well, there's no hope whatsoever." He made such a plea, however, and seemed like such a gentleman that I said I'd come down and see him. He told me that Joseph Pulitzer, of the *New York World*, had put him on this assignment personally and that he was supposed to accompany the family throughout the trip. He was to make daily reports to the *World* on Father's trip. I explained the situation to him. I said that Father did not want to see any newspapermen or have any publicity, that he was going to go to small towns to avoid it, and that there was no hope whatsoever of getting an interview. I said, "There's no use even dreaming of going on the trip with us. You can tell your paper that it's impossible." Valentine just wouldn't take no for an answer.

We headed south for Aix-les-Bains. In those days, an automobile was a novelty, and all the horses were scared and would rear up. These Frenchmen would shock us all with the way they beat those poor animals. They particularly shocked my young brother, who was around thirteen. He would turn around and watch a man beating his horse until they were lost in the dust—there was a tremendous amount of dust in those days. He was looking backward as much as he was forward, because it seemed to be a more or less universal habit that when these horses reared up or started to cut up, their drivers would beat them. It bothered Theodore a great deal.

One time Theodore said, "You know, it's a funny thing, but there's an automobile behind us, and every time we stop the two men get out and look at their car." They were always a long way behind us. We surmised that one of them must be this fellow Valentine, who was trailing us.

We kept trying to give him the slip by stopping in out-of-the-way places. We tried to lose him for about three or four days. Finally, one night I was out in the village. I was walking along, and Valentine came up to me. He said, "Can't I have an interview? Can't I? My paper is riding me, and I've got to have an interview!"

I said, "I told you that Mr. Edison wouldn't be interviewed and that he doesn't want to be followed."

Valentine said, "I know how distasteful it is to you; but, after all, Mr. Pulitzer's put me on this job, and I've got to get something off every day. I've just run dry. Nothing happens that I can write about because I'm not with the family. Furthermore, I never know when you're going to start in the morning, and I have to be up at four o'clock so you all won't leave so early that I'd lose you. Can't you tell me at least where you're going tomorrow?"

I said, "No. I'm sure Mr. Edison wouldn't want me to do that."

He said, "Well, I haven't even been able to have any laundry done. If I could only know where you're going tomorrow or where I could pick you up again, I could at least get a shirt laundered."

I felt sorry for the fellow. He seemed to me such a nice lad. He seemed to appreciate so much that we didn't want to be disturbed. I relented and said I'd try to arrange an interview. But Father was adamant, and he didn't even want me to tell Valentine where we were going. In fact, we didn't always know where we were going because sometimes Father would look at the map and change the route without warning. We'd stop wherever we felt like it; so it was impossible to tell Valentine ahead of time. Finally, Valentine asked me if I couldn't just tell him when we were going to start in the morning, and I did get Father to say we wouldn't start before eight o'clock. At least the poor man got a little sleep.

That sort of hide-and-seek game kept up for a few more days. We went into Switzerland to Geneva and Lucerne. Then we went on into the Tyrol to a place called Bolzano. In the meantime, I had gotten Father to give the man one interview. Valentine was very grateful.

During lunch at a little place way up in the Austrian Tyrol someone came to us and said that our traveling companion (Valentine) was in very bad shape, that he'd had an overdose of something or other and the doctor said he might die.

I rushed upstairs, and there was poor Valentine just about out. He never drank. He wasn't a drinking man. He told me weakly that he had been having to take strychnine to keep going. He had a heart condition, and he'd taken an overdose of strychnine. He'd forgotten he'd already taken some, and it had knocked him out. At that point, the doctor said Valentine would probably be all right and could travel in a little while. He pulled him through—but he couldn't travel right away. Poor Valentine was in tears. "I can't pull off this assignment," he lamented.

I got a very high respect for the power that a newspaper has over these independent people roaming around all over the world—how they are able to instill in them the feeling that they must produce without any supervision at all.

Valentine was a pretty cultured fellow. He'd written several books, and he was a high-grade man, one of the best that they had on the *World*. Since he was so worried about his newspaper articles and of losing us, I finally said, "The family's got to go on, but I'll stay with you until you're able to travel." I spoke to Father about it; and he said, "Well, you stay, and we'll go on to where we're going tonight. You come on as soon as he's able to travel." Father talked to Valentine. That broke the ice, and the whole family broke down and kind of adopted him from there on.

He was lying there weak. All he could think about was the daily cablegram that he had to get off. I said, "If you'll dictate it, I'll write it down and we'll get the cable off." So he started to dictate, and it was

16

pretty bad. He wasn't in any mental shape at all to do it. He said he'd lost so much sleep. He had two big bags of laundry that he hadn't had done.

He said, "I'm going to die anyway, but I do want to get this cable off."

I assured him he wasn't going to die. He gave me all the money he had. He had two pocketbooks—the *World*'s and his own money. He gave me his watch and his wallet and told me whom to notify. He really thought he was going to die. I said, "You relax, and I'll write this article for you." This was the Sunday article. It was to be an illustrated Sunday supplement article. I wrote about amoebas, or something or the other—I forget what it was—but, anyway, it all came out in the *World*. I read it to him after he woke up.

Then he wanted to go on. He said he felt so much better that he could travel.

I loaded him in the back of the car, and I sat up with the chauffeur. We went through the Austrian Tyrol. There was a beautiful big moon, and it was a wonderful experience. From then on Valentine was part of the family. He wanted me to ride in the car all the time, because then he knew he wouldn't lose the family. Later we were joined by my half sister, Marion Oser, and her husband, who was a German army officer—a Bavarian and seemingly a very nice fellow. She told us later that when World War I came along, he suddenly became a perfect boob. She escaped from him and got over into Switzerland and finally back in this country. But he was a very pleasant fellow during the time I knew him.

We got on to Klagenfurt in Austria and then up to Vienna. We finally went down into Budapest, where I had to leave the group. Of all the towns and cities that I knew and saw on that trip, Budapest was certainly by far the most outstanding. It had everything that Paris had, and more. There, Father got involved in a lot of entertaining. They gave him a big dinner. I'll never forget going into that hotel. They showed us to our rooms, and it was the whole side of the hotel—one great palatial room opening up into another palatial room. Father was a little bit leery about the expense of this royal suite. The hotel manager told him, "Oh, no. The hotel is glad to give it to you."

Francis Jehl was there. Mr. Jehl had worked for my father in the early days at Menlo Park and had been sent to Budapest to install the electric system over there in the early days of the electric light. Budapest was a very progressive city. It was one of the first places to have a central generating station. Jehl had installed this, and then he stayed on for a while. Later, Henry Ford put him in charge of the Menlo Park laboratory re-creation at Dearborn, Michigan. Jehl wrote several volumes entitled *Reminiscences of Menlo Park*.

I had to get back to college; so I left them at Budapest and went on up

17

to Berlin and Hamburg and took a ship home. I went back to college. The family motored back through Prague and finally up to Berlin. And then home. It was a very good trip for all of us.

At twenty-one, Charles was entering a new stage in his life, a stage that in no way dissipated filial ties, but one which changed them in many respects. His final year at M.I.T., followed by a year working for the electric utility in Boston and another year roving the West, kept him away from home for three years. Although he was to remain close to his father until his passing in 1931, their association took on a new dimension—Thomas became Charles' boss in Edison Industries. His deep and tender relationship with his mother, who lived until 1947, never waned. Even though Charles continued to live at Glenmont for the three to four years until his marriage in 1918, his daytime duties within the Edison Company in West Orange, combined with late nights spent in Greenwich Village, left little time for him to enjoy the restful luxury of Glenmont. The youth was becoming a man.

Charles was twenty-four in 1914 when, at about the time he was returning from his western ramblings, he penned these lines to his mother on her forty-eighth birthday:

> Back from the world's far corners,
> From mountains and prairie and shore,
> Back to her care and her shelter
> Mother has called us once more.

> Intangible, vague, but yet present,
> She labors without our ken.
> Brooding, quiet, and tender,
> She molds us and makes us men.

> She seeks for the best and she finds it;
> She sifts out the dross from the gold;
> And forges the links of devotion
> For a chain that cannot grow old.

> Here in life's happy springtime,
> Where our thoughts are but of today,
> She prepares us for winter's rude storming
> And quietly leads us the way.

> And when at last we are standing
> Perplexed at the door of the world,
> She gives us a burning emblem
> Never again to be furled.

It is character she has given,
Chiseled and carved from the past;
How little we knew she was working,
But her work will remain to the last.

For her vigilance never relaxes,
Tho' away she watches no less;
As a mother she comforts our failures,
As a mother she cheers our success.

And so, when the lengthening shadows
Steal quietly over the shore,
And from the ocean's wild buffeting
We turn toward the harbor once more.

God grant we can look back with pleasure,
With never a cause for regret,
And give to mother what's due her,
Our honor, our love, our respect.

2

Reading, Writing, and French Governesses

THE EDUCATION OF the daughter and two sons of Thomas Edison's second marriage was in sharp contrast to that of the daughter and two sons of his first marriage. Marion Estelle, the eldest of the three children by first wife Mary Stilwell (sometimes spelled Stillwell), was thirteen when her mother died in 1884, leaving Thomas a widower at age thirty-eight. Thomas, Jr., was ten; and William Leslie, eight.

Influenced, probably, by his own lack of formal academic education, the elder Thomas thought these children should rely mainly on self-learning in the manner that he had with the aid of his mother.

True, Marion attended a New York boarding school for a brief period, but she was to comment later: "My father's idea of my education was that I shouldn't have any. Or, at any rate, that I should get it by reading everything, as he did, perhaps beginning with Gibbon's *Decline and Fall of the Roman Empire* or *Watts' Encyclopedia.*"*

Mr. Edison actually withdrew Marion from the boarding school and substituted, in its place, his own assignments of reading. As for Thomas, Jr., and William Leslie, he wanted them trained in mechanical trades. They spent much of their younger days, after their mother's death, living with an aunt in Menlo Park, New Jersey.

Thomas' remarriage in 1886 to Mina Miller introduced drastically different viewpoints on education into the Edison ménage. Mina was the daughter of Lewis and Mary Valinda Alexander Miller, a well-to-do Akron, Ohio, family. Lewis, an inventor and manufacturer of farm equipment, was a nationally known Methodist layman with strong

---

*Matthew Josephson's *Edison* (New York: McGraw-Hill Co.), p. 301.

views on educational and religious matters. With Dr. John Heyl Vincent, later to become a Methodist bishop, Lewis Miller was a cofounder of the Chautauqua Institution on Chautauqua Lake in northwest New York State. Today, more than a century after its founding, the Chautauqua Institution continues as a populous and popular summer center, heavily oriented toward education and religion.

Mr. Miller's reputation in educational circles was such that in 1868 the governor of Ohio appointed him to a commission to make plans for the organization and curriculum of the Ohio State Agriculture College, now Ohio State University. He served as president of the board of trustees of Mount Union College, in Alliance, Ohio, from 1868 until his death in 1899. Moving to Akron, Mr. Miller served a number of years on the city's board of education, several terms as the board's president.

Years later, Thomas Edison had this to say about Lewis Miller:

If inventing and manufacturing were his vocation, education was his avocation, and he surely accomplished as much, if not more, in the time he spent at the latter as he did at the former.

He should have been a professional educator, for it was this that he loved best to do; and what a wonderful University President he would have made, with his great organizing and administrative ability, his originality and fearlessness of thought, and his great capacity for selecting the right men for important positions and then to keep them working together in peace and harmony.

He was one of the kindest and most lovable men I ever knew, and spent his life trying to make it possible for all mankind to reach the higher planes of living. To me, he seemed to be eternally making money in his factory in order to enable him to better carry on his schemes for education. *

High praise from a world-acclaimed genius whose formal education, delayed until age eight because of illness, lasted only six months.

Thus, Charles Edison was born into a home presided over by a father whose achievements in science and inventions were changing the world and by a mother who, by inclination and upbringing, favored more

---

*This quotation, dated May 1, 1925, was part of an introduction Thomas Edison wrote for the biography *Lewis Miller*, written by Ellwood Hendrick and published by F. P. Putnam's Sons, New York and London.

academic curricula. In the rearing of their children, Mina exercised more influence than did Thomas.

Within Glenmont, the gracious twenty-three-room Edison home in Llewellyn Park, an exclusive and rustic retreat for the wealthy in West Orange, New Jersey, educational opportunities spanned the spectrum of knowledge. At age sixty-three Charles recalled life at Glenmont in these words:

> As far as my education is concerned, we had a French governess and we used to talk French quite as fluently as English. I've completely forgotten my French.
>
> I had an older sister [Madeleine] and, of course, a younger brother [Theodore] who didn't come along until seven or eight years later.
>
> I went to kindergarten at Miss Henning's School, and later to the Dearborn Morgan School. I think most children of the early well-to-do families of the Oranges went to that school.
>
> Then the Carteret Academy was built, and the boys in Dearborn Morgan, when they reached the age of twelve, moved over to Carteret, which, at the time, was at Central and Essex avenues. It has since been moved to the top of Orange Mountain, and the old school building torn down.
>
> My sister and I used to pedal our bicycles down to Dearborn Morgan School, on Main Street, opposite the Military Common.

These schools attended by Charles were private ones, as was the Hotchkiss School, in Connecticut, which he attended for two years, being graduated in 1909, in preparation for entering the Massachusetts Institute of Technology. M.I.T. to its students of the period was generally referred to as Boston Tech. It had not yet been removed to Cambridge but occupied a number of disparate buildings in Boston proper.

These were merely the surface markings of Charles' education. Summer vacations, at least quite a few of them, were spent in Chautauqua at the Miller cottage. Chautauqua now is a National Historic Site; the Miller Cottage is a National Historic Landmark.

Widespread travel to Lake Chautauqua, to the Edison winter home and laboratory in Fort Myers, Florida, and to many other points lent educational values. And life with Father and Father's associates also fed the educational channels serving the Edison children. In his taped memoirs, Charles said:

> It must be remembered that Father worked in his West Orange Laboratory all day long. He used to come home and, perhaps after a nap of fifteen or twenty minutes, would come downstairs to dinner. Then he

would go upstairs and read or think out things. He'd make a list of things he was going to do the next day.

As ideas would occur to him, he'd jot them down. So, really, the home was his thought bench, you might say, as his laboratory was his work bench.

He was surrounded at home by a library of reference books. *Watts' Encyclopedia* was one of them I know he relied on a great deal. There were books on all sorts of subjects. Every once in a while he'd say, "I'm on a campaign, and I've got to get all the references that I can about a certain chemical or process."

Then the whole family would have to go to work, take all these books, go through them, and mark any place where there was reference to the chemical or process Father was interested in.

If there was a reference to some book he didn't have, we were to note that.

We would spend many evenings—my mother and brother and sister—going through these books and inserting slips of paper wherever references were found.

Then Father would sit there maybe until three, four, or even five o'clock in the morning reading all these things to get ready for what he was going to do later that day at the laboratory.

He wouldn't sleep late, either. He would be up at seven-thirty even after reading until five o'clock.

Neither Charles nor his younger brother, Theodore, thought much of these long sessions of looking up references. "I sort of dreaded them," Charles said, "because they were a bit dry and used up the whole evenings."

Theodore, although more of a dedicated student than Charles, shared this viewpoint. "It certainly wasn't very educational," Theodore told the author.

Madeleine, the first of Thomas Edison's children to go to college, attended Bryn Mawr College, in Pennsylvania, where she was a good student. By design, she only went for two years, but even that was quite novel for young ladies shortly after the turn of the century. Within the home, Madeleine also received extensive training in music, particularly in piano and voice. Throughout her long life, she pursued numerous cultural and civic activities with distinction.*

In a 1976 interview with the author, Madeleine (Mrs. John Eyre

---

*At the time of this writing, Madeleine Edison Sloane, still active at the age of ninety, continues to make her home in Llewellyn Park, West Orange, New Jersey.

Sloane) reminisced on the home atmosphere in which her father's second family grew up:

As children, Charles and I, and later Theodore, learned to know quite a few different homes. Naturally, Glenmont, in West Orange, was the number-one home, but starting somewhere about the time I was eleven, the family began almost annual visits to Fort Myers, in Florida, where they would generally stay from around February twenty-fourth, my parents' wedding anniversary, until mid-April. Then, whenever it was possible, we would also spend time at Lake Chautauqua, in upper New York, which had been the summer home of my mother when she was young.

Father was as attentive as his manifold interests would permit, but Mother was the real head of the house as far as the children went.

She was a reasonable disciplinarian. The French nurses and governesses were the martinets who made us young people hew the line.

As a young lady, I pretty much had to be satisfied with playing with dolls and engaging in other girlish activities because, particularly in those days, such things as going fishing, riding in the cab of a steam locomotive, or playing with chemicals were strictly for the boys.

I have always been a little sorry that one of the talents shared by brothers Charles and Theodore was not also vested in me. They both played the piano by ear, whereas what playing I achieved had to come through the dint of very long and arduous practice.

In some respects, it was an unusual family. Father would like to run little quizzes at the dining table to determine whether or not we children were keeping up with our studies in school or in the studies with the governesses. This wasn't too bad because sometimes we could avoid a lot of homework by asking him questions. He seemed to know the answers to everything.

On the other hand, Mother was very serious about education. An example I can remember is that she kept a list of words that Charles and I learned so that she could check on the progress of our expanding vocabularies.

There is little doubt that Madeleine went to college because of Mama's wishes, not because of Papa's.

Theodore, Charles' junior by eight years, graduated from the Massachusetts Institute of Technology with a degree in physics. This was followed by a year of post-graduate work at M.I.T. to study "a wide variety of subjects to give me a broader viewpoint than was possible under the regular physics curriculum."*

---

*From a 1976 interview with the author. He was seventy-eight at the time and, like his sister Madeleine, maintained a home in Llewellyn Park.

Both Charles and Theodore were mavericks in their own ways, as had been so many members of the Edison family. The earliest Edisons to reach America, circa 1730, fled Europe for religious freedom and other reasons. During the American Revolution, one branch of the family joined the rebels and another remained loyal to the Crown.

John Edison, Thomas Edison's great-grandfather, was imprisoned as a Tory and his property confiscated. After being spared execution through the intervention of Whig relatives, John and his family migrated to Nova Scotia. Years later, Thomas' father, Samuel Edison, joined the ill-fated Papineau-MacKenzie Rebellion against the Canadian government and had to flee for his life to the United States. Thus it was that Thomas Edison was born in the United States instead of in Canada.

Because of Theodore Edison's precocious interest in science and invention, father Thomas early had slated him to guide the company's future in these fields. By reverse token, Charles was earmarked by Thomas to be the executive head of Edison Industries.*

Getting back to education, Charles graduated from Hotchkiss School in June of 1909. The following September he entered M.I.T. to study general science. Despite his satisfactory but not necessarily distinguished marks, Charles' college career was to be limited to three years, one short of graduation.

"Father thought the curricula of the engineering colleges of the day were deficient in providing general knowledge to adequately train an engineering candidate to become a well-rounded administrator and executive," Charles explained. "This may still hold true at least in part, because only in fairly recent years have some educators begun to fully appreciate the advantages that insruction in economics and some of the humanities can give to engineers."

The oral history tapes review Charles' three years at M.I.T. in his own words:

At Boston Tech, I took a course called Course Nine, which was elective after the first year. You could sort of pick and choose.

I didn't want to become any specialized type of engineer. Father didn't seem to care whether I got a diploma or not. Mother sort of had her heart set on the diploma business.

---

*In 1926, at the age of thirty-six, Charles became president of Thomas A. Edison, Incorporated, and its subsidiaries, known collectively as the Edison Industries. Principal products of the Industries at the time were phonographs, office dictating equipment, several kinds of batteries, cement, and specialized instruments.

The last year in Boston Tech was a specialized year. You had to decide at that time whether to be a mechanical, civil, electrical, or some other kind of engineer, and then you concentrated on learning that.

I happened to mention my educational dilemma to a Mr. Atkins, an executive of the Boston Edison Company.

"Why waste the year?" Mr. Atkins asked. "Why don't you come down with me and we'll put you through all the departments and show you what makes a business tick."

On being told of Mr. Atkins' offer, father Thomas was delighted. "That's the thing to do," he said. But mother Mina's reaction was another matter.

After a few heartaches, she, too, thought it was all right. So I left Boston Tech and went to work for the utility company.

His year with Boston Edison did, indeed, provide a wide assortment of duties for Charles. Electric automobiles were still in vogue, and he not only had to keep track of their sales in the area to see that recharging equipment and service were provided, but occasionally he had to try his hand at repairing malfunctioning equipment.

In his taped memoirs, Charles recalled:

After going through accounting, sales, and all sorts of different assignments, including the testing of giant turbines, I finally ended up in the Special Service Department, which took care of everything that didn't fall into some particular niche.

There were all sorts of odd jobs. The main reason for the existence of the department was to provide detective service and to police the company's installations.

I had to answer every three-alarm fire any place in the five-hundred-and some square miles of territory the company serviced. The reason I had to go to the three-alarm fires was to make sure a fire was not the fault of electrical equipment but could be traced to the gas company or to some other cause.

Sometimes explosions would occur underground, tossing heavy manhole covers high in the air and occasionally injuring people.

One of my assignments was to try to determine what caused these manhole explosions, whether they stemmed from illuminating or sewer gas.

I had the task of mapping all the manholes and all the outlets in Scollay's Square in Boston. I think there were some two hundred eighty in that one little square alone.

But counting manhole covers was neither as arduous nor as exciting as one of his Special Service Department assignments in which the goal was to assist in the capture of "wire-nappers." Charles recalled that experience in these words:

One night I was handed a sealed envelope. I was told to be at the Dedham police staion, where I would be contacted. My boss—a Mr. Manchester—was a very mysterious guy. I went out to the Dedham police station, and pretty soon a man sidled up to me and secretly slipped me an envelope. I opened it. I was to go to a designated location where I would meet a man, and together we were to go to a certain spot out in the country and watch a power line—a 13,000-volt transmission line— because that night they expected wire thieves to cut pieces out of the live cable.

I thought that any persons who could cut pieces out of a live 13,000-volt line must surely know their business. There must be several of them, I thought. We had been given permits and revolvers by the municipal police to protect ourselves, but they didn't know why. We had no help. We just went out there to spot this very dangerous group of wire thieves. They'd been doing this all over the system, each time knocking out the service for a while.

The way they'd do it would be to put in a small wire that could carry the current for maybe fifteen or twenty minutes before melting.

In the meantime, they would have taken the big wire and made off with it. The splice would last just long enough for them to safely get away.

We laid out there behind a hedge watching the power line. Frankly, I was never so scared in my life. Every time a twig snapped, I jumped. It was a fairly clear moonlit night, although a little cloudy. We could see pretty well. We stayed there all night. Nobody ever showed up, for which I was very thankful.

All we were supposed to do was to watch and then try to get the license number of their car or any other clues as to who they were. We weren't supposed to attack them, but we thought they might attack us.

It was all quite exciting.

Among Charles' fond remembrances of M.I.T. were some non-curricular activities and associations.

Reminiscing on the Oral History Project tapes in 1953, Charles said:

I joined a fraternity known as Delta Psi. It was a relatively small fraternity with only a few chapters. The ones at Yale and Williams were the ones we knew best.

We lived on Boston's Louisburg Square, which was like a page out of Dickens. It was an old, old square with a little lawn in the middle of it. All around it were the old red-brick houses up on Beacon Hill.

27

Number Six Louisburg Square was where we had our fraternity house. We were the only discordant note on this otherwise peaceful square. There were only twelve of us in the group, but they were all individualists. Each was completely different from the other.

One was Luis de Florez, who later became an admiral in the navy's air arm. He was responsible for developing many gadgets now used in airplanes.

Another one of the boys who came in just about the time I was leaving was Donald Willis Douglas, who is now the president of Douglas Aircraft.

My life there was built around the Number Six Club, as we called our fraternity, rather than anything at Boston Tech, which was scattered all around Boston.

Charles also offered this commentary on M.I.T.'s faculty:

The teaching force at that time was recruited from the bright boys in every class who were asked to stay on as instructors whether they could teach or not. Usually, the bright boy is the poorest teacher because he doesn't know what's bothering the boy who isn't as smart as he is.

I remember we had one very brilliant young instructor who taught the elements of electrical engineering. Mind you, this was the elements of electrical engineering—the first freshman course in the subject.

He had a class of about sixty-five or seventy fellows. He would get up before the class and talk calculus, a subject we hadn't even taken yet.

Except for about two men out of the whole group, we didn't even know what he was talking about.

When we came to the examination at the end of the term, the average of the class was only 30 on a scale of 100, except for the two fellows. They hit about 60.

That's the danger of taking the bright boy—the brilliant man—and making him teach the other fellow.

Charles Edison maintained a basic interest in educational processes throughout his life. Both within and outside his business activities, he was an active participant in and proponent of education. With his substantial philanthropic endeavors he encouraged education, particularly among youth.

Within the Edison Industries, he established a program of seminars designed to encourage greater participation in civic affairs among employees at all levels. William F. Buckley, Jr., led the series, which featured a number of outstanding speakers.

After the merger in 1957 that created the McGraw-Edison Company, Charles, as chairman of the board of directors, initiated a special public affairs journal circulated within and without the merged companies.

Active businesswise and in historical preservation and conservation on eastern Long Island, Charles Edison established the Sag Harbor Forum at Sag Harbor, New York. Open to the public, these meetings were held within the large, beautiful 150-year-old Hannibal French House, named for an early-day whaler, which he had acquired and restored. Speakers appearing before the Sag Harbor Forum included such outstanding personalities as Admiral Richard E. Byrd, of polar exploration fame; nationally known columnist Fulton Lewis, Jr., and Dr. Norman Vincent Peale.

Peale does not know it, but he is responsible to a degree for the title of this book. The celebrated Protestant minister had finished an inspirational talk before the Sag Harbor Forum on the evening of August 2, 1948. The hour was growing late as Mr. and Mrs. Edison, Dr. and Mrs. Peale, and the author relaxed over coffee on the spacious veranda of the Hannibal French House. Peale posed a question for Charles in approximately these words: "Charles, you have all the money you'll ever need, and you are the illustrious son of an illustrious father. Why is it you keep working so hard?"

Charles replied, "My father's fame cast a giant shadow. I hope, at least in some small way, to move out from under the umbrella of his fame and cast a small shadow of my own."

Outside of business, Charles was aligned with numerous educational efforts in a variety of capacities. He was a trustee of the Stevens Institute of Technology and Hotchkiss School; vice-chairman of the American Afro-Asian Educational Exchange; chairman of Town Hall; and a leading mover in the broad educational activities of the Thomas Alva Edison Foundation.

Circumstances denied him a diploma from M.I.T., the college of his choice, but in later years he received nine honorary degrees from John Marshall College, the University of Newark, Rutgers University, Upsala College, Hobart and William Smith College, Lafayette College, Stevens Institute of Technology, New York University, and Indiana Technical College. Rutgers University subsequently became Rutgers—the State University of New Jersey, and the University of Newark was absorbed into it.

Perhaps Charles' catholic appreciation of cultural matters explains why these words by Ovid were among his favorite quotations: "Nothing is more useful to mankind than the arts, which have no utility."

29

Within this spacious home called Glenmont, Charles was born on August 3, 1890. In this 1917 photo, Thomas, then seventy, relaxes as he reads on the front lawn of the thirteen-acre tract in secluded Llewellyn Park.

Charles, sister Madeleine and brother Theodore all were born in this ornate bed in the master bedroom in Glenmont.

A chubby child was Charles at age
one.

Judged by his riding habit, Charles should have been riding side-
saddle.

Charles was four in this picture with Madeleine
and mother Mina.

At five, Charles got front-and-center billing in his Sunday school class photo.

Heap big Injun.

Madeleine, Theodore, and Charles celebrate the Fourth of July with an ecstatic father.

A hint of things to come? Perhaps this fancy sailor suit foretokened Charles' becoming secretary of the navy.

Charles was not always as angelic as he appears here.

At nineteen, Charles was an engineering student at M.I.T.

At the tiller of the actual Studebaker electric owned by his father around the turn of the century, Charles shares the two-seater with H. S. Vance, president of the Studebaker Corporation. Vance brought the historic auto into the Waldorf-Astoria as an exhibit in 1953.

3

Westward Ho

A TOUCH OF WANDERLUST, plus strong suspicions that vacations might be few and far between once he returned to West Orange to work for his father, led Charles into a year of travel and adventures in the West after his year of training with the Boston Edison Company.

"I decided to try to get a year off just to take a trip and see the world," Charles recalled in his taped memoirs. "Money in those days was worth quite a bit more than it is now. I had saved up about $400, and at the age of twenty-two I considered $400 to be a large sum, certainly enough to finance me." But his father's wishes still had to be considered. "I contacted Father," Charles said, "and he rather razzed me, saying it was all right for me to go but that I'd be writing home begging for money within a couple of weeks. I took a solemn vow right then that I wasn't going to write home for money even if I was starving. That really set the tone of the entire trip."

The first weeks of the trip were relatively unexciting, considering what was to come.

Before leaving the East, Charles contacted a former M.I.T. buddy, Robert Cox, a mining engineer then in Colorado, whose job it was to determine the economics of reopening an abandoned silver mine near Idaho Springs. Cox was all for seeing Charles and more of the West; but, unfortunately, he was broke. Not to worry, Charles assured him, confident in the purchasing power of his $400 nest egg. The two met in Denver. This probably was in the summer of 1913.

Charles, with misplaced confidence in Bob's knowledge of the Rockies, and Bob, with a misjudged estimate of Charles' resources, soon ran into troubles. They got lost in the mountains near Silver Plume, near an old mining camp called Argentine, an altitudinous 13,000 feet high over Argentine Pass. Charles reminisced in these words:

We had decided to spend the night there, but after climbing the Pass and doing a little fishing in one of the lakes, we found that Argentine was abandoned except for a combination general store and saloon. They told us there were no acommodations there at all, that we couldn't stay there, but that we could find accommodations at a place called Montezuma about five miles down the valley and another two miles up the mountain. That meant a seven-mile walk on top of the fifteen miles we already had covered. We felt we needed a little reinforcement.

After a couple of slugs of good mountain whiskey, I covered those seven miles faster than any time in my life.

Montezuma offered a night's lodging, but came the dawn and the two tenderfeet were still miles from nowhere without a compass. Blistered heels, empty stomachs, and bottoms wet from sleeping on the ground were to be experienced before the dauntless duo reached Colorado Springs, via Cheyenne, where they witnessed one of the early rodeos.

In Colorado Springs, Charles and Bob rejoined civilization by checking into the Antlers Hotel, which, some sixty years later, remains a landmark.

"There," Charles reminisced, "I ran into a friend of mine, Graham Douglas, who had a ranch near there of about 30,000 acres and 6,000 sheep. He wanted us to go out to his spread even though he had other commitments for a day or two. So he left us his Model T Ford."

Douglas' directions to his ranch were unusual, to say the least. "You go down here about two blocks, turn to the left, and turn to the right," Douglas said. Questioned about the clarity of his directions he added, "They're right. When you come to that second turn, check your odometer; and after you've gone exactly sixty miles, you turn to the right. There are some tracks across the prairie there; you'll see 'em. Go about a mile and a half and you'll get to my gate."

After they left Graham Douglas, Charles and Bob, still operating off Charles' initial grubstake of $200 (he had left the other $200 on deposit in a Boston bank) decided to shove further west.

They purchased train tickets for San Francisco by way of the Grand Canyon and Los Angeles.

"At the Canyon," Charles recalled, "we decided we had to take the trip down to its bottom. It occurred to me to ask Bob if he had any money left. He had eight dollars, and I had something like seven. We skipped the trip down into the canyon; but even so, after paying our bill at a canyon-side hotel, we only had a dollar and a half between us when we boarded the train. We couldn't even use the dollar and a half for food because I would need it to telegraph Boston for my other $200. But we really had to eat, so Bob hocked his belt, a really fine one with a silver buckle, with the Pullman porter. By such tactics we managed not to starve before reaching San Francisco.''

With only the dollar and a half left for a telegram, Charles and Bob decided to put up a bold front of prosperity.

"If we went to a cheap hotel," Charles reasoned, "we'd probably have to pay in advance. So we decided to go to the St. Francis, get a room, and wait for the $200.''

Being a son of Thomas Edison denied Charles anonymity. The pair had scarcely entered their room when the phone rang. It was a *San Francisco Examiner* reporter who had jumped to the conclusion that Charles was in town to arrange for exhibit space for the Edison Industries at the forthcoming Panama-Pacific Exposition.

"I told him that that was not the purpose of the trip," Charles said in his taped memoirs, "and that I was there strictly on a pleasure trip. Nevertheless, a little squib appeared on the front page of the *Examiner* to the effect that Thomas A. Edison, Incorporated, had sent me there to engage a lot of space for an exhibit.''

It was fortuitous for Charles and Bob that the squib reached print, because it was spotted by a good friend of Charles. The friend, Francis Upton, wasted no time in phoning Charles at the hotel.

"Remembering our financial straits," Charles said, "we invited him to the hotel and stuck him with the breakfast check.''

Francis and his brother Curtis were sons of Francis Upton, a mathematician who had worked with Thomas Edison back in the Menlo Park days. The brothers Upton, as it turned out, were practically without funds and were scratching out a living doing any jobs that turned up.

Charles recalled his adventures with the Uptons in these words:

We had a wonderful time when the $200 arrived, but it wasn't going to last long. The Uptons were living in an inexpensive apartment on Bush Street; so Bob and I moved in with them, and the four of us "bached" it.

We got to thinking about what we were going to do when the money ran out. On one or more visits to the beach, I had noticed a whole raft of automobiles out there with people sitting in them just watching the ocean. There were no boardwalks or amusements, except a place called the Cliff House, but the lower end of the Golden Gate Park still attracted hundreds of people. It occurred to me that there should be some sort of

40

development there to encourage these people to spend money. Something like Atlantic City, maybe.

The more we talked about it the better the idea seemed. Despite our approaching bankruptcy, we conceived the idea of building a pier there.

The Uptons already had a tiny office, and we located a lawyer who would work on speculation. He drew up papers of incorporation for the Ocean Pier Amusement Company.

When news of this hit the newspapers, we were played up as capitalists from the East in San Francisco to build a great pier at Golden Gate Park. It was heralded as a great thing.

The next day, a fellow named Crowley showed up. He was with the firm of Coates and Travers, architects for a number of buildings planned for the Panama-Pacific Exposition.

"Boys," Crowley told Charles and his friends, "I don't know who you are or anything about you, but you've got the greatest idea that's hit San Francisco in a long time. For years, we've talked about such a thing in our office, but we never got around to doing anything about it. We want to be your architects."

Charles' taped account continues:

They made a beautiful colored rendering for a magnificent pier, which was to cost $750,000, a lot of money in those days. It was to be an amusement center with such things as a steeplechase and other rides, roll-a-ball games and wheels of fortune, a dance hall, a swimming pool, and a large restaurant.

We had to get permission from the War Department, but that was not long in coming. Then, of course, we had to get permission from the Golden Gate Park Board. At the start, members of the board seemed quite enthusiastic.

Meanwhile, the newspapers were playing up the idea, and the amusement park became a much talked about thing. Then one day we were informed that the Park Board was not favorable, that its members were bothered by the thought that the pier, if financially unsuccessful, might become an eyesore.

We went to great lengths to get together all figures and facts. They showed such a glowing probability for success as to be almost unbelievable. We even went to the extent of finding out the estimate of increased revenue to the Gary Street municipal streetcar line to show the city's interest in the amusement pier.

There was more than met the eye behind the Park Board's reticence. Fortunately for Charles and his fellow incorporators of the Ocean Pier

41

Amusement Company, that "more" reached their ears, thanks to a friendly newspaper reporter. He had learned confidentially that the Park Board planned to turn down the project, not because of its merits but mainly because they believed its fruits should go to San Franciscans, not to "greedy carpetbaggers" from the East. These greedy carpetbaggers, so reduced in funds that each was living on fifty cents a day, immediately withdrew their petition so that the Park Board would have nothing before it to act upon.

Inasmuch as the Park Board was subsidiary in authority to a body known generally as the San Francisco Supervisors, Charles and company redirected their application to them. Meanwhile, public interest in the project continued to flare. Said Charles:

> The matter got so hot between the Supervisors, the Park Board, and the press that Mayor James Rolph, Jr., called a public meeting in his office in city hall in an attempt to reconcile differences. It was a very hot meeting. At one point, Judge Curtis H. Lindley, a Park Board member opposed to the project, and Supervisor Andrew Gallagher were on the verge of fisticuffs.
>
> Mayor Rolph had a way of smoothing things over. I guess that's why he was mayor for so long. After calming down Lindley and Gallagher, he asked the representatives of the public to speak.
>
> Sid Grauman, later to become a big figure in the west coast amusement field as operator of the famous Grauman's Chinese Theater and other enterprises, spoke as a public representative.
>
> The burden of his story was that eastern bloodsuckers were trying to sap the financial strength of San Francisco and that it was an outrage that San Franciscans would be deprived of the right to have the amusement pier for themselves. He gave a Californian's regular "native son" story.

Sensing the futility of pursuing their efforts, Charles and his cohorts reluctantly decided to abandon their efforts. Their disappointment was heightened by the fact that the public had exhibited a strong desire to invest in the enterprise.

"Here we were," Charles said, "resorting to nickel beers and free lunches to keep within our fifty-cents-a-day budgets, while people were trying to buy shares of stock in the Ocean Pier Amusement Company. We didn't dare take a cent, however. We would promise to let them buy stock when and if the project was approved. It was heartbreaking not to take some of the money. Altogether, I think we received unsolicited pledges of something like $380,000."

An ace in the hole for Charles was that he had purchased return-trip tickets to Denver for Bob Cox and himself.

"I remember one very fine dinner we all had on Bob at Tate's Restaurant," Charles said. "I didn't know where he had gotten the money to feed us until I started looking for the tickets back to Denver. They were missing, and I accused Bob of taking them. 'Yeah,' Bob admitted, 'you ate the Denver tickets at Tate's the other night.' "

That was not an isolated instance. After Bob had treated on another occasion, Charles discovered that a revolver he treasured was in hock at a pawnshop.

Things were soon to take a turn for the better for Charles. In his words, this is what happened:

We were in the St. Francis Hotel bar, sitting around with some other people. These other folks got to talking about some land they were interested in acquiring near Marysville, California. Our group had been joined by a fellow named Dudley Moulton, who was a horticultural expert employed by the government. So, we decided on the spot that we were land experts. Among us, we could count a civil engineer, a mining engineer, a horticulturist, plus a couple of others. We made a deal to examine the property and report back to the people we were by that time sitting with in the bar.

As I remember the facts, it was a tract of 1,300 acres of good land they wanted to buy, plus some additional acreage that wasn't so good. It was the price that bothered them. They couldn't understand why the tract was being offered so cheaply.

In a very informal way, without any fee being agreed upon, my group grabbed at the chance to examine the property. We scraped together enough to go by train to Sacramento, where we visited a banker named Henderson who had property for sale.

After getting facts and figures from Henderson, we proceeded to Marysville. The property was all as represented. It was fine bottomland by the Sacramento River, a lot of it fertile. And the upland was covered with oak.

After examining it for farming possibilities, for minerals and the like, we couldn't see anything wrong with the tract. Just as we were about to return to San Francisco, I happened upon two fellows with high puttees and ten-gallon hats. They turned out to be government surveyors laying out a flood-control plan for the Sacramento River.

We smelled a rat right away. Evidencing great interest in flood control, we were invited to view their plans. Sure enough, the plans for flood control would have inundated the more valuable farmland, leaving only the white oaks in the uplands. We got them to give us blueprints of the places and hurried back to San Francisco.

43

To display their "seasoned professionalism" at the expense of fully depleting their funds, Charles' group bound their findings, with the blueprints, in an impressive brown leather cover.

"We presented the report to our sponsors, and they were delighted," he said. "The facts were quite obvious when you understood what the flood-control program was. They gave us a thousand dollars for the report. I used my share for a ticket home."

Months had elapsed since Charles had left West Orange; but, true to his vow, he had not wired home for money.

4

Bohemia and the Man

THE DIVERSITY OF Charles Edison's interests—and talents—constantly amazed newcomers to his wide circle of friends, associates, and acquaintances. That a business leader, a Cabinet officer and a governor could also have been a Greenwich Villager when the Village was truly a cauldron of burgeoning genius, could pen acceptable poetry and write the words and music to publishable songs, somehow did not fit preconceptions of the man.

Charles' love affair with Greenwich Village was just one facet of his flair for the arts. It was 1914, and his engineering studies at M.I.T. were only a couple of years behind him. His first out-of-college year had been spent as jack-of-all-trades, learning the ropes as an employee of the Boston Edison Company, the Hub City's electric utility named for Thomas Edison and established years earlier under the original Edison licensing agreements. His second postcollege year was, in Charles' words, "a vacation, something I was afraid might be a long time coming once I settled down and went to work for Father in the Edison Industries." Most of the vacation year was spent traipsing the great West.

His western adventures at an end, Charles went to work in the Edison Industries in West Orange, New Jersey, on November 19, 1913. His first assignment was to develop cost figures for the new Edison disc phonograph records. Theretofore, Edison phonographs used cylinder records.

"I went on the payroll as an assistant to Father, with general duties he hadn't bothered to define too clearly," Charles recalled on tapes recorded in 1953 as part of Columbia University's Oral History Project.

Although accounting had not been among his college subjects—"I

45

couldn't even balance my own checkbook at that time"—Charles came up with quite accurate figures, thanks at least to some degree of help from the firm of Lybrand, Ross Brothers, and Montgomery, auditors for the Edison Industries.

Another of his early assignments was to ferret out activities and assets detrimental to the Edison Company's profit picture. This led Charles to New York City and to his fascination with Greenwich Village.

"My aim was to examine into certain odds and ends to see if I couldn't turn them into profitable things or cut them off entirely," Charles recalled, adding:

> Among these odds and ends was a building at 10 Fifth Avenue, in New York City, which was incurring sizable expenses. At one time it had been a private home; but when we wanted an uptown office, we bought the house. Father had put the building in Mother's name, but nevertheless he was paying the taxes on it.
>
> Even though the building was no longer used to any substantial extent, the cost of janitor service and repairs, plus the taxes, was involved.
>
> At the time it was purchased—10 Fifth Avenue was at the corner of Eighth Street and Fifth Avenue—the area was considered uptown. The building was opposite the Brevoort Hotel. Nearby Wanamaker's department store, on Eighth Street, was the center of the uptown shopping district. Union Square was about as far north as many people got.
>
> Cable cars were running and horsecars were still operating on Eighth Street when I was a boy, which was about the time we acquired the building. The only thing it was being used for by 1914 were small offices for our export business. Other than that, this old five-story building was unused.

At the time Charles was seeking ways to avoid unnecessary expenses, the Edison Company was introducing its new Diamond Disc Phonograph using virtually indestructible plastic records, approximately a quarter-inch thick, and a real diamond stylus. As part of its promotion program, the company put on a series of "tone tests" across the country to demonstrate the fidelity of the recordings.

This was in the days before electronic recording, so the diamond disc selections were acoustically recorded and mechanically reproduced. Their fidelity was remarkable. During a tone test, the actual recording artist would appear on the same stage as the phonograph and sing a duet with the recorded selection. The lights would be turned off, the music would be performed solo, and the audience would be asked to guess whether they were listening to the artist in person or the recording. Most of the replies were that it was the real artist singing "live."

46

But when the lights went back on, the phonograph would continue playing, but the artist would be gone from the stage.

"You'd hear a gasp go over the audience," Charles recalled, "so it really was high fidelity recording.

"It was my thought that we could at least put in a phonograph record shop in that location to pay the taxes and let the rest of the place go. So I started a little phonograph store there on my own."

At about the same time in 1914, Charles' sister, Madeleine, married John Eyre Sloane. At the outset, they lived in an apartment in Greenwich Village. In his reminiscences, Charles said:

I would drop in to see them, and they told me about this interesting section; so I started to look around Greenwich Village. The poet or whatever there is in me reacted favorably to that Bohemian type of atmosphere. "Here is an undiscovered section of New York which really has atmosphere," I said to myself. "Isn't there some way I can combine this commercial venture within the atmosphere of the Village and make it a kind of unusual store or operation and bring in people that way?"

I conceived the idea of having a little theater on the second floor and of giving these tone tests on a sort of talent-scout basis. The more I fooled around in Greenwich Village, the more I discovered a lot of very talented young people who could either play or compose or act or something, but who couldn't get a hearing because they didn't have the funds necessary to hire press agents. Or they had American names and not Italian or foreign names, or they couldn't hire Carnegie Hall for their initial recitals. In other words, they didn't have the money to do the required things to get the necessary press notices to have attention called to them. They had come to New York from all corners of the country expecting to make their way in whatever their chosen fields were, only to find they couldn't get started. They ended up as waitresses or just about any old thing.

Determined to pursue his ideas for a little theater, Charles looked around the Village for someone to run it, because he was working in the daytime at the West Orange plants and tending to the Village commitments at night. If candles had three ends, all three would have been burning brightly at this period in his life.

His search for an assistant in the little theater venture (which, he hoped, might even produce future artists for Edison phonograph records) led him to a whole new series of new adventures, as recounted on the oral history tapes:

In wandering around the Village, I encountered a place at the corner of Washington Square South and Thompson Street. It was an old farmhouse. I saw a lot of automobiles, some of them limousines, parked

47

nearby. I couldn't imagine what was going on, so I entered. Inside, there was a tall, swarthy fellow about six foot three. The walls were covered with manuscripts, pamphlets, and one thing or another. In a room upstairs, the big fellow would give readings of Oscar Wilde and translations from the Russian of one thing or another. It seemed to go over big with the carriage trade.

I conjectured that if he could get all these people to come down here, why wouldn't he be a pretty good man to get them to come to my proposed theater and introduce Greenwich Village atmosphere into 10 Fifth Avenue?

The tall, swarthy fellow was Guido Bruno. A Serbian, he could speak six or seven languages. He'd been with the Hearst organization and was nobody's fool. He was a good publicity man, and he'd made a hobby of collecting all sorts of manuscripts.

He had trunks full of them. He gave his readings in what he called Bruno's Garret. His readings were going over well, and, additionally, he was selling pamphlets and other things he'd write, plus books and treatises by others.

To shorten this recounting, I made a deal with him for three months to come up to 10 Fifth Avenue and put this theater over. It was so small that we called it the Thimble Theatre. We fixed it up very nicely. The walls were of blue material. We had a stage built, a very small stage. Some of the local artists helped out. Clara Tice, for instance, made a silk curtain with peacocks on it that was beautiful. Because of the help of the local boys and girls, the whole thing didn't cost much. Chairs were the most expensive thing. The theater had about a hundred seats.

Then we sent tickets to a selected list of art critics and music critics and others. Much to our delight and amazement, on opening night the place had standing room only, partly because it was free, of course.

Youngsters were asked to come in to put on their acts. First we made a little spiel. Bruno (no one ever seemed to call him Guido) would talk about Greenwich Village, what was there and how these young people needed a start in life. We didn't take any responsibility for their talent or lack thereof; it was up to the critics to evaluate their efforts. It was sort of the original talent-scout idea. We put on shows, sometimes two or three a week, somewhat hit and miss. And then, as I say, we'd bring in the phonographs.

The Thimble Theatre began to take hold. The *Morning Telegraph* made quite a stir about it. That was a little later, after it had gotten going. I was working for $35 a week at the company, which for the times wasn't too bad. Yet it was fairly expensive to do all these things. I was trying to do it on my own to persuade the big brass in our company that I had something. While I might borrow some equipment from the plant every once in a while, I never got any money from it for the Thimble Theatre. We were up against it for mailing out announcements and sending out tickets because of postage and the like. Bruno and I were talking things over downstairs in the Brevoort late one night and came up with the idea of publishing a little magazine so we could get second-class postage rates instead of having to use first-class, two-cent stamps. We decided to print a small four- or six-page Greenwich Village magazine. We never expected to have any subscriptions, but we put a dollar-a-year subscription price on it. Anyway, Bruno would write up something about Greenwich Village and maybe a little translation from some Russian work. Of course, we put in an announcement for the theater.

Much to our surprise, subscription dollars started coming in. Then we went to eight pages and later to twenty-two pages. Yearly subscriptions rose by stages to $2.50, and we put a cover on it. Finally it got to be quite a little magazine going out on a weekly schedule. By that time, the uptown critics started coming down and writing about Greenwich Village. The newspapers started exploring the Village.

In the meantime, Bruno began to think, "Here's a rich man's son, and there'll be some easy pickings." He tried playing me for an angel. He was always at me to get money for this or that, and I kept telling him I was working for $35 a week and that was all there was to it. Finally he believed me, but he kept on working with me just the same. He and I had a really good time together. I enjoyed it; and after he got through thinking I was going to be an easy mark, he enjoyed it, too.

So we built up this little magazine as a separate operation, while still using it for the theater announcements. We built it up until it had a circulation of about 4,000 a week. It was also sold on the newsstands. And it was full of very interesting things that Bruno would translate from different languages. He had trunks full of original stuff. He had original stuff, for instance, from James Whitcomb Riley. So it was quite an interesting magazine.

Charles, using the *nom de plume* of Tom Sleeper, became a fairly regular contributor to *Bruno's Weekly*.

"I don't remember why or how I got the name Tom Sleeper," Charles recalled on tape. "I think it probably had something to do with the small amount of sleep I was getting at the time, what with working all day in West Orange and spending nights into the wee small hours in the Village.

"I kept this up for about two years—1915 and 1916—but it finally got so tough that I couldn't take it any more. Not only that, I was being given more responsibilities out at the plant."

Tom Sleeper's input to *Bruno's Weekly* covered doggerel and more serious verse, plus prose. Examples:

I rarely care to eat my shoes
Or mix cornstarch or pickles with my booze;
Nor yet to munch a salad dressed with rope,
But I do confess—I do like soap.

The bloomin' buds are bustin' on all the bally trees
And the robins come a-wheezin' and a-snortin' down the breeze;
The donkeys are a-brayin' and the jays begin to sing
'Cause they know without our tellin' 'em
It's Spring—Sweet Spring.

The fishes in the ocean are a-jumpin' and a-splashin'
And the water bugs are actin' in a most peculiar fashion.
The cats are yowlin' choruses a-sittin' in a ring
'Cause they know without our tellin' 'em
It's Spring—Sweet Spring.

The mushrooms in the cellar'll be bloomin' pretty soon
And the neighbor's puppies whinin' and yappin' at the moon.
The April skies are leakin' and wettin' everything,
So come on and join the chorus—Here's to Spring—
Sweet Spring.

An example of Tom Sleeper's prose, titled "Religion," came out this way:

And it came to pass that I pondered on the reason for my being. And as time passed my spirits drooped within me—my days became sunless and my nights abysmal—for I knew not my purpose. And lo! as I sat, brooding by the margin of the pool, watching the pale white lilies nodding one unto the other, the figure of a man appeared unto me coming from out of the hemlock grove. And he came close to me and spoke words of counsel. And I thought unto myself, "I will do what this man counseleth," and arose and went straightway unto mine own house.

Then it came to pass that after three days I stood before the oracle and spoke unto him three questions: "Whence came I? By what rule must I live? Whither do I go?"

And the oracle answered unto me, saying: "These are mighty matters of which ye speak."

Then drew away the oracle unto himself. And after the moon had risen I went again to him for an answer. And he replied, saying: "O ye of little faith! Know ye not that the Kingdom of Heaven is like unto rare gems that are hidden, and that he that liveth by the spirit shall have everlasting life? Let thy faith circle thee round about like a coat of armor. Believe, because in believing lies all virtue."

And I prostrated myself before him in reverence and in worship. And after I had made offering of gold and of silver—of sandalwood and of rare spices—I returned unto my own hearth exalted.

Yet I knew not the meaning of that which was spoken to me.

Tom Sleeper's outpourings—frequently composed on makeshift stationery, such as envelopes and the backs of unpaid bills while Charles wearily rode a Delaware, Lackawanna and Western "owl train" from Hoboken to Orange at 2 or 3 a.m.—were forerunners of his lifelong interest in the written word, whether it was poetry, prose, or lyrics to a song. His contributions to *Bruno's Weekly* at least shared space with numerous famous, possibly infamous, names of the times. A review of the thirty-seven copies of *Bruno's Weekly* available to the author, each bearing 1915 or 1916 dates, frequently attributed authorships to Oscar Wilde and, of course, to Guido Bruno. Other attributions included such luminaries as Edgar Lee Masters, Stephen Crane and Violet Leigh.

As an editor, Guido Bruno appears suspect of being a copyright violator. There is no record of fee payments.

Interestingly, *Bruno's Weekly* of December 11, 1915, carried the following:

This is the famous [Woodrow] Wilson limerick which is making the rounds:

> As a beauty I am not a star,
> There are others more handsome by far;
> But my face, I don't mind it,
> For I am behind it—
> The people in front get the jar.

The Thimble Theatre and *Bruno's Weekly,* although each in its own way left its mark on the Village, were not to survive, for a number of reasons. Even though the United States was not to become officially involved in World War I until April of 1917, much earlier it was apparent that we would be. As early as 1915, Thomas Edison had to restructure operations in his laboratory and industries to compensate for shortages of materials formerly imported from Europe. The same year, in response to an urgent request of Secretary of the Navy Josephus Daniels, the great inventor became president of the newly created

Naval Consulting Board, whose membership included the nation's outstanding scientists and whose mission was to prepare the nation for possible contingencies up to and including war. These extra demands on Thomas Edison naturally threw additional burdens on Charles, already selected by the father as the son to direct the destinies of the Edison industrial empire.

One of the later issues of *Bruno's Weekly*, dated May 16, 1916, carried within a ruled box this announcement:

THE MEXICAN BORDER
A poem by Charles Edison
250 copies printed—27 cents each

This is what your twenty-seven cents bought:

She was pretty enough and I like her,
But her dad was a queer sort of ass;
Taught Greek to the kids of the ranchers
In the mountains near Donegan's Pass.

I flattered her some and I got her.
She was small—just a slip of a thing,
And her eyes had a queer fascination;
So I bought her a wedding ring.

We moved to the Mexican border.
Rough place, but we built us a shack.
She hated the plains; I the mountains,
And I swore that I'd never go back.

She bore me a poor race of pygmies,
A joke that I didn't enjoy—
Two girls and a kid with a hunchback—
My God, how I hated that boy.

The girls both went under as babies;
It broke the old woman all up,
But she still had the grinning young cripple
And would cry half the night for the pup.

She got white and pasty from crying
And lost what I liked in her eyes,
Slunk round the house like a phantom
In a way that I got to despise.

Then I took to riding to "Dobe"
To try and lose track of her face.
But its whiteness was sickly and haunting;
I'd see it all over the place.

Then one day I came back from Adobe.
She met me with eyes blazing red.
"John," she says, sort of husky,
And motioned her hand towards the bed.

There was the crippled kid, lying
With his face turned away from the light.
I knew he was dead—she showed it.
Maybe she wasn't a sight!

Well, I rode for more hock to Adobe
(Lord, I was glad he was gone)
Then back to the shack the next evening,
With all but my pony in pawn.

I found her rocking and crying
With the kid in her arms by the door.
I was drunk and I grabbed for the carcass
And chucked it away on the floor.

God, what a look she gave me;
It'll follow me down to the last.
But I laughed at her then, I remember;
What a brute I was. But that's past.

That night when the liquor had dropped me
As dead to the world as a stone,
She tied me in bed with a lasso
And struck out in the night all alone.

Next morning I woke up and called her;
Then I tumbled to what she had done.
Mad? I could almost have killed her
As I picked up my saddle and gun.

I knew she would head toward Fort Donner,
And at noon I fell in with her track.
Straight trail she was making and lively,
But I swore that I'd fetch her on back.

By five the footprints were staggers;
There were spots where she'd dropped to the ground.
And I'd smile, tho' the heat scorched my eyeballs,
As I tracked her down like a hound.

At last, along about sundown,
I found her, half-dead, and half-wild.
When she saw me she clutched after something;
I'm damned if it wasn't that child.

But she didn't have strength left to hold it,
And her courage was leaving her fast.
She dropped on her face in the sagebrush.
The desert had got her at last.

I buried them there in the sand hills
With a cactus set up for a mark.
Then I plodded along after moonup
With a queer feeling lump in my heart.

From Cape Nome to the Mexican border
I have sweated and stolen my way,
But that face that I left in the desert
Has never left me for a day.

I've learned what a woman's love means.
She loved me, but God knows why;
And I'd give you my life this minute
Just to hear her tell me good-bye.

In this poem, Charles was attempting to emulate Canadian Robert
W. Service in his "Face on the Barroom Floor."

Of his many experiences during his Greenwich Village days, two
stood out more vividly than all others. Both involved women, including
his mother, his wife-to-be, Carolyn Hawkins, and poetess Edna St.
Vincent Millay.

Charles' mother, the patrician Mina Miller Edison, whose family were
pillars of Methodism, quite naturally was interested in her son's activities. She spoke frequently of wanting to visit 10 Fifth Avenue to
learn more about the Thimble Theatre, but months went by without
her plans materializing.

The date she finally chose to visit the Village was far from a
propitious one from Charles' viewpoint. The two-act play being per-

formed was "The State Forbids," an avant-garde production by Sada Cowan, the theme of which daringly (for the period) espoused birth control. "So mother, much to my horror, happened to pick that one out," Charles commented in his taped oral history reminiscences. "I thought she was going to be very much shocked by it all. But she told me afterward, 'I think this is one of the finest and strongest little plays I've ever seen.' " Mother's ideas were not quite as Victorian as Charles had thought them to be.

The young lady destined to become Mrs. Charles Edison in 1918 occasionally was part of the Village scene.

"It was 1916, I think," Charles recalled, adding:

I wasn't married to Carolyn then. We were courting. She had come down from Boston, and I was showing her the Village.

We went over to Sheridan Square to a fourth-floor "joint" called Romany Marie's. There we met up with Edna St. Vincent Millay, her sister, and another woman named Peggy St. John. We all sat together in a booth, sipping mocha coffee. The room was lighted only by candles, one of which was on our table.

Suddenly Edna exclaimed, "Oh, have you got a piece of paper? I just thought of something."

I gave her the envelope that I had, and she wrote on the back of it:

My candle burns at both ends;
It will not last the night
But, ah, my foes, and, oh, my friends—
It gives a lovely light!

We thought it was wonderful. So I put the envelope in my pocket, and I still have it somewhere.

His Greenwich Village days as a steady diet drew to a close for Charles, but he never fully recovered from his love affair with the area. For vitually the rest of his life, he made periodic visits to such Village bistros as Jimmy Kelly's, there to relive old memories and lament the passing of many landmarks and individuals who, because they were characters, had lent character to the Village scene.

As a child, Charles' exposure to a musical education was limited to a series of private piano lessons given by a teacher whose tenacity was less than a match for the resistance she encountered in her young charge. A student of the piano Charles was not, but as a performer thereon, he was almost unique, provided the word *unique* will submit to a modification such as *almost*.

Charles learned to perform by ear on the piano. He also had an ear—

despite the intensifying deafness that plagued him from his youth—and a knack for composing music and supplying the words thereto.

Charles not only learned to perform on the piano by ear; he learned to perform on it by orange. An explanation is due.

As previously indicated, Charles certainly was no José Iturbi, but then it is highly doubtful that even Iturbi could have performed Edison's "Orange Symphony" with equal gusto and éclat. His performances of this "classic" were infrequent but overwhelmingly acclaimed. Since his living room always featured a grand piano, guests uninitiated in the mystery of his artistry would occasionally ask him to play. After a show of reticence, he would seat himself and slowly, softly launch into an unfamiliar melody. The tempo and volume would quickly rise to a frenetic crescendo. The bass notes of his left hand left something to be desired, but, ah, those treble notes. They poured forth in such profusion and exuberance that had his audience worn hearing aids, as Edison did, theirs, too, would have been turned off. All the while his remarkable "finger" work would be concealed by the piano's tilted top. Upon conclusion of his performance, the guests would be invited to assemble around the instrument. Only then would they learn that his unique right-hand expertise consisted of rolling an orange back and forth over the keys.

In a letter dated March 25, 1940, to his close friend and counsel, Albert R. Jube, a distinguished New York lawyer, Edison wrote from Washington, when he was secretary of the navy:

Dear Al:
Enclosed is a contract for a little song (Don't Ask Nothin' of Me) I put together. A man heard the organist at the Hay-Adams playing it and sent it to his publisher.

The contract looks pretty standard in form and I suppose the amounts mentioned are fair enough for a "rookie" in his first attempt. Please look it over.

I have another song that I am sending the publisher to listen to which seems to be more on the commercial order. No contract involved yet— merely a submission of the piece to see what he thinks of it.

Between running for Governor, writing songs, being president of a business and running a navy—it's a busy world for me but a grand one!

"Don't Ask Nothin' of Me," a slow foxtrot, was published by the Braun Music Company, of New York and Chicago, as was Edison's "Wicky Wacky Woo."

The words to "Don't Ask Nothin' of Me" follow:

Grass is green,
Sky is blue,
Sunshine shining on the dew;
Sittin' quiet
All the day;
Trouble, don't you come my way.

Chorus

I'm in my cabin,
God's in his Heaven,
Just watchin' the river roll by,
I ain't doin' nothin',
Just sittin' way up in His sky.
We're just as happy
As happiness can be
Tho' we ain't got nothin'
But a river and a tree;
And I don't ask nothin',
God don't ask nothin'
So don't ask nothin' of me.

Composing poetry and prose, whether frothy or serious, was a hobby that Charles pursued throughout his life. In 1967, just two years before his passing, he bowed to the urgings of friends and arranged for the publication of numerous of his manuscripts in a handsomely turned out sixty-page hardcover booklet titled *Flotsam and Jetsam*. Much of its content was made up of items which had appeared in *Bruno's Weekly* during his Greenwich Village days.

A couple of selection from *Flotsam and Jetsam* are as follows:

AD INFINITUM

Worry, worry, fret and trouble,
Nothing's right and all is Change.
Facts are but a phantom bubble;
Truths today—tomorrow strange.

Changes bring but other changes;
Progress runs in Error's ring;
Plans are made but Change deranges;
Hail the master; Change is king.

O QUAE MUTATIO RERUM
(O! What Changing Times)

"Of course you can go"—and I had told her so on many occasions. She always kissed me and went, leaving me to my books and researches. It was pleasant to feel that her youth was enjoying the things she craved—and Sam was really quite a delightful fellow—

Ah, yes, books and researches. My mail reaches me now at the University Club.

Being a rhymester seemingly served as therapy for Charles when not feeling up to par. In March of 1938, for example, when he was assistant secretary of the navy, he dashed off a bit of verse to Louis Johnson, his army counterpart as assistant secretary of war. He composed the following while recuperating from fatigue at the Bethesda Naval Hospital:

> Dear Mr. Secretary:
> I thank you for you letter;
> It did me lots of good;
> I may be down but I'm not out—
> I want that understood.
>
> Just "check-ups," "tests," and thumpings round,
> And gargles and X-rays,
> Examinations, tonics, drugs,
> And fluoroscopes and sprays.
>
> "How old are you?"—"Where were you born?"
> "What is your mother's name?"
> "When did that happen? How and why?"
> "Today? You feel the same?"
>
> From early morn 'till late at night
> The medicos troop by:
> "I'll order this for you tonight;
> Today give this a try."
>
> They poke a hole in your left arm,
> Draw so much blood away
> You wonder if anemia
> Will set right in today.
>
> They hitch up wires to your leg
> And arm and back and chest

58

To see how goes the pump today,
And if you need a rest.

They do a lot of other things
Indelicate to tell
'Till you begin to speculate
"God! Was I ever well?"

But after all is said and done,
And though you fuss and spout
This place is "tops," but better yet,
They know what they're about.

So trust not in your ARMY "Meds,"
And when you get the urge
To have some overhauling done
Let NAVY give the "purge."

The Bohemian part of Charles Edison's makeup camouflaged, to some degree, the underlying intensity with which he attacked the more serious aspects of his careers in public life and business. Perhaps it was this lighter side that fed and nourished his other abilities.

5

Enter Carolyn

THE LOVE AFFAIR between Charles Edison and Carolyn Hawkins spanned the half century from 1912 when they met in Cambridge, Massachusetts, through their marriage six years later, until her death in 1963. It was a love affair fraught with parental problems, beset by individual doubts, unblessed by progeny, but blessed by a tender and abiding spirit of mutuality that deepened with the years.

Carolyn was the youngest of three daughters of Dr. Horatio Gates Hawkins and Ada Jane Woodruff, both of early Vermont stock. Pretty, petite, and personable, Carolyn was a popular member of the younger set in Cambridge when she met Charles. She was working as a secretarial assistant to Dr. Hugh Cabot, a prominent medical doctor, and was neither "society" nor wealthy in the sense that Charles was.

Charles was introduced to Carolyn when he visited the doctor's office. The following day, he was riding on a streetcar in the vicinity when he spied her waiting on a corner for a trolley going in the opposite direction. He jumped off, reintroduced himself, and then accompanied her home, where he met her mother.

Charles was a relentless suitor. He and Carolyn dated nightly for three weeks. The string was broken only because he had to return temporarily to West Orange.

While her own father also was a medical doctor, his practice dwindled as his affection for morphine and liquor expanded. The Hawkins family was living in Springfield, Massachusetts, in 1906 when Dr. Hawkins, overwhelmed by problems, drowned himself in the Connecticut River. Mrs. Hawkins, who died in 1943 at the age of ninety, was a close companion to her daughter over the years.

This family background played a part in the resistance that Charles' mother, the patrician Mina Miller Edison, and his father displayed toward their romance. Father's resistance was not as deepseated as mother's, however.

There is little doubt that if Mina Edison had had her way, Charles would not have married Carolyn. This letter to her, written by Charles less than four months before the date of his marriage, demonstrates his determination to wed Pony, one of the pet names he reserved for Carolyn throughout their lives. Others included Dilly, Dearie, Bunch, short for Honeybunch, Sweetza Rose, Bunt, and Chebunt. On December 6, 1917, he wrote:

Darling Mother:

Your sweet letter touched something in me very deeply. I shall always keep it.

You say "be sure there is only one person for you." How can I be sure, by what must I judge? If it were not for the fact that I wanted to be sure, I probably would have married Pony three years ago at least. But I have tried to be sure. I have met others and lots of them. There are two or three I have had so-called "cases" on and am still very fond of. But these seem always temporary and in the long run Pony seems to be the one I always come back to. I have purposely put her out of my mind and stopped writing or seeing her, but someway I always get back on the old trail sooner or later. I have purposely treated her miserably at times just to see how she would act. In fact, I've never treated her as most men would if they were courting a girl. Possibly a book at Christmastime and a letter now and then with an occasional brief visit. No daily bunch of flowers or box of candy or any of those little attentions that so frequently expire with the honeymoon. In other words, we have not "courted" each other into false affection but we have rather merely grown together over the last six years.

I have gone house hunting with a number of different couples and every time I find myself unconsciously fitting Pony into the surroundings. Is there any significance to this? Why shouldn't I once in a while fit some of the other girls I am fond of into the scheme of things? Houses, as you know, have always been more or less of a hobby of mine and I have built a good many of them in my mind's eye. But why is it that Pony is always sitting around on the porches of them or before the open fire? These are unconscious things that I have often come to myself with a bit of a start when I realized she was there again.

But the other side of the story. The unromantic cold-blooded side of conscious reasoning. Many and many a time I have pictured to myself a future with her, and oftentimes have been a little bit ashamed of this brutal dissection. I might be inclined to think that I could not be in love with her and still think of things the way I have.

But all this thinking or dreaming or whatever you call it only gets me to the fact that the practical side of cards or business or getting married is all a matter of chance and that in the case of Pony, the chances are more for me than against. I can conceive of being entirely happy with her as an invalid but from what I know of her I'm reasonably sure she won't be one—as I am reasonably sure that none of the other gloomy pictures I have sketched will come true. However, in any event I don't think that it would exactly wreck my life if they did.

You said that you were afraid to write all that you felt because it might hurt me. I don't think you could say anything now that would hurt me but you could after we were married. Probably the thing that has worried me most is the thought that you and she could never get on together—that she would always be a thorn in your side and Father's side. I hate the thought of you sitting at home regretting and regretting that you had not followed me up closer in Boston. What I want most is that those I love should love each other. I have seen John Constable estranged from his family because of his wife and I don't want this to happen to me, as you are and always will be my "first love." But Pony isn't Wanda, is she, Mother? Tell me your "first impressions" of her—it won't hurt. She wouldn't embarrass you with your friends or make you feel that you have to apologize for you son's choice, would she? From what you know of her, do you think she has instincts toward "culture" and "refinement"? Do you think she would be offish, self-centered, selfish, or sulky? What makes you believe she would not mix?

Tell me truly, Mother, please do. I want to know.

Pony and I have had many talks together on many subjects. During those talks and arguments I've had a chance to find out how she looked at the world pretty thoroughly. Her expressed views were not bluff, either, as she got far too "earnest" for bluff. Sometimes when you want to know how a person really feels it pays to pass out a few "beliefs" of your own that you don't believe. You've become quite earnest once or twice yourself by this method so you know what I mean. I think it is quite true that Pony is a man's girl rather than a girl's girl, fundamentally, but from the way old ladies have of mothering her and from the way other girls have of confiding in her most of their troubles, she must get along with women pretty well, too. She has shown me a letter from Dr. Cabot, who is now one of the great surgeons in charge of hospital work in France— shown it to me because of what it told her about conditions at the front. But in it he mentioned what a great comfort it was to him to feel that there was someone at home so devotedly looking after his interests. She is conscientious almost to a fault when she believes it is her duty. I have often remonstrated with her when her "duty" interfered with something I wanted to have her do, but never yet have I gotten away with it. She always says, "I promised, so I have to."

62

One time an old lady gave her a perfectly hideous dress and she wore it a number of times, even tho she felt embarrassed every time she did, rather than to hurt the old lady's feelings. She knows and likes good books. I know from the volumes she has in her little library and from those she has sent me to read and those that we have discussed. She likes music—good music and dance music—she loves to dance.

They bought an Edison Diamond Disc [phonograph] some three years ago, which ought to establish her musical discrimination, don't you think? Ask Father. And they bought it without ever hinting to me that they wanted one or that they would like a discount as many of our more affluent friends have done—which shows, I think, that they have at least a little good taste. In numerous ways, by chance remarks and little unconscious actions, she has expressed traits in her that I both like and admire. I can't put my finger on particular instances perhaps, any more than you can describe or say, "just this makes this shade of green pleasant and this one unpleasant—or this perfume preferable to that." It is the thousand and one little things that make a person react or not to another, as the case may be.

When I was sick it didn't occur to me that any other girl than Pony would drop in and say hello. There was nothing conscious about the wishing—just a vague sort of thing. Girls have given me presents at Christmas, etc., and as I write I can't for the life of me think of what any of them are except the ones that Pony gave me.

I suppose I could go on and on in this strain, but this poor letter is so incoherent and jumbled up already, and probably doesn't say or express what I want to express at all, that to go on might make it all the more incomprehensible. But, Mother dear, don't you think I have tried to be sure, that I do appreciate all or at least some of the unpleasant possibilities as well as the pleasant? Who can ever be sure? I have known her for six years and for the last two or three my state of mind is very adequately expressed in only slight exaggeration by a certain ghost as he looked at the headstone over his grave. This meditative shade remarked, "I have studied many times the marble which was chiseled for me—a boat with a furled sail at rest in a harbor. In truth, it pictures not my destination but my life. For love was offered to me but I shrank from its disillusionment; sorrow knocked at my door, but I was afraid; ambition called to me, but I dreaded the chances. Yet all the while I hungered for meaning in my life. And now I know that we must lift the sail and catch the winds of destiny wherever they drive the boat. To put meaning in one's life may end in madness, but life without meaning is the torture of restlessness and vague desire. It is a boat longing for the sea and yet afraid."

It isn't that I read this and was so impressed with it that I want to act on the advice. I casually happened on it yesterday while I was reading in bed—and it seemed to rather fit my case.

Well, Mother dear, this has been a long rambling letter, and as I said before, it probably doesn't say what I mean to say, but I guess one never can really.

Last Sunday I caught cold in some curious way in the back of my head and it thrummed and pounded away in good shape for a couple of days. It made my neck stiff and made me feel generally under the weather all around. I stayed in bed most of Tuesday and yesterday. I stayed home all day. I'm now out and feeling very much rested up and altho my neck is still a little stiff, Dr. Bradshaw says it probably will be for a day or two. Except for this I feel splendid. It is fine to know you are coming home next Thursday. We've missed you a lot—

Write me quick and love me a little—
Devotedly
Charles

In this letter about Carolyn to his mother, Charles used the words "I have met others and lots of them." He was being forthrightly honest. Coupled with his position of wealth and social standing were his wit, his overall ingratiating personality, and his good looks. Charles was fully as handsome as some of the matinee idols he was to brush shoulders with in the burgeoning motion picture industry—another of the great industries created and launched by his father.

Young ladies, in spite of the supposed primness of the times, vied for his company and attentions. He was not noted for rebuffing such overtures.

Despite occasional dalliance on Charles' part over the years, Carolyn was his one and only true love.

The date of their marriage—March 27, 1918—was influenced by the course of World War I. Even before America entered the conflict, Thomas Edison had been summoned to Washington by Secretary of the Navy Josephus Daniels. Daniels asked that Edison, America's best-known scientist and foremost inventor, turn the running of the Edison Industries over to others and devote his energies to helping the nation's preparedness efforts. Edison's acceptance of this challenge naturally placed additional burdens on other Edison Company executives, including Charles, then twenty-seven.

In his taped memoirs, Charles recalled this period in these words:

The reason I didn't get into the war in active service was my deafness. It worried me a great deal that I was not carrying a gun or sailing on a ship. It worried me so much, as a matter of fact, that when I was down in

Washington one time, after talking to Secretary Daniels and my father, I took occasion to tell Newton D. Baker, the secretary of war, about my worry about not being in uniform. I had been rejected by the army on account of ears, but I said I felt I ought to be in uniform. He told me that since my father had been drafted, and also because of my ears, I would be much more valuable in helping operate the Edison businesses, which were doing a lot of war work, while my father was running the Naval Consulting Board. He persuaded me that that was the smartest thing to do, and that I could make a better contribution there. So during the war years I spent my time trying to run the business, creating departments to handle war work, leading Liberty Loan drives, and selling bonds and one thing or another.

We had several successful bond drives in West Orange; in fact, we won an award for one of them, because it had the biggest percentage per capita, I believe, of any of the New Jersey towns. In that work, Mr. Nelson Durand (an Edison vice-president) was of great assistance. We worked it out together; we had parades and all kinds of stunts to sell bonds. It was a different kind of a thing from the way it is now. It had to be run by generating enthusiasm—mass meetings, parades, and all that kind of thing. It was a real sales job, because this was the first time that it had been done on such a large scale. That occupied some of my time.

Also, in the middle of the war I had gotten pretty well tired out. I had asthma attacks and neuralgia rather badly. I persuaded my mother to invite Carolyn to Florida for a short visit. Carolyn was doing her bit in the war in Massachusetts by assisting doctors and nurses in seeing that they got overseas for the Harvard medical unit, which operated a large overseas hospital for service people. She had been working with Dr. Cabot of Cambridge on this project. He later went over himself to take charge of the hospital unit—I think it had 2,200 beds. Anyway, it was a large establishment. Dr. Cabot's leaving multiplied the demands on her energies. So she was getting pretty tired. We decided that we both needed a rest, and I got mother to invite her to come down to Fort Myers, where my father and mother had this winter place called Seminole Lodge. After we got there, I thought it was a good time to ask her to be my wife. So one moonlit night, out on the end of the Edison dock, I popped the question by saying, "Do you want a large wedding"? She said no; so we decided that we would get married right away, down there in Florida.

At that time, the families of both of us were pretty well scattered. My mother was the only one in Fort Myers. My father was out on a ship, off Key West somewhere, doing Naval Consulting Board experimental work. My younger brother, Theodore, had an idea which was considered of military importance. It involved use of a small gasoline motor on a frame, and a shaft on which a wheel revolved. The wheel, about four inches wide, was filled with TNT.

Designed for use in trench warfare, the machine operated on a flywheel or gyroscope principle. When the stationary motorcycle-type engine got the wheel revolving at an extremely high velocity, the axle shaft would be removed and the spinning wheel, loaded with TNT, would be aimed toward the enemy's trenches. On account of the speed at which it was turning, the wheel had a gyroscopic action. It could not be diverted from its course. It could hit a shell hole, for instance, dig its way out and go right on in a straight line.

Theodore was working on this project near Morristown, New Jersey, but the army moved him to an uninhabited island, one of the Florida Keys, to continue his experiments. That's where he was when I decided to get married; and, of course, he couldn't attend.

My sister, Madeleine, and her husband were in Washington, D. C., where he was serving in the army. Consequently, they couldn't be present.

Carolyn's family also was scattered around.

Our minds made up, Carolyn and I left the dock, which ran from my parents' property about a tenth of a mile into the Caloosahatchee River, approximately fourteen miles inland from the Gulf of Mexico, to seek out my mother. She took our announcement rather well.

We told her we wanted to get married right away, right there in Florida. When she asked what date we had in mind, we suggested two or three days from then.

We did want to send telegrams to people to let them know about our plans. Mother finally agreed, and we sent off the wires. I well remember the reply Father sent me from the ship he was on. It read: "If it's going to be, then the sooner the better. Anyway, it won't be worse than life in the front-line trenches. You have my blessings."

Naturally, we had a lot of ground to cover in just three days. Getting the license. Arranging for a minister.

My bride-to-be got a white dress and a wedding bouquet. I've never seen a wedding bouquet as lovely as that one.

A rather amusing incident occurred in getting our marriage license. The night before Carolyn and I had attended a dance. There was a young man there who took a shine to Carolyn and gave her quite a rush. He wanted to call on her.

When we went to get the license, who should be the official to issue it but this same young man who had given Carolyn such a rush. Flabbergasted, he counted himself out of the running right then and there.

Seminole Lodge rests in the middle of a botanical garden filled with strange trees and exotic plants. We decided to be married outdoors, in front of a camphor tree and a cinnamon tree, with a huge Japanese umbrella tree serving as a backdrop. It made for a lovely setting.

We rolled out a little carpet from the house to a small altar with two burning candles.

Mother gave the bride away. Only two others were present—my old baby nurse and the butler. They served as witnesses. Carolyn was as nervous as if the ceremony were being held in a cathedral.

After the ceremony, we decided that we were going to take a honeymoon. It consisted of getting into a Model T Ford with a few prepared goodies. We were to drive down to the Gulf, where I was supposed to catch a couple of fish for me to cook on the beach, then return to Seminole Lodge. Well, everything went all right except that when we got to the beach the mosquitoes were so thick that we just couldn't stay there. So we moseyed back to town through roads of sand. That's all they were then. I then took my bride to Hunter's Drugstore and bought her an ice-cream soda. That was our honeymoon.

From Fort Myers, Carolyn and I went on to Key West and were guests in the house of a Captain Krout, who had previously visited in Seminole Lodge. After that, we returned north. She had to go right back to Boston to wind up her work with the Harvard Unit, and I had to go back to the plant in West Orange. So almost as soon as we were married, we were separated for six weeks.

Then we got an apartment on Park Avenue near Prospect Street in East Orange. It was a furnished apartment and was rented as such; but we hadn't been there more than a couple of weeks, I think it was, when the landlady decided she wanted her furniture and yanked it all out. We were left with a bare apartment. We scrambled together some old chairs from the Edison shop and a couple of beds from somewhere. We literally camped for a while until we were able to buy some furniture of our own. That was that. We still had a Model T Ford, not the one in Florida—which, by the way, is still there on exhibition as part of the Edison museum in Fort Myers—but another one which I had gotten in 1914. It was far from new.

After six years of courtship, Charles and Carolyn "settled down"— hardly a truism in their instance—to suburban living, he to prepare himself to take over his father's executive duties in the Edison Industries, she to grow into a life-style unknown to her before. Both served their apprenticeships well.

As Charles rose within the hierarchy of the Edison Industries, the life-style for him and Carolyn improved commensurately. Their furnished-to-become-unfurnished apartment in East Orange was supplanted not too long thereafter by a modest home of their own in West Orange's exclusive Llewellyn Park, hardly more than a stone's throw from Glenmont, the magnificent home of Thomas and Mina Edison. After several years of dreaming and planning, Charles launched upon the building of a grandiose home, also in Llewellyn Park. Construction began in 1929, just prior to the economic crash, and was completed in 1931, at a time when the Great Depression had engulfed the nation. Called Landmore, this rather austere house—built with limestone blocks hauled fifty miles from the Edison Portland Cement quarry in the hills of Sussex County—contained twenty-two rooms and rested on a six-acre tract.

Although it was a monumental structure in a monumental setting, Landmore never really became a home of warmth. Even though Charles retained ownership of Landmore until his death in 1969, the diversity of his activities so changed the course of the lives and life-style of him and Carolyn as to permit little more than a veneer of permanency to enshroud Landmore.

Following Charles' introduction to public life during the early days of Franklin Roosevelt's first term as president, the Edisons began living more and more in hotels and less and less at Landmore as he became more and more caught up in the ungossamer webs that tend to bind persons in the public eye.

Hotel living became virtually a way of life for the Edisons, starting with Charles' becoming assistant secretary of the navy in 1937. The Hay Adams House was their principal address in the nation's capital. The three years of Charles' governorship (1941-1944) marked the last extended period that Landmore served the Edisons as home. Shortly after his term as governor ended, the Edisons transferred the base of their activities to New York City. For somewhat brief periods they rented apartments, first at the St. Regis Hotel and then at the Ambassador Hotel. For the two decades preceding his passing in 1969, the Waldorf Astoria Towers, at Park Avenue and Fiftieth Street, was home. There were occasional weekends spent at Landmore, but they became less and less frequent with the passing years.

Life in New York City held greater charm for Carolyn than it held for Charles, particularly up into the early 1950s, when he was still intimately involved in the day-to-day operations of the Edison Industries. In May of 1950, Charles became chairman of the board of Thomas A. Edison, Incorporated; and Henry G. Riter 3rd succeeded him as president in a move engineered by Charles as the company's majority stockholder.

This change provided Charles with greater freedom from business details and permitted greater attention to the many civic and philanthropic activities in which he was involved.

Many of the intimate friends of the Edisons held the opinion that

Carolyn was the real reason for the move to New York City. She loved the social life of the big city and the prestige of living in the Waldorf Towers, where the neighbors were to include former president Hoover, General MacArthur, Jim Farley, and a host of other luminaries, including, from time to time, the former king of England—the Duke of Windsor and his "woman I love."

Although fifteen years earlier Charles had switched from ingrained Republicanism to New Dealism, his subsequent disenchantment with many of FDR's policies nudged him from the slight left to the slight right, even to the slight right of the slight right. This, coupled with his propinquity within the Waldorf Towers to Herbert Hoover, plus a mutual interest in cardplaying, revived an old acquaintanceship and solidified it into warm friendship. Charles and Carolyn were usually once-a-week opponents at canasta of the former president and "Bunny" Miller, his secretary, who filled in after the death of Mrs. Hoover.

The relationship between the Edisons and President Hoover (who died one year after Carolyn Edison and five years before Charles) became increasingly cordial. Their friendship, however, was not without its whimsical aspects. Mr. Hoover enjoyed one or two dry martinis "up" before dinner at this stage in his life, whereas Charles was fighting with virtually uninterrupted success a years-old battle with drinking. All liquor—but particularly gin—revived within him a latent tendency toward alcoholism, something he fought—and, to his credit, mastered—over many years. The Edisons would have been just as happy if the sedate Mr. Hoover had not indulged his taste for a martini in the face of Charles' inclination. Personally, it didn't bother Carolyn, because a smidgen of dry wine was the usual extent of her intake. Charles came to learn that a bottle or two of ale or beer, preferably ale, really was the extent of his tolerance for alcohol.

Another aspect of the Edison-Hoover card games was this: "Mr. Hoover liked to win," Charles confided to the author. "Once in a while, I fear, he and Bunny Miller benefited from some rules of the game known only to Mr. Hoover, certainly not to Mr. Hoyle."

As a businessman, Charles moved among the elite of industry. Not only did he head the Edison Industries and, later, serve as chairman of the board of the McGraw-Edison Company, he also sat on the boards of a variety of big businesses, such as the Jones and Laughlin Steel Company, International Telephone and Telegraph, and the United States Life Insurance Company. Socially, Charles and Carolyn were members of the "400." But there was a side to living in the Waldorf Towers far removed from the likes of Hoover, MacArthur, and Farley. Charles literally was loved by the bellboys, the bartenders, the elevator girls, the maids, and the other employees.

Reminiscing on the two decades Charles lived in the Towers, Ray Peteracki, forty-two years with the Waldorf, mostly as a bartender in the Bull and Bear restaurant, used these words: "I was here when the Edisons moved in somewhere around 1948. He was a beautiful person.

"In the early years, I was tending bar at the old Men's Bar. The governor would come in frequently for a rum and Coke. He'd never have more than one. When there weren't too many customers, we would have long talks. He always was interested in what other people were doing and thinking.

"He certainly looked like his father, even to using a hearing aid.

"In later years, he switched from rum and Coke to ale.

"He was tops."

Anthony Mormando, a thirty-six-year veteran of Waldorf service, was a bellboy during most of the years the Edisons lived there. Later, as bell captain, he recalled those days. "There was only one Charles Edison," Mormando commented. "He liked to talk with everyone here, not just to pass the time of day, but to really find out what others were thinking. He was a friendly man.

"I was a bellboy at the time and we chatted often, as he also did with the doormen, elevator operators, the maids, and all the others.

"Mr. Edison was a generous tipper. He frequently would say, as he handed me a tip, 'Have a ham sandwich on me' or some similar words.

"Did you know that when he died, Mr. Edison left each of us in the Waldorf who in any way had served him and his wife an amount based essentially on the individual's number of years with the Waldorf during their long stay here? It was in appreciation of courtesies and services rendered.

"All of us genuinely loved him, not just because of his generosity, but mainly because he was so kind, so thoughtful, such a gentleman."

Carolyn Edison, on occasion, could be as imperious with help as Charles was gentle. Charles once commented that, "When provoked, she can react like a Bourbon."

There was nothing imperious about Carolyn, however, if a friend or even a casual acquaintance, irrespective of station in life, was sick or troubled. She was the epitome of thoughtfulness and compassion under such circumstances.

The forty-five years of their marriage were unusual in a number of ways, not the least of which was Charles' superabundance of concern over Carolyn's health, happiness, and welfare. He never ceased courting her over those four-and-a-half decades.

Even when they were in their sixties and seventies, he frequently continued his habit of leaving little love notes around the apartment for her to discover. These notes often contained tender but impromptu poetry. Sometimes they were in recognition of a birthday or an anniversary; at other times they marked no particular occasion.

Many of Charles' little *billets-doux* were addressed to Sweetza Rose, Bunt and Chebunt, and other pet names he had for Carolyn.

One such note on the occasion of her birthday, Charles directed to "Darling Bunt." It read:

> A stomach they say
> Is the way to a man.
> If you want to make hay,
> It's the very best plan.
>
> But a woman is different
> And so I confess,
> I'm using the line
> Of a pretty new dress.
>
> Mainbocher, Carnegie—
> Anything goes
> When I reach for your heart
> Via swanky new clothes.

The envelope contained $1,000.

Another note, this time in an envelope containing $5,000, used these words:

> The North Wind doth blow
> And we shall have snow,
> And what will my Bunty do then?
> Poor thing.
>
> She will sit in her room
> Only covered with gloom—
> No coat, since Heaven knows when,
> Poor thing.

71

But this little note
Is a good antidote
For all of the gloom and the chill,
Poor thing.

It's a new mink for you
From your head to your shoe,
And your best beau is footing the bill.
Poor thing.

That note was dated November 9, 1950, when Charles and Carolyn were in their sixties.

When Charles was away on business trips, as happened frequently, never a day passed but that he would phone her at least once, more likely twice, and occasionally three times.

Nothing pleased Charles more than to plan and execute elaborate surprises for Carolyn on special occasions such as birthdays or anniversaries. One of the most unusual of these occasions was "staged" in their expansive apartment in the Waldorf. *Staged* is the proper verb for the occasion. The evening started as though it was to be a rather routine birthday dinner. A half dozen or so guests, including the author, were present.

The surprises started immediately thereafter. Charles had composed a special song, both words and music, to Carolyn, which was performed by a talented professional pianist and vocalist hired for the occasion. The author chipped in with another original song, "Sing a Carol to Carolyn," which also was performed. In combination, Charles and the author produced a script and acted out a fifteen-minute skit taking off on a then current comedy show on network radio. The finale was a fashion show put on by Hattie Carnegie's exclusive shop with the assistance of professional models. At the closing curtain, after a play-on-words tribute to the good works of the (Andrew) Carnegie Foundation, one of the shapely models entered garbed only—but discreetly—in a Carnegie's foundation garment.

The play on words actually contained a triple twist, because both Carolyn and one of the guests of the evening, Alice Stevenson, had just completed a Dale Carnegie course in public speaking.

Neither Charles nor Carolyn was athletically inclined. Consequently, their pursuits were rather sedentary. Bridge and canasta were among their favorite pastimes. Chinese checkers was another.

Sedentary diversions, yes, but since both Charles and Carolyn were essentially night people, it is probably good that they did not try to combine little sleep with robust activity. It was more usual than unusual for them to stay up until 2 or 3 a.m., and even later, on just run-of-the-mill nights. Neither seemed ever to tire of the other's company. Frequently, of course, they were surrounded by friends.

Late hours posed less of a problem for Carolyn than for Charles. She could generally sleep in as long as she desired. Charles was something of an insomniac; so maybe his late hours and busy day schedules were not as abrasive to him as they might have been to others.

His father was renowned for requiring less sleep than most men. Perhaps some of this quality rubbed off on the son.

Carolyn's welfare was so near to Charles' heart that, despite his wealth, he went to extreme lengths to make certain she would not want even under emergency circumstances. Remembering the closing of the nation's banks by presidential order at the outset of FDR's first term, Charles established a cash fund of $200,000 in a safety deposit box in her name so that even if regular deposit accounts and savings accounts became frozen, she still would have access to the funds in her private safe deposit vault. With customary meticulousness, Charles left with the funds in the vault certified proof that all Internal Revenue Service taxes had been paid on the money therein.

The poignancy of their union extended to the grave. Together they planned a marble mausoleum in Rosedale Cemetery, Orange, New Jersey. Carolyn saw the finished mausoleum before her passing on June 28, 1963. While she admired it in its entirety, there was a special touch added by Charles that particularly pleased her. At the cost of $2,000, he had arranged for a stained glass window depicting a beautiful woman administering to the sick. It symbolized her volunteer work over the years in which she assisted patients in the recovery room at the Columbia-Presbyterian Medical Center in New York City.

6

Learning the Business

UPON HIS RETURN to the East from San Francisco, Charles began his duties at the Edison Industries in November of 1913. He was made assistant to his father, an assignment intended to expose him to all facets of the diverse businesses. Although Thomas Edison's direct connection with the power-and-light industry was by 1913 pretty much behind him, his operations, headquartered in West Orange but with multiple plants and nationwide offices, ran the gamut from research to phonographs, from cement to office dictating equipment, from batteries to motion pictures.

This assignment was no small order even for a young man capable and eager to learn, conceding the fact that this particular young man was more attuned to the arts than to the sciences. Charles' almost immediate fascination with Greenwich Village and its bohemianism might just as well have been directed to the Edison motion picture studio in the Bronx, had it not been for the fact that picture making there was about to give way to Hollywood and other pressures. He never ceased being enamored with the glamour of the filmmaking industry. Years later, on visits to the west coast, he seldom failed to visit the film capital to cement old friendships and make new ones. Mary Pickford—known as the Biograph Girl during his days at M.I.T.—remained one of his idols and dear friends until his passing.

Indirectly, at least, the motion picture portion of the Edison enterprises almost put an end to them. Charles had been on the job less than thirteen months when a catastrophic fire destroyed much of the sprawling manufacturing complex in West Orange.

In the late afternoon of December 9, 1914, spontaneous combustion ignited containers of highly flammable motion picture film in storage.

The flames spread rapidly to adjacent factory buildings, several of them of steel-reinforced, concrete construction and ostensibly fireproof.

Fanned by a brisk breeze and fed by the old-fashioned nitrate films, tons of celluloid used in making phonograph records, large supplies of chemicals, and huge tanks of alcohol, the fire became a holocaust. Twelve firemen were overcome, and one Edison employee died. More than 10,000 persons crowded adjacent streets and fields to watch. Several acres of buildings were burning at the same time.

Twenty-four hours later, the flames reduced to smoldering embers, only Thomas Edison's laboratory group of brick buildings and one large five-story concrete factory structure remained unscathed.

In dollars it was costly. Because the concrete structures had been considered fireproof, the amount of fire insurance was sorely inadequate. But as a lesson in fortitude, it was a valuable experience for Charles. His admiration for his father rose to new heights.

In his taped memoirs, Charles recounted events during and after the fire:

> Father was in the cement business with a plant out in New Village in New Jersey. He pioneered in the construction of steel-reinforced, concrete factory buildings. One of the things claimed for these structures was their complete fireproofness. In fact, one of the talking points was that one needn't insure them because they wouldn't burn.
>
> That was a fatal mistake as far as our fire was concerned. The window sash were wooden. And of course there were wooden partitions, wooden desks, and wooden bins, tote boxes, and stockroom shelving. So, whereas the buildings themselves were not flammable, the contents were. Also, the machinery required oil, some of which would soak into the pores of the concrete.
>
> All the non-fireproof buildings seemed to survive the fire, and all the fireproof buildings were completely gutted.
>
> An interesting point is that none of the fireproof buildings collapsed. Refurbished with metal window sash and other refinements, they're still there today. *
>
> The insurance we carried, as I recall it, was $287,000; but our fire losses were over $2 million.
>
> The fire was still smoldering when Father began planning how he would rebuild. He was almost sixty-eight at the time, and most men of

---

*Later, in 1974, all but one of these concrete structures were razed as part of an urban renewal project.

his age would have been crushed and stunned by such a catastrophe. I don't think they would have reacted as he did.

He had been up for well over twenty-four hours, and after giving decisive orders for starting to clean up the tons of debris, he rolled up his coat as a pillow, stretched out on a table, and was asleep in a minute. He just turned things off and went to sleep.

He had great gameness and an optimistic outlook, plus an important quality called guts. He never thought of the fire as a great calamity. He said to me, "We'll have a much better plant after we get through. We've swept away all the old shacks, and now we can have a good plant."

Mind you, he wasn't a young man facing up to misfortune. Here was a man you might expect to be thinking about retirement and leisure.

Out of the wreckage of the whole thing, with all the machinery having to be repaired and set up elsewhere, on New Year's Day—just three weeks later, mind you—we presented Mr. Edison with the first phonograph turned out with this reconditioned machinery. It took a little longer to get into regular production, but we produced in less than a month the first phonograph out of the ashes. Things then took shape rapidly, and it wasn't long until we were in full production.

Charles' youthful career had undergone baptism by fire.

His chores with the company remained relatively nominal until the approach of World War I whisked his father off to Washington to organize and head the Naval Consulting Board. The absence of Thomas as the directing head of the Edison Industries naturally placed added burdens on other executives, including Charles. As his responsibilities expanded, Charles began to develop his own philosophies on managing a business.

"I had come from the big Boston electric utility, the Boston Edison Company," he said, adding:

It was a little ahead of the times.

They had put in things like dispensaries and first-aid stations. They built an employees' recreation hall, but the employees grumbled about it, saying in effect: "We don't give a hoot about that. Why don't they just put it in our pay envelopes?" In other words, the Boston Edison Company was a paternalistic organization, with the management doing things that they thought the men and women would or should like.

But when I was working there, I was down at a different level. I could hear what the employees were really saying, and so I said to myself, "We must never be paternalistic, because that does not satisfy the people."

It soon became evident to me that a company should be responsible, first, for good wages; second, for good buildings and working conditions, good sanitary facilities, a reasonable number of safety precautions, first-aid and dispensary services, and things like that. Things such as a clubhouse or tennis courts, I decided, should be done as an employee movement, rather than as a company handout.

By and large, but with a few major exceptions, father Thomas held son Charles on a loose tether. The extent to which Thomas let him make major decisions even impressed Charles.

Despite his youthfulness and short experience, Charles began the initiation of a number of changes with a view to modernizing the administration of the Edison Industries. "I was always amazed," he said, "that he gave me such terrific latitude. But he could be a very exacting master, too. He insisted that I know the answer to any question involving our business. Occasionally, he would ask me a question out of the blue. I knew he expected me to know the answers; so I had to do a lot of detail work just to keep ahead of the questions he might ask me. He was testing me out by letting me flounder around and make my own mistakes. He told me once, "How are you going to learn if you don't make mistakes, if you don't try something? Go ahead, try it.' "

Charles proceeded to implement some of his ideas for improvements, such as improved medical service. Much earlier, when a summer vacation job was his only firsthand contact with the Edison plants, he was astounded—and almost nauseated—when a workman asked his foreman for some cotton waste and carbolic acid. The workman was holding a severed finger in his good hand. He wanted cotton waste and the carbolic acid for a do-it-yourself medical treatment.

"At the time," Charles said, "we had no first-aid stations; no dispensaries. We had nothing. If an employee got hurt, we would call an ambulance and send him down to the Orange Memorial Hospital. Nobody paid any attention to such things in those days."

The Edison Industries had been established and operated through strict centralized control, due, no doubt, to the commanding leadership of Thomas Edison, who, individually, held virtually all stock in the various affiliated Edison companies. Young Charles became an exponent of decentralized authority, a viewpoint that was to carry over into his later excursions into public officeholding.

Quoting from his taped memoirs, Charles said:

As I studied the Edison organization, I became convinced that we could not continue to make a profitable go of things as long as it was a centralized organization.

We were in the motion picture business, and it had grown to such a degree that we had built a studio up in the Bronx, near the Botanical

Gardens, and were making pictures there. That was one kind of business.

Father was also working on the nickel-iron-alkaline battery, getting that started—an entirely different type of business. He also was making a better battery for the railway fraternity in a plant several miles away in Bloomfield and Belleville, New Jersey, quite another type of business.

We were making phonographs, our largest business at the time. We also had an office equipment business, making things such as dictating machines. We had a cement mill and we also were making fans and other appliances and a variety of instruments. We even had woodworking plants to produce phonograph cabinets.

It was a mixed-up type of business, comprised of businesses dissimilar in nature, but all run from one central point. Everything went up to one accounting office, one general manager, and only one of this, that, or the other.

I decided that we weren't making enough money because responsibility was too far removed from the actual products. So I advocated pulling these businesses apart, placing a vice-president or a general manager in charge of each logical division of the business, and then tying them all together by having a central service organization which each division could draw upon. These centralized services would consist of such things as a legal department, traffic control, purchasing, personnel, and the like.

To accomplish this radical changeover took about five years and a lot of reeducation of entrenched management dedicated to centralization. Charles remembered it this way:

Finally it was set up and operating smoothly. It became known as the divisional system and is the one that is still in force in the company today [1959].*

I think one thing that assured me the theory was sound was General Motors. When formed, its organization was predicated on centralization. A huge office building was built in Detroit, and everything was centered there.

Mr. William C. Durant was the head of the company. His managers in all the different places had no local autonomy. They were all subservient to this central organization in Detroit. But when Mr. Durant was, let us say, forced out of the management of General Motors, the company was reorganized. The new management sent men down to our place in West Orange to study our setup. GM's setup is now based almost exactly along

---

*Thomas A. Edison, Incorporated, merged with the McGraw Electric Company on January 2, 1957, to form the McGraw-Edison Company. The combined firms operated on a decentralized divisional basis.

the practices we follow here. They had men in our place studying us for more than a week.

They adopted our type of decentralized organization, so that they now have their Buick, Chevrolet, and other organizations separate, but they still have their central laboratory, proving grounds, styling outfit, and so on, whose services are available to all divisions. That's about the way we operate.*

Thomas Edison backed up Charles in putting the divisional policy into effect, but the "old man" kept a constant eye on all facets of the business. On one or more occasions, he stepped in and overruled his son.

One such instance related by Charles in his taped memoirs follows:

The divisional policy occupied me for quite a while, what with trying to reorganize the company on that basis. I was considered something of a maverick because I wanted to put in such things as an employee cafeteria and a personnel department.

When I went to work, we only had one personnel man who would hire and fire. Otherwise, hiring and firing was done ad lib by any foreman. If some foreman needed a man, he would call up this fellow in the "personnel office." There were always people lined up at the gate waiting for jobs. He'd go outside, and yell something like this: "Hey, you! Come in. What do you do?"

"Well, I do so and so."

"Sorry, you won't do."

He'd keep calling in men until he found one with the proper skills. He'd send the man up to the foreman, and if the foreman didn't like him, the foreman would fire him.

It seemed to me that we ought to have a better system, that we should remove the hire-and-fire right from the foreman, so that the foreman could not actually fire a man, but only return him to the personnel department. There the man would be interviewed and treated like a human being. If he had just been fired for lack of work or something like that, then we would find perhaps that he would be useful in another one of our divisions looking for help. So we started trying to put the business on a little more human basis.

Don't get me wrong, however; we were as good as anybody else around there. People liked to work there. We had never had a strike. The plant was completely nonunion, and everybody liked working there, but we

---

*The divisional policy was set forth in a formal memorandum, fourteen pages long, dated April 26, 1920. Many facets of the decentralized organization policy already had been in operation for a number of months.

were falling behind the times.

I introduced quite a number of new things, and Father usually was perfectly willing to go along with them. He didn't pay too much attention to them, because he was buried in the storage battery, the phonograph, and other things. He kept a very close eye on the sales end of the phonograph business, because he was more or less running that himself, on the technical end particularly. He read all the salesmen's reports and things of that kind. He would have a bag full of all kinds of reports, and if I didn't also know what was in them, it was just too bad. He would ask me a question like "How many records did we reject today?" If I couldn't answer him right away, I was chided. Or he would say, "What's the name of our dealer out in Dubuque, Iowa?" or something like that. He knew the answers. So I used to sit up half the night reading these reports and boning up on things just to answer any possible questions that he might ask. It was all good training.

I built up quite a sizable personnel department and other service organizations. This central group grew quite a bit. Our business was growing, and I felt that this divisional idea would more or less be an automatic check on the growth of overhead. In other words, if, for example, the head of the storage battery division found it too expensive to use the central legal department, he just wouldn't use it; and that would automatically keep the legal department down to a reasonable size. Or if he didn't like the way personnel was being handled, he would probably yell about it. I thought that was the way to keep overhead down.

It didn't turn out that way; there's no substitute for everyday management. As a result of too much reliance on the theory of automatic checks, some of the departments got a bit out of hand. They grew considerably. That was all right as long as we were making money. But when the tight-money time came and a depression followed World War I, business dropped off suddenly. We found ourselves out on a limb, and Mr. Edison gave instructions to cut the payroll. I knew I had built up this beautiful organization and I didn't want to see it destroyed. Father and I had some pretty heated arguments. Finally, he virtually relieved me of the responsibility and took over himself. He started going through the shops like a bulldozer. Sometimes the good went out with the bad. But if he hadn't done that, we probably would have been bankrupt.

I remember I went through a very, very tough time there. Radio had come in on top of the depression to hurt us, since we were in the phonograph business. Mr. Edison resumed command and ordered drastic cutbacks, and it almost broke my heart. I would lie awake thinking, "How can I stop him from making these terrible mistakes? What can I do? He just doesn't understand." Things got tougher and tougher between us, and every time I urged him not to do something or other, he

80

would say, "I've been through half a dozen of these depressions. I know how they work, and it's got to be this way or we'll go broke."

I just couldn't see it that way. I knew we wouldn't go broke. I thought I knew better than he did. That was the only time in my life that a strain developed between Father and me. It got so bad at one point that I thought I had better leave the company.

Then one night, while lying in bed, I had a sudden thought. I said to myself, "You know, there's a possible chance that he may be right and I may be wrong." I resolved that I wasn't going to let this stand between Father and me. Father meant more to me than holding out for what I thought was right; and the thought that he might be right, after all, rather swung me around to another viewpoint. So I decided that I would go down and tell him that I would do anything that he told me to do. If he told me to burn the laboratory down, I would burn it down—anything at all! So, with that, he turned right around and said, "All right, you're going to learn a big lesson out of this depression," and I joined him in the pruning of the business.

We were $6 million in debt beyond what we should have been. That was quite a lot for us—we weren't one of the huge companies. We even had to have our suppliers finance us by taking notes for our purchases. We had $2 million worth of those out. We had long ago reached the limit of our credit at the banks. We were teetering on the edge of bankruptcy. If father hadn't stepped in, we would have been completely broke.

I think that punctured my swelled head, and I've always been grateful to him for it. It was a tough lesson, and I had learned it the hard way, because I thought I had been pretty successful up to that time in building up this organization from about $6 million-a-year thing into about a $30 million proposition.

Effects of the postwar depression of the early 1920s on the phonograph business, the major segment of the Edison Industries, were aggravated by the growing popularity of radio. Over a period of several years, sales of all phonographs—not just the Edison brand—dwindled almost to zero. Radio took over. This circumstance lured Charles into a misadventure in business, over his father's objections. Charles recalled the period in these words:

We were left with our largest business, phonographs, practically gone. We tried various ways of whipping it up, but we finally had to face the fact that it just couldn't be whipped up at that time. Neither Mr. Edison nor any of us felt that the phonograph was dead; we felt that it would come back for the very fundamental reason that once you heard radio, you couldn't play it back, whereas with a phonograph, you could have what you wanted when you wanted it. We felt the phonograph business would revive; but in the meantime, since there just wasn't any business, we couldn't keep a large organization waiting for the hoped-for upturn.

Father got very much worried about business. He became more and more concerned about it because, as a young man, I thought I knew all the answers. I thought I was cutting down to meet the situation. I felt that if Father would ever let us go into the manufacturing of radios, it would solve everything. He didn't want to get into it, but all the rest of us had been bitten by the radio bug. Here was a big dealer-jobber organization—we had something like thirteen thousand dealers and forty jobbers—that were starving to death for something to sell. We were fast losing the dealers to radio. With all this wonderful organization, it seemed to me that we ought to get into radio. Mr. Edison said, "In three years, it'll be such a cutthroat business that nobody will make any money. Furthermore, those large cabinets that they are selling now at high prices will be reduced to a little box, and there won't be any money in it for anybody; you'll go broke if you get into it."

I couldn't see it that way; neither could the rest of the organization. I remember seeing Father off on the train going to Florida. As he was leaving for his winter vacation, I made another appeal to him: "Won't you let us go into radio?"

He turned to me at the station and said, "Well, if you want to be a damn fool, go ahead with the radio. You've got my permission, but I'm telling you that it's no good."

That was all I needed. My brother Theodore also wanted to go into radio, so we got the wheels turning immediately. He worked night and day developing the Edison radio; and even today, I will say that I know of no radio with a better tone or one that performs better than the one he and other engineers got up at that time. It's still good and will stand up with any of the modern ones that I've heard.

Good, bad, or indifferent, the Edison radio, as a business, did not fare well. Even though Edison men, including son Theodore, achieved certain patents, it really was necessary for success to hold a license from the recently established Radio Corporation of America to have access to the pool of patents created under governmental edict. It should have been easy, but it wasn't. Thomas, as a result of his discovery of a basic principle of wireless telegraphy—called the Edison effect—and his other scientific contributions, had received an implied promise from industry leaders that when and if he wanted an RCA license, one would be available to him. This didn't turn out to be true, but this hurdle was cleared by the Edison Company acquiring the already issued RCA license held by the Splitdorf Electrical and Radio Company of Newark, New Jersey, a firm far from prospering.

82

Radios bearing the Edison trademark and the prestige of the name were large, expensive for the times, and handsomely cabineted in wood.

"We were going lickety-hoot," Charles recalled. "We were selling a lot of high-quality instruments. We were, of course, in competition with General Electric, RCA, and other companies manufacturing radios, but we were getting established very well. Then along came Bill Grunow, of the Griggsby-Grunow Corporation. Griggsby-Grunow brought out a good-looking model at about half the prevailing price. It scooped the market, and almost overnight Griggsby-Grunow grew to tremendous proportions. Everybody else had to build down or fold up.

"That started the price war, and the whole industry became demoralized. The large cabinets gave way to those little boxes that father had prophesied. Our losses mounted tremendously. We dropped about $2 million in about two years. We decided radio was not for us. Reluctantly, we concluded that Mr. Edison had been right again and that we had better get out of the radio business."

On more than one occasion Charles told the author that one of the manifold fond memories of his father was that Thomas, after failure of the radio business, never said, "I told you so."

Despite dropping out of the phonograph and radio markets, the Edison Industries prospered in other directions under Charles.

The heavy-duty nickel-iron-alkaline storage batteries came into their own. Originally created by Thomas Edison to propel electric passenger cars and trucks, they found their real niche as suppliers of standby power for air conditioning systems on railroads, for specialized lighting and signaling requirements on subways and related forms of transportation, for propelling forklift trucks, and for providing safe and sure lighting for miners working underground.

One of the old standbys of the Edison Industries—wet-celled primary batteries—expanded its profitability and virtually held a monopoly on the huge railway signaling market.

Over his father's objections—Thomas looked down on lead-acid storage batteries—Charles launched a line of such batteries at a new plant constructed in Kearny, in the New Jersey Meadows. These batteries used the brand name E-Mark because Thomas Edison did not want the Edison name to appear on them. Organized to supply original equipment for Ford automobiles, the E-Mark operation rang up consistent profits over many years.

A line of medical and industrial gases was introduced successfully by Charles.

An offshoot of Thomas Edison's invention of the musical phonograph was a phonograph recorder and transcriber for office dictation purposes. Known generally as the Ediphone (later as the Voicewriter) this line of products played second fiddle to the musical phonograph when that part of the Edison Industries was riding high. Like the nickel-iron-alkaline storage battery, the Ediphone came into its own under Charles. It developed into a worldwide, multimillion-dollar business.

In one area, Charles and those in management under him literally fashioned a silk purse out of a sow's ear. When economic and competitive factors closed down the phonograph works, the Edison Company was left with a large woodworking plant in New London, Wisconsin, which had been devoted to making phonograph cabinets. This plant was New London's largest employer. Rather than close it down and wreck the local economy, Charles and his staff of executives looked for a different product line. A young man named Tom Fitzgerald, sent to Wisconsin more or less to hold the fort, developed a line of juvenile furniture—cribs, highchairs and the like. Edison Little Folks Furniture proved highly profitable and was looked upon as the Cadillac of the trade.

Charles' stewardship of the Edison Industries—official since his assuming the chairmanship in 1927 and vitually absolute after the death of Thomas at the age of eighty-four on October 18, 1931—had had its ups and its downs. He was looked upon by many peers as an up-and-coming executive with a great future. He was forty in 1930, and the Great Depression was not just around the corner; it had turned the corner.

Charles lost an idol with the passing of his father. He was moved to compose a prayer that was spoken by Dr. Stephen J. Herben at the funeral three days later on October 21, the fifty-second anniversary of Thomas' invention of the electric lamp. The prayer read:

Eternal God, who art within Thyself all things, take now his soul, and in High Heaven blend it once more within thine own.

We that remain give thanks that he has shared our toil—even for all too brief a time. A kindly, noble leader and our friend.

Grant now our prayer that, in the march of history to come, our sons and daughters still will feel the deep enrichment he has given. May he live on in hallowed memory, forever honored and forever loved.

Hard-line Republicanism as a way of life for Charles gave way to liberally oriented New Dealism. Although he had voted for Herbert Hoover in November of 1932, by the time Franklin Roosevelt took the presidential oath on March 4, 1933, Charles was volunteering his administrative expertise to the New Deal. He had launched himself on new careers which would separate him from direct management of the Edison Industries until 1944.

BRUNO'S WEEKLY

Five Cents   December 11th, 1915

Typical of the art carried in *Bruno's Weekly* is this front-page drawing by Clara Tice.

Charles and Carolyn, shortly after their marriage in 1918, in the solarium of his father's and mother's home, Glenmont.

85

Carolyn, one month after her marriage.

Resembling a World War I ad for Arrow collars, Charles was as handsome as many matinee idols of the era (1917).

Looking more mature with wide-brim felt hat and pipe (1917).

Two years later, Charles had turned from pipe to cigar.

Learning under the "master," Charles listens as his father makes a radio talk from his laboratory in 1929.

The young executive at work.

Carolyn Edison as the young matron.

Charles, as created by Paul Ford in his syndicated feature "Private Lives" in the *Washington Evening Star* on June 8, 1944, demonstrates his "orange symphony."

The real Charles at his grand piano.

MEDIUM

In Eb

DON'T ASK NOTHIN' OF ME

SONG

WORDS AND MUSIC
BY

CHARLES EDISON

PRICE 35 CENTS

IN U.S.A.

Braun Music Co.
PUBLISHERS
1619 BROADWAY. N. Y.

Printed in U.S.A.

"Don't Ask Nothin' of Me," one of two published songs with words and music by Charles Edison. He composed many others as a hobby.

7

Apologia[*]

*A*N *APOLOGIA IS AN* apology with frills and can mean an admission of error accompanied by an expression of regret; or it can mean a desire to make clear grounds for some belief or course of action. It is within this latter context that I use the word. The good Lord knows I've made manifold mistakes in my lifetime, but I feel that future readers should be given the opportunity to understand in advance that, at least through my own eyes, my public career was not as vacillating as some critics have implied.

An overly constant mind can be so rock-ribbed as to produce intransigence. An overly inconstant mind can produce chaos.

"Foolish consistency," Emerson said, "is the hobgoblin of little minds." It does not necessarily follow that foolish inconsistency is the hobgoblin of big minds. I have encountered many so-called big minds in public life that were eerily inconsistent.

There was little in my background to hint that, from 1933 to 1944, I would for all practical purposes take a sabbatical from business in favor of public offices, appointive and elective, at both the federal and state levels. The onslaught of the Great Depression was the pivotal factor causing this change.

When the economic crash broke into the open in 1929, I was thirty-nine and, as president, the operating head of Thomas A. Edison Industries, a complex of diversified manufacturing enterprises based in large part on the inventions and scientific developments of my father.

---

*This chapter was set down by Charles Edison shortly before his passing on July 31, 1969. It was intended as a prefatory statement to that portion of his memoirs treating with his career in public office.

By training at M.I.T. I was an engineer; by predilection I was an administrator.

The gravity of the depression, which was worldwide in scope, fertilized seeds of social consciousness lying dormant, sometimes completely unsuspected, in the breasts of untold thousands of Americans. From adulthood forward, with the notable exception caused by admiration for Woodrow Wilson, I had practiced what might best be described as passive Republicanism. The Great Depression ended my passivity; and *Looking Forward,* a book by Franklin Delano Roosevelt published on the eve of his inauguration on March 4, 1933, as our thirty-second president, detoured me into the Democratic party, even though I had cast my vote only four months earlier for the reelection of President Hoover.

Looking Forward was essentially a recapitulation of positions taken by FDR on public issues during the campaign and of his earlier actions as governor of New York. Much of it was—and is—good reading. Some salient parts of the book, however, brought into bold focus the differences between what he said he stood for and what he ended up doing.

A professed admirer of Thomas Jefferson—and who isn't?—Mr. Roosevelt espoused the cause of states' rights in his book, but in the end his administration was responsible for the greatest concentration of power in Washington our nation had ever known.

Mr. Roosevelt stated, "We do not want the government in business"; yet by the end of his twelve-plus years as president, and even discounting the exigencies of World War II, government was deeper into business and exercising far greater control thereover than ever before.

President Roosevelt, at the outset, proclaimed that the "regular" costs of government must be pared, and once the economic depression was conquered, those irregular costs and controls necessary to this accomplishment should be phased out. Looking backward on his *Looking Forward,* one finds little in FDR's later actions and attitudes or, for that matter, in those of some of his successors, to enamor anyone who came to feel that the federal government, like a snowball rolling down a steep and endless slope, fed and fattened on its own momentum.

These lines of mine are not an appeal to turn back the clock. Rather, they are prologue to a hoped-for understanding of many of the whys and wherefores of my own activities during and subsequent to my ventures into public service. Should this recounting stimulate, even to some small degree, revised thinking or new approaches to any of the problems besetting our beloved nation, then it will have served as more than the whim of a member of the older generation who, as many others have done, has taken autobiographic pen in hand.

Autobiography, as contrasted to a day-by-day chronicling of events and attitudes such as might be set forth in a diary, has both its perils and its compensations. Autobiography is perilous in that memory and honesty of declaration are taxed almost beyond credibility. Its compensations lie in the leeway the form provides for retrospective evaluation of the whole—as contrasted with life's isolated component parts as they occur.

I am reminded of what was said by Benvenuto Cellini, the celebrated Florentine sculptor and goldsmith, when nearly 250 years ago he undertook to tell of his own career. He wrote:

> All men of whatsoever quality they be, who have done anything of excellence, or which may properly resemble excellence, ought, if they are persons of truth and honesty, to describe their life with their own hand; but they ought not to attempt so fine an enterprise until they have passed the age of forty. . . . Many untoward things can I remember, such as happen to all who live upon our earth. . . . I can also bring to mind some pleasant goods and inestimable evils which, when I turn my thoughts backward, strike terror in me. . . .

I lay no claim to excellence or that which may properly resemble excellence. But being almost twice forty, I am qualified at least in this respect, under Cellini's rules, for autobiographical effort. The "pleasant goods" of a lifetime conjure many happy recollections both of persons and events, but the "inestimable evils," if any, which came within my ken, fail to "strike terror in me."

Cellini also warned that in writing about oneself "there will always be found occasion for natural bragging." It should be easy for me to avoid this pitfall.

One does not want to turn back the clock nor for the time to stand still in its flight, but in this same metaphorical vein, I have often commented that the swing and sway of politics, and its effect on society, could be likened to a clock's pendulum. When the pendulum swings too far to the right—or to the left—counter forces should bring it back into proper synchronism. The pendulum should not be permitted to stop, however, for then the stilled hands of time congeal into an immutable status quo. Change—always, one hopes, for the better in the long pull—has characterized man since his primeval beginnings.

When Franklin Delano Roosevelt emerged from his party's national convention as the Democratic nominee for the presidency in 1932, the pendulum was far to the right, and had been so since the days of Wilson and Theodore Roosevelt. Big business had been riding high and wide but not so handsomely. The mighty leaders of industry and finance, with some notable exceptions, had little or no conception of the gravity of the times and even less understanding of what to do about it. President Hoover was no more the architect of the depression than was Marat the underlying cause of the French Revolution. Nevertheless, Hoover for many years, until the leavening action of time removed this unwarranted stigma, was made the archvillain of the era.

Over the years, my long acquaintanceship with Herbert Hoover ripened into a deep friendship, a friendship heightened on my part by strong admiration, which, at least to some degree, I believe, was reciprocated by Mr. Hoover. I am still convinced, however, that in 1933 Franklin Roosevelt was better able to meet the needs of our nation than Herbert Hoover would have been, not because of any lack of ability on Hoover's part, but, rather, because he would have been sorely restricted in planning any action by the forces and personalities then dominant in the Republican party. Whether such a conviction would have still held true eight, twelve, or more years later, what with changing times and a changed Roosevelt, is a question on which, a quarter century later, many have opinions but no one knows the answer for certain.

Few persons now under the age of fifty, unless they are students of the period or at least have listened intently to their elders, have any real comprehension of how deep and drastic were the effects of the Great Depression. Subsequent ups and downs in our economy have been mere ripples on a millpond compared with the surging, angry seas of want and privation during most of the Thirties. Self-proclaimed messiahs, each with his own panacea to peddle, were a dime a dozen. Factories and businesses, large and small, closed down by the thousands, or severely curtailed operations. Foreclosures of mortgaged homes and farms accelerated beyond belief as financial institutions pursued a will-o'-the-wisp solvency, all too often to discover that repossessed assets, having no market, were as valueless as the mortgage paper. Bank closings and a plummeting stock market wiped out the life savings of hundreds of thousands of families. Bread lines became a familiar sight in most urban areas. And, tragedy of tragedies, many Americans, including some important political leaders, began to lose faith in our form of government. Some in high places, including at least one United

States senator, spoke glowingly of Italy's Benito Mussolini and, by indirection, at least, implied that America's problems could only be solved by a dictatorship.

Even the name of Al Capone, lushly rich from the proceeds of his bootleg liquor and beer empire, was bruited about as presidential timber by a handful of possibly well-meaning crackpots who, blinded by their own fears, could not, or would not, look beyond Capone's "soup kitchens" for Chicago's indigents into the sordid world of rackets and murder that made his largesse possible.

With such fears prevalent in the land, small wonder that America elected a man who could cock his head, tilt his elongated cigaret holder, fix his smile, and say, "The only thing we have to fear is fear itself."

Any number of things other than the gradual erosion of principles I sensed in President Roosevelt contributed to my equally gradual disillusionment with the Democratic party. There was, among the Democratic "ins," a growing lust for power which frequently concealed itself behind a facade of humanitarianism.

In this respect, I am reminded of an incident that occurred during my years as assistant secretary of the navy, later as secretary, under Roosevelt. The navy's important armor plate mill in Charleston, West Virginia, had been long unused and was threatened with abandonment for lack of work. The lengthening shadows of approaching war made this unthinkable; and since the Navy Department had no funds available for use there, I approached Aubrey Williams, director of the federal government's National Youth Administration, with the idea of using the facilities as a school for training young men in heavy mechanical skills. This, I thought, not only would preserve the installation for later use in building the ships that unquestionably would be needed, but in the interim it would provide valuable training for hundreds of the unemployed. Williams cottoned to the suggestion, although he was something less than enthusiastic when I proposed that the necessary federal funds be disbursed locally in the interest of efficiency and economy.

"Charlie," Williams said to me, "you just don't get the idea. If we can get enough millions of persons getting checks directly from Washington, whether for things like this, for school lunches, or you name it, they'll never get us out of office."

The training program was activated, and the armor plate installation later resumed regular operations in support of the preparedness effort. But the checks went out from Washington. To some it may be all right to ride the devil's back if the purpose of crossing the river is a good one, but I have never become reconciled to such a philosophy.

One obvious approach to combating increasing centralized authority in Washington was, and is, to revivify and strengthen the role of state governments. The better the job the states do, the less excuse there is for stringent federal control. So it was with some degree of satisfaction that circumstances presented me with the opportunity in 1940 to run and win election as governor of New Jersey. My goal, an ambitious one to say the least, was to make New Jersey's state government a model for all other states to emulate, hopefully thereby to stem, or at least slow down, the flow of power to the federal government.

These circumstances were rooted in FDR's desire to demonstrate to the world at large, and to Hitler and the Axis powers in particular, that the United States was united behind what has been called "our neutrality in favor of England and her Allies." One of the methods employed by the president to accomplish this was to remold his cabinet into a bipartisan body. Frank W. Knox, the Chicago publisher who had been the Republican vice-presidential nominee in the 1936 election, succeeded me as secretary of the navy in August of 1940. Henry L. Stimson, who had been secretary of state in Hoover's Republican administration, was named secretary of war to replace Harry R. Woodring. Alfred Landon, the G.O.P.'s 1936 standard-bearer, originally was offered the post of secretary of war, but the conditions for acceptance he laid down were unacceptable to Roosevelt. Thus, by these moves, President Roosevelt placed minority party members in the two Cabinet posts most closely involved in international affairs, excluding, of course, the office of secretary of state, which Cordell Hull continued to hold.

With FDR as head of the Democratic party's 1940 national ticket, and with the reluctant support of Frank Hague's Democratic organization, I was elected New Jersey's governor over Republican State Senator Robert C. Hendrickson by a plurality of 64,000 votes, a margin considered to be somewhere between slim and comfortable. It was no landslide. FDR carried New Jersey by 72,000 votes over Wendell Willkie.

No discussion of New Jersey politics of that period can be meaningful without reference to Frank Hague. Although his highest elective office was that of being the perennial mayor of Jersey City, the state's second largest city, Hague's influence within the Democratic party at all levels was highly disproportionate to just being the mayor of a city of 300,000.

He was a vice-chairman of the Democratic National Committee; and, strange as it may seem to the uninitiated, he exercised a strong but muted voice in the afairs of New Jersey's Republican party.

I offer the following as being somewhere between typical and atypical of this interparty byplay. One of my Republican predecessors as governor of New Jersey, Harold G. Hoffman, who was a master quipster, tried to write off his own *sub rosa* entente with Hague by saying, "To me he's like Haig & Haig; I can take him or leave him alone." This was true up to a point, because Harold controlled any affinity he may have had for Scotland's Haig & Haig, but prior to his death as an admitted defalcator of state funds, he had played a brash game of political "footsies" with Hague and Hague's machine.

President Roosevelt, as part of his plan for bimetalizing his cabinet, had asked me to run for New Jersey's governorship. He said he could promise me Hague's support. I, in turn, told the president I would run for the office, and not refuse Hague's support, provided there was an advance understanding that Hague would stick to his knitting in Hudson County, of which Jersey City is the county seat, while I functioned as governor of the State. Thus it was that, throughout the campaign, the Charles Edison camp maintained a state campaign headquarters separate from the party's regular state headquarters.

I am as certain of Romeo's love for Juliet as I was of Hague's lack of political love for me. I was a candidate little to his liking, but one who was satisfactory to the president and who was available at a time when Hague's old-time wheelhorse, A. Harry Moore, was not. Unfortunately for Hague, New Jersey's then century-old constitution forbade a governor to succeed himself, and Harry Moore was finishing up the last of his three three-year nonconsecutive terms.

Later, when someone bold enough to inquire asked him why I wouldn't bend to his will, "Boss" Hague reportedly replied, "That deaf little SOB only hears what he wants to hear." But the whole story of my running battles with Hague is reserved for later. Sufficient for the time that I merely point to the woes of a Democratic governor trying to clean up and modernize a state with a Tweed-type boss in command of his party's apparatus and with tentacles of power reaching deep into the party of the opposition.

Judicial reform, tax reform, and a broad overhauling of the antiquated state constitution formed a part of my campaign promises to New Jersey's electorate. Another pledge made by me included freedom from bossism, which, I can say, was accepted with several grains of salt by thousands of Hague's faithful, to whom such promises were an old, old story. How well, or how poorly, I performed during my three-year term has been the subject of partisan, nonpartisan, bipartisan, superpartisan, and sometimes superficial, controversy. In my own mind, the record of those three years was one of some accomplishment, some defeats. But best of all, I left the office with the feeling that at least in some small measure decency in government had been given a boost, not so much by anything I did or didn't do, but rather by the many fine men and women who responded to my pleas for greater public participation. The man-in-the-street had reason to believe that politics in New Jersey were at least a little less tawdry than they had been before.

When my term as governor expired in January of 1944, I welcomed, for selfish reasons of home and business, New Jersey's then constitutional restriction against self-succession. Never again did I seriously bid for elective office, although once, in the early Fifties, I toyed with the idea of becoming an independent candidate for the governorship. That was, however, essentially a maneuver to encourage certain actions and reactions within the established parties. I never had to make good on my threat to run, if threat is a proper word to use.

Subsequently, with the exception of occasional service on quasi-official bodies such as the Hoover Commission on Reorganization of the Federal Government, my activities relating to public affairs were channeled in the main through nonpartisan organizations such as the National Municipal League, the Committee of One Million (against the Admission of Red China into the United Nations), and other comparable groups. Also, in varying degrees of involvement, I have supported certain Democratic candidates, certain Republican candidates, and certain Independents, almost all of whom were dedicated conservatives. Irrespective of any good I may have accomplished, I have felt repaid by the things I have learned, things such as that "liberal" and "conservative" can be synonyms or antonyms, depending upon who speaks the words—that any basic difference between Democrat and Republican is infinitesimal, if, indeed, any difference exists—and that "progress" can not be defined in terms of taller buildings, larger companies, bigger unions, greater budgets, etc., *ad infinitum.* Some way, somehow, somewhere along the line, values more worthy than sheer bigness must gain ascendancy if the tomorrows are to be better than the todays and yesterdays. I believe that good tomorrows will win out in the end.

The future belongs not to septuagenarians such as I. Rather, America's destiny resides in the restlessness and strivings of the young. The good of the past should be preserved, but to the exclusion of old second-rate, or worse, values and practices.

In the words of George Santayana, "Those who cannot remember the past are condemned to repeat it!"

8

Depression Reflections *

THE GREAT DEPRESSION, which broke into the open with the stock market crash in 1929, and the election of Franklin D. Roosevelt to the presidency in November of 1932 were two of the most important factors that led me to divert my attention from running the Thomas A. Edison Industries to taking a more active part in public affairs. Politically, I had a background of Republicanism. I voted for Herbert Hoover in the 1932 election. But the sweeping changes initiated by FDR after his inauguration on March 4 of 1933, coupled with my reading of his book *Looking Forward,* spurred me into direct action.

Prior to the 1932 election, in the late spring and early summer of that year, I made a six-week swing around the nation in an attempt to assess the depth and breadth of the business depression, and to determine what progress, if any, was being made toward recovery. As president of the Edison Industries since 1926, and with an increased burden of responsibility since Father's passing in October of 1931, this cross-country sampling of the economic climate was most illuminating. Arthur Walsh, a vice-president of the Edison Industries, made the trip with me. A spirit of defeatism pervaded much of the East, particularly in and around New York City. This defeatism lessened the farther west we went. Starting in St. Louis and westward through Oklahoma, Texas, the Pacific Northwest, and elsewhere, our contacts with business leaders both big and small reflected an optimism for the future even though immediate effects of the depression were as apparent as in the East.

At the risk of seeing levity in conditions of despair, I am reminded of what an official of a mining center in Montana told us. "Things are so

---

*Written in 1969 by Charles Edison in conjunction with the author.

102

bad," he reported, "that even the prostitutes are applying for relief." Arthur and I, may I be quick to add, regarded this as an economic commentary rather than as social news.

A summary of my reactions to the trip appeared under date of July 3, 1932, in the *New York Times* as follows:

EDISON SEES SLUMP DEFEATED IN WEST

West Orange, N. J.—Belief that the bottom of the business depression had been reached was expressed today by Charles Edison, son of Thomas A. Edison and head of Edison Industries, Inc., following the return to his home here from a six weeks' tour of the United States.

"If the East had the pioneer spirit of the West," Mr. Edison said, "I believe I am sure in stating that business would return to normal at a faster rate. In the West I found that businessmen in that section who have taken it on the chin came back fighting for more, and as a result licked the depression to a frazzle. They are now on the way up.

"East of the Mississippi River, I found that businessmen, to some extent, are still bemoaning their fate in the business world but are more optimistic about the future than they were several months ago. New York City is the zero point, the gloomiest spot in the business world. In my estimation, New York City businessmen are too busy watching the ticker tape."

In retrospect, perhaps I was a little too optimistic about prospects for a quick economic recovery; but our findings on this trip, which covered 10,000 miles and 400 places, at least had the beneficial effect back at the Edison Industries of focusing our sights on the future instead of merely bewailing business conditions.

Two weeks before the general election of 1932, although playing an inactive role in the campaign, I took it upon myself to urge the Edison Company's several thousand employees to vote, irrespective of their political persuasions, an attitude not pursued by many industrial leaders of the times, nor by union bigwigs. In bulletin board announcements and in the public press, I reminded them that "under the Constitution of the United States every citizen has the right to vote according to his own ideas and opinions and without coercion and interference from others. For this reason the Thomas A. Edison Industries, as a business institution, have no political faith. They are neutral politically. They support no one party any more than they support any other party. Furthermore, we do not follow the practice of opening up our buildings to the representatives of any party for political purposes such as speech making and electioneering.

"However, we are desirous of having our people take a personal interest in political matters to the extent that they will vote and that they will exercise good judgment when they vote. For this reason we usually cooperate with any party representatives who desire to address our people or who desire to distribute pamphlets, provided they do so outside the company's buildings, in an orderly manner, and in such a way as not to interfere with the ordinary operation of business.''

In a small way, I was starting to think about public affairs and the democratic process.

A month later, on November 20, 1932, mindful of the widespread bitterness engendered by the Roosevelt-Hoover election, I wrote anew to our employees, urging them to "forget politics and the heat of the last campaign" for the common good of the country. "The election is over," I said, "and the result cannot be changed. The battle was ended when the ballots were counted. Now it is time for everybody to buckle down and get down to hard work."

"Our country needs criticism based on intelligence," I added, "and not on heated political emotions."

The bank moratorium FDR declared at the very outset of his administration seemed to me to be a highly necessary step to help restore some sort of order and confidence during a period when bank failures were almost daily topics in the headlines. President Roosevelt, on March 6, 1933, two days after he took office, closed the banks for an indefinite period, which turned out, however, to be just five days. Like other companies, the Edison Industries found themselves short of liquid assets at the time of the moratorium; so we did something about it. Working through the local chamber of commerce and with the cooperation of local merchants, our company issued its own paper money, called scrip, to meet its payrolls. This private paper money was issued in denominations of $1, $2, $5, and $10, bore the likeness of Thomas A. Edison, and carried a promise of redemption in full five days after the end of the bank holiday, or any time thereafter. According to press reports, we were the only company in New Jersey, and perhaps in the nation, to take such action.

Our employees were delighted to receive the scrip, and the local merchants unhesitatingly honored it. Redemption at full value followed on schedule. Although publicity was not my reason for deciding to issue scrip, it certainly did result in a lot of favorable publicity both locally and nationally.

A somewhat humorous sidelight of this scrip episode is that the Edison Industries ended up making a little profit on it. Some of the employees, those with some ready cash on hand, I assume, treasured the scrip as souvenirs and never cashed in all of theirs. Percentagewise, the uncashed scrip was small indeed. I do not recommend this as a method of making a profit.

As a businessman just starting to wet his feet in the eddying pools of public affairs, I felt there were at least two areas in which I might prove helpful. Number one was to direct our company in a manner consistent with the immediate needs of our economically depressed nation; and number two—this was not to start until a little later—was to serve in some public capacity, whether at the local, state, or federal level. As a consequence, the Edison Industries undertook a variety of activities, in addition to issuing scrip, intended to bolster the public spirit as well as the public economy.

In late March of 1933 the company launched a campaign, both among our employees and among the public at large, to encourage private spending. One of the devices we employed was a cartoonlike picture showing an amalgam of workers pulling together on an imaginary rope, which represented the sagging economy, trying to restore the economy to normality. The headline read, "President Roosevelt Has Done His Part—Now YOU Do Something!" Accompanying the cartoon was this further text: "Buy Something . . . Buy Anything—Anywhere . . . Paint Your Kitchen . . . Send a Telegram . . . Give a Party . . . Get a Car . . . Pay a Bill . . . Rent a Flat . . . Fix Your Roof . . . Get a Haircut . . . See a Show . . . Build a House . . . Take a Trip . . . Sing a Song . . . Get Married. It doesn't matter what you do—only get going. The old world is beginning to move."

Later that year, in October, our company backed this up with an even more direct approach. As our part in a broad "Now Is the Time to Buy" campaign, we presented each of our 3,000 employees, regardless of his or her job, with a check for $5 and this message:

"President Roosevelt is doing his part. NRA was the first step in his great recovery program. The 'Now Is The Time To Buy' campaign, now being conducted, is the second great step. I urge all members of our organization to support it to the limit of their ability. Start with buying something with this check—something that you would not have bought unless you received it."

If memory serves correctly, I even presented myself as company president with a check for $5.

A year or so later, in support of the federal government's efforts to energize the building trades, the Edison Industries initiated a modernization program costing $500,000—big money during those dark days.

Very early in Roosevelt's first term the National Recovery Administration with the Blue Eagle as its symbol came into being, one of the first of the alphabetical agencies soon to proliferate in Washington. One feature of the NRA was the creation of State Recovery Boards, whose members were appointed by the various state governors. New Jersey's governor, A. Harry Moore, selected Colonel J. Lester Eisner, a Red Bank clothing manufacturer, as chairman of our State Recovery Board. Moore chose two vice-chairmen—Harry L. Tepper, a Newark lawyer, and me. That was in August of 1933.

Those were hectic days. Colonel Eisner's headquarters were in Newark, at the Industrial Building on South Broad Street. Events were moving so rapidly and areas of responsibility were so loosely delineated, that one was never quite sure today what he might be doing tomorrow.

As an example, the office space assigned to me on the first day I met with Colonel Eisner was occupied by a couple of strangers when I got back from lunch. He assigned me new offices, but these, too, were preempted by the following day. So, rather than become enmeshed in red tape and bickering, I personally rented a small office in the same building to maker certain that I had my own desk, chair, and file cabinet.

Harry Tepper, whom I have always considered to be a fine man, and I weren't absolutely sure just what our duties were, but we wasted no time getting busy. One of the facets of NRA was the creation of codes for different industries. These codes established minimum hours and wages and were also intended to control selling prices. Naturally, this brought on a rash of management-labor grievances. So Harry and I set out on a merry-go-round of hastily held meetings with dissident parties. Our theory was that if disputes were allowed to fester for days or weeks, then their susceptibility to settlement lessened in geometric proportion because of the bitterness that the passage of time could engender. We would dash to trouble spots and conduct on-the-spot hearings, not always according to strict parliamentary procedure, I fear. Or, if indicated by the facts, we might summon the disputants to our Newark headquarters, both of us, Tepper and me, keeping tongue in cheek because we weren't sure that a summons on our part was enforceable. But neither were the battling parties sure; so they usually showed up.

Labor disputes are, of course, serious matters; but they are not always without humorous angles. Such was the case when a group of shochtim, those men whose blessings precede the slaughter of animals intended for the kosher trade, decided that, like other groups in Newark, they, too, needed a union to help guarantee minimum hours and wages. The shochtim's dispute was with the wholesalers of beef and poultry. Harry Tepper and I "subpoenaed" the warring factions to our offices. Fortunately, they decided to honor our summons. The black-garbed, bearded shochtim, a dozen in number and looking not unlike the twelve biblical disciples, plus a sizable contingent of kosher wholesalers, were just too many for our meager-sized "courtroom" to accommodate; so we asked each side to reduce its ranks by designating representatives to act on their behalf.

Harry Tepper, who was Jewish, held a distinct advantage over me in this case. At least he had some appreciation of the ritualism involved. In my naiveté I asked a shochet why it was considered necessary to bless a chicken before it was slaughtered for market, to which he replied, "It permits the chicken to die happy"—a not-so-kosher answer, I suspect.

Because Harry Tepper was the "expert" in this particular case, he was assigned the questionable honor of giving the decision. Harry ruled that since the shochtim were holy men, they were ineligible for unionization.

The case of the underpaid "chicken pluckers" was another hot potato, if I may mix my metaphors. These chicken pluckers, all Negroes, unquestionably were being exploited by the white retailers and wholesalers of dressed poultry in one of Newark's roughest, toughest areas. The pluckers' efforts to improve their lot were being rebuffed by the employers, no holds barred. Tactics such as the throwing of stink bombs were not unknown.

Despite warnings from Newark detectives that we were asking for trouble if we intervened, Tepper and I decided to see what we could do about settling the dispute. We summoned both sides to our South Broad Street headquarters.

Testimony revealed that for something like a ninety-hour, seven-day week, the pluckers were being paid $6 and a few cents in change. Even for the depths of the depression, such an amount was unconscionably low. And since the applicable NRA code called for no more than forty hours a week, with minimum wages of $12.50, which was the equivalent of thirty-one and a fraction cents per hour, Harry and I were prepared to rule that the NRA standards should apply. Imagine our surprise when the chicken pluckers' union spokesman called us aside to say that if we tried to enforce the NRA formula the employers would be "busted" and there would be no jobs at all. He suggested a six-day, fifty-six-hour week, at $12.50.

Harry and I realized this would be blinking at legality, but we decided to go along. However, that still left one of the knottiest problems unsolved. The employers not only distrusted the chicken pluckers, they distrusted one another; and the pluckers were equally distrustful of everybody. Questioning by Tepper and me finally brought out the fact that there was a poultry wholesaler—his name escapes my memory—who was *persona grata* to both sides. So Harry and I appointed him the "czar" to see to it that terms of this somewhat illegal arrangement were lived up to.

A recurring problem of the times was that the more honorable employers, while personally willing to abide by NRA standards, justifiably insisted that their competitors also be forced to comply. Unless this was done, they argued, complying employers could be forced to the wall by unfair competition from the chiselers. Our problem, to put it simply, was that there wasn't enough manpower to police everyone, even if we had authority to do so, which was extremely doubtful.

I'm reminded of a case in point that occurred in the little town of Manville, New Jersey. There, a small manufacturer of ladies' dresses, a Cuban, was trying his best to maintain NRA minima, but he kept running up against situations such as this: a fly-by-night operator would rent a loft, move in a number of sewing machines, and then advertise for women to run them. The fly-by-night would promise the women that once they became sufficiently adept they could make good wages under a piece-rate system to be installed later. In the meantime, being an "altruistic" fellow at heart, he would pay them a couple of dollars a week as learners. After a couple of weeks, when he no longer could put them off, he'd put the women on piece rates, explaining, however, that it was "company policy" to withhold their first week's wages until such time as they left their jobs. Then, at the end of the second piece-rate week, a truck would pull up behind the loft building in the dead of night, be surreptitiously loaded with the sewing machines, finished dresses, and raw materials, and then spirited away to some other loft in some other town, where the whole process would be repeated. Needless to say, the women received only a pittance for their first several weeks of work and nothing for their final two weeks.

Those were restless days indeed. From August through December of

1933, my appointment calendar shows almost daily NRA conferences or hearings, covering scores of different cases, details of which for the most part have blended into a oneness over the intervening thirty-five years.

The NRA, like many other of the mushrooming agencies of the New Deal, was created under the broad aegis of the National Industrial Recovery Act (NIRA), a keystone piece of legislation enacted during Roosevelt's "first 100 days," as history has termed this dramatic and eventful period. Napoleon's Hundred Days, between Elba and St. Helena, were no more world-shaking by comparison.

In an effort to provide stature and better defined authority for the labor-management activities of the State Recovery Board, the New Jersey Regional Labor Board, another NIRA offshoot, was organized in November of 1933 as an eleven-member body chaired by Prof. David A. McCabe, of Princeton University. Harry Tepper and I were the vice-chairmen. Other members were Edward D. Duffield, of Newark, president of the Prudential Insurance Company of America; Theodore Boettger, of Lodi, president of the United Piece Dye Works; Clinton L. Bardo, of Camden, president of the New York Shipbuilding Company; Peter A. Smith, of East Orange, treasurer of A.P. Smith and Company; Thomas B. Eames, of Millville, president of the New Jersey Federation of Labor; Louis Marciante, of Trenton, president of the Mercer County Central Labor Union; John J. Hart, of Newark, president of the Typographical Union, Local 103; and John J. Dowd, of Jersey City, of the Workmen's Compensation Commission. Organizationally, we were better equipped to perform our assigned duties of mediating labor-management disagreements; but from a practical viewpoint, I couldn't help but feel that, on many occasions at least, delays brought on by increased red tape made our efforts much less effective than during the preceding two to three months when Harry Tepper and I, almost literally, were operating out of our hats.

Somewhat parenthetically, I'd like to mention that as early as April of 1934 several overly kind New Jersey newspapers mentioned me as a possible candidate for the Democratic nomination for United States senator. The mention may have been flattering; but as far as I was concerned, I had no intention then, or later, of trying to become a member of what some wits have described as the "world's most exclusive club."

Events following Roosevelt's "first 100 days" kept up their feverish pace. In January of 1934 I was named compliance director for the NRA in New Jersey and state director for the New Jersey Division of the

National Emergency Council (NEC). The NEC and its counterparts in the various states exercised planning, coordinating, and administrative functions over and for many New Deal agencies. By May of 1934, these fast-moving events whisked me from New Jersey to Washington, where the NEC, under Frank C. Walker, later to become postmaster general, was seeking ways and means to stimulate an important segment of the American economy, the construction industry. On my arrival in the nation's capital, Walker told me in so many words that my task was to "dream up something that will get the construction trades back in gear and open up the mortgage market."

A somewhat nebulous assignment, I admit, but it was not as obscure to me as Walker's next immediate set of instructions. He told me the first thing I had to do was to find a million dollars to carry on the project, which, like any governmental undertaking, would require office space, personnel, etc. As a neophyte on the Washington scene finding a million dollars for something that had not even been thought of yet seemed to me like the insurmountable mountain. But those were free-wheeling days; so as a starter, I made an appointment to see the director of the budget, Lewis W. Douglas, a man who looked askance at some of the government's spending practices, somewhat as I did.

On entering his office, I haltingly set forth my case, which went something like this: "Mr. Douglas, I've just been brought down here from New Jersey to help dream up ideas for stimulating the construction trades and the mortgage market. Frank Walker tells me we'll need a million dollars to get the show on the road. I'm here today to ask you just how I should go about getting this much money."

Mr. Douglas looked at me, stroked his chin, gazed off into space, and then replied: "Mr. Edison, everybody else in this madhouse is getting such sums; so there is no reason we can't find a million dollars for you."

With this assurance, I went back to the real problem of my assignment under Frank Walker. And when I say "I went back," let me explain that in this narration, with appropriate exceptions, the use of "we" instead of "I" probably would be more accurate, as frequently many other persons were involved. For example, my compatriot from the Edison Industries, the ubiquitous Arthur Walsh, came down to Washington to lend a hand. Then there were such men as Eugene S ("Red") Leggett, bless his soul, a staff man whose talents were many and whose loyalty and enthusiasm were beyond example. There also were many others.

The impelling and appealing idea born out of hours of thought and

110

conference turned out to be what became known as the Federal Housing Administration (FHA). Other housing agencies already had been created, the Home Owners Loan Corporation being an example; but the HOLC was only designed to lift the burden of the high interest rates of the opulent 1920s from the sorely beset mortgagors of the 1930s still saddled with those high rates. By contrast, the FHA was intended not only to stimulate the construction trades by opening up the mortgage market; it was to function as an insurer of mortgages, operating through regular banking channels, on a self-liquidating basis. This insurance feature required banks to lower their interest rates and pay a fraction thereof to the government in return for the privilege of having repayment of their loans guaranteed by the government. The FHA was designed specifically to avoid being just another giver of governmental handouts.

This incipient legislation occasioned my first appearance before a Committee of the Congress. The date was May 24, 1934. It was the Committee on Banking and Currency of the U.S. Senate, of which Sen. Duncan Upshaw Fletcher, Florida Democrat, was chairman. In my testimony I described the pending FHA bill as "the most important part of the (recovery) program left."

"Unless we solve this problem," I said, "we are going to face next winter the most staggering problem of unemployment in those industries that we have yet faced."

Shortly thereafter the FHA was enacted into law, not just because of my testimony, naturally, but essentially because at the time, under the conditions existing, it was good legislation. The fact that the FHA originally was intended as emergency legislation, designed to meet specific needs for a limited period of economic depression, may easily be overlooked three-plus decades later, when, by some strangeness of political reasoning, our nation is still using antideflation pills to try to cure inflationitis.

[An updated opinion of the worth of the FHA was offered by eminent economist Eliot Janeway in the December, 1976, issue of the magazine *Business*. Mr. Janeway wrote: "Roosevelt's New Deal met the crying need to make homeowning cheap and safe. The most effective of Roosevelt's reforms worked out to be the one that enabled the greatest number of voters to make the most money for themselves: the Federal Housing Administration. It financed long-term mortgages on low down payments."]

If the preceding paragraphs make it appear the formulation of the

111

FHA legislation and its introduction and passage were easy and n
fraught with maneuvering and intrigue, then my recounting
deficient. Let me elaborate. Washington in those days—and, I assume
also in these—was a bubbling cauldron of machination. Frank Walke
a smart and levelheaded man in my book, was doing the best job I
could as head of the National Emergency Council. He not only had th
ear of the president, but he was in close contact with most members
Roosevelt's Cabinet, including the "back door" variety, reminiscent
Andrew Jackson's "Kitchen Cabinet" of a hundred years earlie
Harry Hopkins was one who qualified as *a*, if not *the*, prime member
Roosevelt's "back door Cabinet."

Unofficially, it was pretty well understood that Hopkins would hea
up the FHA once appropriate legislation was formulated and enacte
into law. Although unquestionably brilliant in many respects, Hopkin
as a behind-the-scenes manipulator, operated in devious ways.

Unbeknownst to me or Frank Walker—and presumably to Preside
Roosevelt, too—Hopkins was clandestinely assembling a staff to dire
the FHA even before the legislation was passed, a staff that w
duplicative of Walker's and mine. Furthermore, he was doing th
when, without any doubt in my mind, he had no intention of ev
openly running the FHA show, even though the assignment probab
could have been his for the asking. Hopkins' irregular metho
eventually led to an amusing confrontation between me and James A
("Jimmy") Moffett, who ended up as the first director of FHA in pla
of Hopkins but presumably with his blessing. More about this later.

In the meantime, Washington greenhorn that I was, passage of th
FHA legislation was not going smoothly, at least to my way of thinkin
Several members of the Congress, one of them extremely powerfu
within committee councils, were outspokenly opposed on the mistake
grounds that FHA was just another "give-away." The most recalcitra
member of the opposition was a senator, who was proving to be a re
stumbling block; so I talked the problem over with Frank Watson, leg
advisor to the NEC's housing committee. Watson, a young, smart an
intrepid operator, was one of the Harvard men known collectively :
Justice Felix Frankfurter's "boys." As a result, I drafted a set
arguments to refute, or at least rebut, the good senator's position. M
plan was to submit these arguments to him in person. Imagine m
surprise when, a day or two later and before I could contact the senato
Washington newspapers carried an announcement from the senator
office that he now favored the FHA bill and for the very reasons I ha
enumerated.

112

Far be it from me to suggest that Frank Watson had anything to do with this senatorial change-of-heart, but I was given to understand that it would not be politic for me to congratulate the senator on his revised opinion of FHA because maybe his reported about-face would be denied by him anyway, and why run the risk of compromising a contact within the senator's staff known to be a close friend of Frank Watson? Suffice it to say, the legislation passed.

Now to get back to Jimmy Moffett. Shortly thereafter he became the first Federal Housing administrator, to the surprise of many who thought the job would go to Hopkins. Moffett, on the few occasions we had met, had been extremely cool to me. It was as though neither Frank Walker nor I had had anything to do with the creation of FHA. He apparently had been led to believe that Hopkins and his "secret" staff had done all the work and if Walker and I had done anything, it had been more harmful than helpful. Moffett felt the need for holding a conference on FHA matters in New York City; and I, now back in New Jersey after my Washington stint under Walker, attended. It was at that conference that Moffett learned for the first time the actual roles played by Walker and me. His coolness ended abruptly, and almost immediately thereafter I was named the FHA regional director for the states of New Jersey, Pennsylvania, Delaware, and Maryland. That was on August 13, 1934. Moffett, an ex-oil man, and I remained friends for many years.

As regional FHA director, a position which required being the state director for New Jersey, my assignment was essentially that of promotion, of "selling" the merits of modernizing old homes and plants, of building new ones, and in helping to establish local FHA offices in cities, towns, and counties. By November 30 of 1934 the job was pretty well in hand, and I resumed my old duties as the New Jersey state director of the NEC.

The year 1935, like the preceding two of Roosevelt's first administration, was one of eventful activity for the nation as a whole and for me as an individual. The federal government had embarked on so many new ventures in so many different areas that I, like the NEC directors in other states, had trouble just keeping track of the alphabetical creations while, one hopes, helping to coordinate their activities. Any huge crash program such as undertaken during the early New Deal days could not be expected to operate flawlessly. Actually, I was surprised that this potpourri of agencies functioned as effectively as they did. In several areas, the higher-ups in Washington were beginning to take time to reexamine and reevaluate the various programs.

This trend toward reexamination resulted once again in my returning to Washington on a special but temporary assignment.

President Roosevelt, on April 26, 1935, appointed me to the National Industrial Recovery Board, of which Donald R. Richberg was the director. I succeeded Arthur D. Whiteside, president of Dun and Bradstreet, who had resigned; and my appointment by prearrangement with Mr. Roosevelt was to extend only until July 1, after which I would resume as the NEC head for New Jersey.

Along with Mr. Richberg, other members of NIRB and I launched upon our immediate assignment, that of studying weaknesses in the overall NRA setup and suggesting remedies. Little did we know that just one month later, on May 27, the United States Supreme Court would declare unconstitutional the National Industrial Recovery Act upon which the whole NRA operation relied for its authority. Some of the NIRB members and I were in the courtroom that day when the justices announced their decision in the case known as *Schechter Poultry Corporation* v. *The United States of America.* In essence, the ruling was that extraordinary conditions (to wit, the Great Depression) do not create or enlarge constitutional power and cannot justify governmental action outside the sphere of constitutional authority. That the ruling was a bombshell is an understatement.

Richberg, other NIRB members, and staff assistants, individually and severally, rushed feverishly to work, trying to draft new legislation that would overcome the court's objections. In fact, everybody and his brother, inside and outside the government structure, scurried to get into the act, including both union and industrial leaders. Lights in our offices burned throughout the night. Richberg arranged an early emergency meeting with the president to chart a course of action.

When the NIRA members assembled in the White House, each of us except one, took turns expressing opinions. Summed up, they all agreed that something should be done Now, with a capital N. Richberg finally turned to the president and, pointing to me, suggested that my views would be welcomed, although he didn't think they would coincide with his. They didn't. For better or worse, I said that new jerry-built legislation thrown together in manic heat and haste probably would be no better than the original legislation. I suggested a waiting period of several months so that all facets of the problem could be thoroughly digested, analyzed, and corrected.

Keeping mum about his own feelings, President Roosevelt thanked us for our opinions and said he would announce the administration's official viewpoint later the same day. So at the appropriate hour our NIRB group assembled around a Western Union teleprinter to get first word of the president's position. I would be less than honest if I didn't admit to being pleased when the president advised against undue haste and proposed a wait-and-see approach almost in the same words I had used.

One NIRB member, on reading the teletyped message, growled something to the effect that "we've been double-crossed again," and stomped out of the room. Parts of what had constituted the NIRA were never reassembled as new legislation. A notable exception was that section dealing with labor's right to bargain collectively. This section, known as 7(a), was pieced together, enlarged upon, and rushed through the Congress as the National Labor Relations Act, commonly known as the Wagner Act in honor of its sponsor, the late Sen. Robert F. Wagner. The Wagner Act became law on July 5, 1935, less than six weeks after the Blue Eagle had been shot down by the Supreme Court.

After my short-lived stay in Washington, I returned to New Jersey to my old NEC post; and for the first time in my life, events made it necessary for me seriously to consider running—or not running—for elective office. The office in question was that of United States senator, and the man who forced me into making a decision was Frank Hague, New Jersey's Democratic boss. Years later he was to be a protagonist turned antagonist who, by any method known to gutter politicians, tried to ruin me politically, financially, and characterwise. Fortunately for me, Hague failed in this latter-day battle. But that is another story in itself.

In late 1935 New Jersey's Democrats began casting around for a candidate to run against incumbent Republican Senator W. Warren Barbour, whose try for reelection would come up in 1936. My name started cropping up in political columns as a logical opponent. Attributes assigned to me included my being an industrialist in an industrial state, a person acceptable to the White House, a reasonably well known public figure because of my NEC and related activities, and—let's face it—a son of Thomas A. Edison. This speculation led to the one and only time that Frank Hague was in my home in Llewellyn Park, West Orange.

Dinner guests that evening of December 9, 1935, in addition to Mayor and Mrs. Hague, included seven or eight friends of my wife, Carolyn, and mine. The story of that evening has never been told publicly before.

Hague, stern-visaged and imperious, used that occasion to corner me outside the earshot of others to "offer" me the Democratic nomination for the United States Senate. One thing that he did not understand, among many other things, was that I had arrived at a predetermined decision not to be a candidate, then or later, for an office in which I would serve as a member of a large body, such as the Senate or the House of Representatives. This was not because I wanted to run a one-man show; rather, it was because of faulty hearing.

Since childhood, following a siege of typhoid fever, I suffered from a degree of deafness which, as I grew older, became more pronounced. Working with, or conferring with, individuals or small groups was not a great problem. But large chambers, of varying acoustical properties, filled with many voices, left me at a distinct disadvantage, even with the help of a hearing aid.*

One of Hague's mannerisms when he wanted to put over a point consisted of rigidly extending the index finger of his right hand and punching it soundly against the chest of his "victim"—an irksome, if not painful, form of physical punctuation. Even after I explained to him why I chose not to be a candidate, Hague persisted; and, with his extended finger tattooing my chest, he said, "This is Frank Hague asking you. Me, Frank Hague. People don't say no to me."

People did. At least I did.

Later that evening Hague drew Mrs. Edison aside and tried his persuasive powers on her, even to the point of the extended-finger routine. Carolyn was equally disinterested in my running.

---

*On more than one occasion, Charles Edison amplified to this author-collaborator on his lack of interest, because of faulty hearing, in running for the U.S. Senate. "It's one thing to operate as the governor of a state or to head a corporation," he said, in so many words, "because most of one's activities are either in face-to-face meetings with individuals or with small groups, or through correspondence. With my hearing aid—and sometimes without it—I usually can get a clear understanding of what is being said by an individual or by members of a small group. But in a large body such as the Senate, I would be lost." Like his father, Thomas, Charles became increasingly deaf as he grew older. One of the widely printed versions of the origin of Thomas' deafness—and the verson supported by Thomas himself during the late years of his life—was that a trainman on the Grand Trunk Railroad, running between Detroit and Port Huron, Michigan, had picked young Tom up by the ears to help him board a moving train. Medical opinion, as reported by Matthew Josephson in his biography *Edison,* held that the aftereffects of scarlatina probably were the underlying cause, even if the story of the grabbed ears was true. Even though Charles thought his hearing loss stemmed from typhoid fever, there is also the hypothesis that it was an inherited trait brought to acuteness by some accident or illness.

Concurrently, I was, as NEC director for New Jersey, seeking ways to dramatize the activities and services of all the varied federal and federal-state agencies, both New Deal and pre-New Deal, operating in the state. I decided that a good method of accomplishing this goal would be to stage a public exhibition in which each agency would be invited to participate, with booths, explanatory literature, and the like. Newark's Robert Treat Hotel was selected as the site and Saturday, January 18, 1936, as the date.

What the affair needed as a topper, I decided, was an appearance and a talk by a really big name from Washington. The biggest attraction, obviously, would be Franklin Delano Roosevelt; so, on the theory that one might as well start at the top and work downward, if necessary, I decided to invite him.

Frank Walker and Red Leggett agreed, after consultation, to process the invitation through White House channels. Their spadework produced encouraging results. The president said he would try to work into his busy schedule a visit to Newark on January 18. In the meantime, I was cautioned, absolute secrecy must surround his tentative acceptance. Not only that, but I was given to understand that if he was able to make it, his visit should be treated as a last-minute decision, with no advance publicity.

As things turned out, equal caution should have been prescribed for Frank Hague. Jersey City's mayor journeyed to Washington to attend, among other things, the Democratic party's annual Jackson Day Dinner on January 6, an affair also attended by President Roosevelt. The next day, being interviewed by the press in Washington, Hague let the cat our of the bag by reporting that the president planned to attend the January 18 exhibition I was arranging. This set off a chain of events which, in retrospect, may be somewhat humorous but which at the time sorely complicated my planning for and coordination of exhibits by something like seventy federal and federal-state agencies. Hague also indicated that one of the purposes of Roosevelt's visit would be to urge me to run for the U.S. Senate, a matter I considered as having been settled weeks before.

As a further complication, the White House would neither confirm nor deny that the president would visit Newark. Nebulous "maybes," while I was still under an interdiction of secrecy, didn't exactly add to peace of mind. It is one thing to arrange such a meeting without a presidential appearance and quite another ball of wax when the nation's chief executive is to be the star attraction.

Not until the night of January 13, leaving less than five full days to

117

alter arrangements, did confirmation of the president's intended visit come through. Demands of the Secret Service for guarding the president were paramount. This necessitated rapid-fire meetings with Newark officials to arrange for some 300 local police to stand guard at the Pennsylvania Railroad station, within the Robert Treat Hotel, and along the streets the president's motorcade would traverse. Because of the earlier dictum of secrecy, in the event the president came, I had made special arrangements for his unobtrusive entry through the rear of the hotel. Now the rules were changed, and a grand entrance through the front necessitated the last-hour construction of a ramp to accommodate his wheelchair.

President Roosevelt, accompanied by Mrs. Roosevelt and the normal entourage of his office, arrived in Newark on schedule, reviewed our exhibits at the Robert Treat, spoke, and departed for New York City for another engagement, all without major incident. I emphasize *major,* because his remarks at the affair were unusual, to say the least, and possibly prophetic of the ultimate course of his terms in office.

Boondoggling, for those too young to recall, was an epithet pinned on the activities of various New·Deal agencies by detractors who considered them absolutely worthless. I quote from the front page of the *Newark Evening News* of January 18, 1936: ''President Roosevelt told the National Emergency Council here today that 'if we can boondoggle our way out of this depression, the word will be enshrined in the hearts of the American people for a great many years to come.' ''

Three decades later the word *boondoggle* is still part of our idiom, but I feel certain that the prediction of its enshrinement missed the mark by a large margin.

At the risk of immodesty, I also quote from the *New York Times* report of FDR's Newark speech:

I have been wanting to come to one of these meetings for a long time to see how they were conducted, and when I heard of the first meeting . . . under the chairmanship of Charley Edison, I wanted to see how New Jersey works. And I am very proud of New Jersey. You have been one of the first states in the Union to carry through the coordination, the tying together of all of our government activities. You pointed a lesson that is being carried out in every other State in the Union, with the objective within a very short time of having an excellent organization similar to this one operating in all the other States.

Two days after the Newark meeting, the *Jersey Journal,* the daily newspaper serving Mayor Hague's home bailiwick of Jersey City, ran a headline that read "Edison Balks at Senate Race," and then went on to say: "The President and Mayor Hague have been trying for some time to get Edison to consent to run, but he has, thus far, always refused to make the race."

As far as I was concerned, the question of running or not running had been decided by me weeks ago. In all fairness, however, I should add that at the Newark meeting President Roosevelt made no direct mention to me about my possible candidacy, although many persons regarded his public remarks as an endorsement.

Again somewhat parenthetically, may I speculate that had I run against Senator Barbour in 1936 and won, I certainly never would have been appointed assistant secretary of the navy on November 27, 1936; nor would I, in all probability, have become secretary of the navy three years later; and had I run and lost—who knows? A defeated candidate for the United States Senate is not exactly an exciting gubernatorial possibility. But that was early in 1936, and the possibility of becoming a cabinet member and a governor of New Jersey had not really entered my mind. Be that as it may, and any speculation on my part to the contrary notwithstanding, the Democratic candidate who opposed Republican Barbour in November of 1936 was William H. Smathers, a state senator seeking to move up to the United States Senate. Smathers, from Atlantic City, had been the first Democrat to be elected to the New Jersey State Senate from Atlantic County in sixty years. Frank Hague made the announcement of Smathers' candidacy for the nomination. Smathers not only got the nomination; he also defeated Barbour in the general election.

Franklin D. Roosevelt overwhelmed Republican Alfred Landon in the same election. Only Maine and Vermont ended up in the Landon column.

This segment of my personal narrative has covered some seven years, from the depression's Black Friday of October 29, 1929, through the general election of November 1936. The nature of the next four years, as they applied to me personally, was so different in character that they must be treated separately.

9

The Short-of-War Years *

A

THE UNITED STATES Navy had a name for the several years immediately preceding Pearl Harbor. Called the "short-of-war" years, the period, while it had no exact starting date, encompassed not only America's initial preparedness efforts as the threat of a major new war in Europe deepened but also the war's actual outbreak in Europe when Hitler's legions invaded Poland on September 1, 1939. The period ended, of course, with Japan's sneak attack on Hawaii on December 7, 1941. Circumstances were to cast me in the role of secretary of the navy, *de facto* or *de jure*, for the most of these short-of-war years. My stay in the Navy Department extended from January 18, 1937, to June 24, 1940, to cite exact dates.

Events leading up to my civilian tour of duty in the Navy Department had a somewhat macabre origin. A death and an illness preceded my appointment as assistant secretary. The death was the passing on February 22, 1936, of Assistant Secretary of the Navy Henry Latrobe Roosevelt, a cousin, somewhat removed as I understand it, of both FDR and Eleanor, and coincidentally, like me, a New Jerseyan (from Morristown). This death created the immediate vacancy. The illness involved Secretary of the Navy Claude Augustus Swanson, whose loss of vigor and mental concentration was apparent in 1936, and possibly earlier. Mr. Swanson was two months shy of his seventy-fifth

---

*The portion of this chapter labeled "A" is in the first person because it was put into words by Charles Edison prior to his death on July 31, 1969. That portion labeled "B" is a second-party recounting of materials related by Mr. Edison to the author.

rthday when I took the oath of office as assistant secretary. But let
ere be no misunderstanding. Mr. Swanson had served with distinction
navy secretary since President Roosevelt had taken office in 1933.
ior to that, as a member of the United States Senate and chairman of
5 Naval Affairs Committee, he had long espoused a strong navy.
laude Swanson was an able and dedicated public servant—and a
ghter.

Small wonder, then, that at that time of my nomination, he reacted
ther strongly to unfounded rumors that a man thirty years his junior
as to replace him within a few months. In newspaper reports of the
1y, Mr. Swanson was characterized as a "swashbuckling" scrapper who
eferred "decapitation" to resigning for ill health or any other reason.

The speculation that was upsetting to Secretary Swanson also was
nnoying to me. So on December 5, 1936, between the time my ap-
ointment was announced and my taking office, I wrote Mr. Swanson
e following letter:

My dear Mr. Secretary:
Acknowledgment is made of your letter of December second in regard
to Mr. Lewis Compton.
I am very glad indeed that you could find a way to make it possible for
us to have his help and thank you for going to so much trouble to accomplish it.
[Lewis Compton, another New Jerseyan, served as my special assistant
until I became secretary, at which time he was advanced to assistant
secretary. Later, when I became governor of New Jersey, he was to perform valuable services as state commissioner of finance.]
Mr. Comptom is assisting me now in pulling up roots, to the end that I
will be pretty well cleared away by the first of the year.
It is remarkable how many things that have quietly been sleeping in
pigeonholes and various other places suddenly bob up for attention now
that it is known I will be out of general circulation for some time. I never
knew I had so many roots until I started to cut them.
Lately I had an opportunity to look over some of the newspaper
comment on my appointment and was considerably annoyed to see
frequent speculation on the future course of my "path to glory."
Any man who takes a job with the idea that it is simply a springboard
for something else is a chump. His attention will be more on the other
things than on the job at hand and so he will fail.
[Newspaper speculation, in addition to posturing me as an early
replacement for Swanson, also had suggested that my appointment was
merely part of a buildup to launch me as a candidate for the United
States Senate or the governorship.]

I want you to believe that I harbor no delusions of grandeur, in spite of the press, and that if I can turn out to be a good Assistant Secretary of the Navy, and especially a good assistant to you, my cup will be full.

Sincerely yours,

Charles Edison.

Mr. Swanson continued to hold the title of secretary of the navy unt his passing in July of 1939.

Being the civilian head of the Navy Department for much of 1937 1938, 1939, and 1940 turned out to be a fruitfully significant period fo me and, I hope, for the nation. The times in which we live and wor unquestionably control, at least in part, the role, or the effectiveness o the role, we play. Benedict Arnold would not have been a traitor ha the Revolutionary War not occurred; but by the same token, Georg Washington could not have been the Father of Our Country. The time in which they lived helped shape their destinies.

At the very time I was tapped by President Roosevelt to becom assistant secretary of the navy, I had decided for impelling persona reasons to sever my ties with the federal government to devote my ful energies to running the Thomas A. Edison Industries. Three and a ha years of double duty, of trying to do justice to a succession of govern mental assignments while, at the same time, attempting to devot adequate attention to private business, had left me tired and rather ru down. Consequently, in September of 1936, my wife, Carolyn, and journeyed to White Sulphur Springs, Virginia, for an extended vacatio that, because of an ensuing illness, kept me there beyond the genera election in November. It had been my intention, a decision solidifie during my recuperation at White Sulphur Springs, to resign at an earl date from my then current post as state director for New Jersey of th National Emergency Council. Informal overtures about my availabilit for the navy post had been extended prior to my vacation, but I ha turned them aside. I was determined to return to the life of a privat citizen. Circumstances were to delay this return to privacy for anothe seven years, until the conclusion of my term as governor of New Jerse in January of 1944.

A few days after the 1936 election, Carolyn and I left White Sulphu Springs for our return to New Jersey. Depending on how one looks at it I made the mistake—or the right decision—of stopping off i Washington to gather firsthand reaction to the Democratic ad ministration's sweeping election victories.

Word reached me at the Mayflower Hotel in Washington that President Roosevelt wanted to see me immediately. This meeting at the White House resulted in the formal proffer of the assistant secretaryship. I tried to decline, but the president insisted that I at least withhold the final decision until after a meeting to be arranged for me with Secretary Swanson.

"Claude wants you as his assistant," Mr. Roosevelt told me. "He also needs you."

This meeting with Mr. Swanson followed in a day or two, and while I heard the secretary's health was not of the best, I was totally unprepared for what I found. As I entered his office, he looked at me with a vague expression and, as though groping to assemble his thoughts, tried ineffectively to identify me or the reason for my visit. Our meeting was brief, and during one period of lucidity Mr. Swanson assured me that he did want me to become the assistant secretary.

I returned immediately to my New Jersey home. Mr. Swanson's debility was most alarming, particularly so because, along with many Americans, I was convinced that war in Europe was inevitable and, just as inevitably, that the United States would be drawn into it. The following day, after a night of soul-searching that left no time for sleep, I contacted the White House and told the president I would accept the post.

On November 17 the president announced my appointment and said the formal nomination would be sent to the Senate for confirmation in January, at the outset of his second four-year term. I was sworn in as assistant secretary of the navy on January 18, 1937.

Good luck, I think most persons will agree, can be an important factor in success. One of the fortuitous things that happened to me was that, virtually simultaneously with my becoming assistant secretary of the navy, then Rear Admiral Ben Moreell was named to head the department's Bureau of Yards and Docks. His offices were adjacent to mine in the old Navy Building in Washington.

Ben Moreell was—and is—a most unusual man. Best remembered as the man who conceived and directed the navy's legendary Seabees during World War II, Ben holds many distinctions. To cite just a few, he was the first non-Annapolis man to achieve the rank of full admiral since the United States Naval Academy was founded in 1845; and he was the first staff officer, as distinguished from a line officer, to become a full admiral. Ben was and is a friend and confidant. Furthermore, the consanguinity of our physical offices in Washington and in our mental attitudes led to an interchange of ideas and mutually arrived-a decisions over and above the normal contacts between a bureau chie and an assistant secretary of the navy.

The Seabees, Moreell's baby, reached a highwater mark of more that 250,000 personnel during World War II. Their slogan, "Can Do," wa justly earned as, time and time again, they accomplished the seemingly impossible by putting airstrips and dock facilities into operation almos before the marines or other fighting units had secured beachheads or Pacific atolls.

Perhaps a personal recollection can best explain the "Can Do' philosophy of Ben Moreell and his Seabees. I had been assistan secretary for a year or two; and at no time had a problem, however big stumped him. So, one day feeling somewhat in a pixieish mood, decided to propose a problem of such magnitude that even Moreel would quail.

"Admiral," I said, with tongue in cheek, "the army engineers are having so much trouble with the Alcan (Alaskan-Canadian) Highway that I think we should help out. Instead of a highway, why don't we build a giant two-way conveyor belt from the state of Washington to Alaska? Then, come hell or high water, snow or sleet, trucks, tanks, or any other kind of vehicle can just be placed on the moving belt and traffic will move unimpeded."

Admiral Moreell squinted, looked at me quizzically, and replied, "Mr. Secretary, I'm not saying the idea is sound, but if you can get Congress to appropriate the money I can build the damn thing."

That was Ben Moreell.

In those days, one of the principal duties of the assistant secretary of the navy, as a civilian administrator, was that of supervising shore establishments, such as naval bases. The secretary, as the civilian directly over the chief of naval operations (always a line officer), held sway over ship construction, ships afloat, and many other matters. I was not long in learning, however, that President Roosevelt, possibly because of his Navy Department background, was no respecter of normal channels of communications. To my surprise, President Roosevelt, only ten days after my assuming the assistant secretaryship, summoned me to the White House to explain why the navy's shipbuilding program was behind schedule.

Even today, some thirty years later, I have the feeling that FDR was employing a bit of psychology on me as a newcomer of less than two weeks. Further, it obviously was a tip-off that my duties were to transcend those normally handled by an assistant secretary. In any vent, here is my recorded summary of that meeting, held January 27, 1937, at the White House:

At the request of the president, I visited him today. He wanted to see me in connection with a report prepared by Admiral [Emory S.] Land, giving the reasons why ship construction has been and is being delayed.

The president said he had read the report and it "left him cold," that it gave the reasons for the delay without giving any recommendations as to improvement.

I explained that the report had not been completed and that it was merely intended to give the reasons anyway and lay the foundation for future discussion as to ways and means of improving conditions.

I explained Admiral Land's concern about the apparent impression that he had merely prepared an alibi, which was in no way in his intention. The President assured me that he was not provoked at Admiral Land in the least—he went on to say, "Well, we have the reason; so what?"

He said it was one of my jobs to visit navy yards and find out and that he hoped I would undertake this at a very early date.

Then he urged that in constructing vessels more speed be attained in their completion. Among other things, he said that European shipyards produced ships in less time. That we had produced destroyers in ten months in this country during the war [World War I], but that now it took three years and at that we were late in delivery; that I would meet arguments against the use of two shifts, but to him it seemed foolish not to employ this method towards speed; that I would meet arguments about a stable work layout but that with proper coordinating of repair and new construction this could undoubtedly be attained without the sacrifice of speed. That private shipyards use navy vessels as fill-in work, favoring always commercial ships. That machinery builders such as General Electric had never been urged to speed except by occasional letters.

That speed was not necessarily more expensive and finally that he wanted me to see if we could not produce ships in less time.

I principally asked questions to bring out his ideas on points he made in further detail. Towards the end of the conference I asked him if he wanted emphasis put on speed even though it might entail some additional expense or substantial revision of methods, and he said yes. He again emphasized that speed and additional expense were not necessarily partners in this. I agreed.

We discussed the three navy vessels allocated [for construction] today and I asked him if he thought that the two destroyers might not be two yardsticks to use on this question of speed. He was most heartily in favor of doing so.

The net result of the conference was that he asked me to use my best efforts to overcome the difficulties in the way of speeding construction of vessels and to do everything reasonably necessary to accomplish this end.

Returning from the White House, I reported to Secretary Swanson, who also told me to follow along the line the president had indicated.

President Roosevelt's weighted interest in the Navy Departmen should have come as no surprise to me. Theodore Roosevelt, later t become president, had served as an assistant secretary of the navy. Th same post was held by FDR during both of President Wilson's terms and, as mentioned earlier, I had succeeded Henry Latrobe Roosevelt i the position. This triumvirate becomes a quadruplet when one adds th name of Theodore Roosevelt, Jr., who was the assistant secretary of th navy from 1921 to 1924. Being an assistant secretary of the navy almos seemed like a prerogative of the Roosevelt families.

Oddly enough, when FDR was assistant secretary under Secretary o the Navy Josephus Daniels during World War I, my father, Thomas A Edison, was president of what was called the Naval Consulting Board which, essentially, was a pulling together into one body of America' leading scientists and inventors so that collectively, and individually they could lend their brains to thwarting Kaiser Wilhelm's dream o conquest. The most lasting achievement of this body occurred after th war, when, on Thomas Edison's recommendation and urgence, th Naval Research Laboratory was established as a permanent arm of ou navy's might.

A colossal bronze bust of Thomas Edison now graces the mall at th Naval Research Laboratory at Anacostia, Maryland, serving as a constan reminder of his contributions to naval research.

B

In the earliest years of our nation the secretary of war represented both the army and the navy in the president's Cabinet. However public dissatisfaction with inadequate naval preparedness, following depredations by Barbary pirates on American shipping in the Mediterranean in 1794, led Congress to establish the office of secretary of the navy as a separate Cabinet post in 1798. The office continued to enjoy full Cabinet rank until the unification of the armed services unde the secretary of defense in 1947, following World War II. Thus it wa when Charles Edison became the assistant secretary of the navy unde.

Claude Swanson in January of 1937. His counterpart in the army was Assistant Secretary of War Louis Johnson.

From the day Edison became assistant secretary he was one of the most persistent advocates of a strong navy. Some of the steps necessary to strengthen the naval establishment could be undertaken within the limits of existing budgets; other steps, however, required increased spending, which, obviously, necessitated larger congressional appropriations. But adequate military appropriations were difficult to come by during this period for a number of reasons, some valid, some not so valid.

The nation was still gripped by the depression, but since governmental spending—PWA, WPA, etc.—was one approach to seeking improved conditions, economy for economy's sake was not the greatest bar to proper preparedness. Rather, a spirit of isolationism, enhanced by reaction to World War I as evidenced in part by our refusal to join the League of Nations, was a decisive factor. It must be remembered that even though Hitler had usurped supreme authority in Germany, a fighting war was still two and a half years away; and the Neville Chamberlain–type leaders of England and western Europe had many adherents in the United States, both in and out of Congress. Broad segments of our population honestly believed that steps leading to military preparedness would be provocative of war rather than a deterrent. In other words, stepped-up appropriations for the military were slow and painful to attain. This was particularly true within the navy because funds for shipbuilding purposes were held at low ebb by the nation's Naval Armament Limitation Treaties. When we abrogated these treaties as of the first of 1937, after Japan's flagrant refusal to abide by their terms, the nation was free to embark on a naval construction program that had languished in neglect for fifteen years.

Edison's navy feet were hardly wet with salt water when his new duties threw him into the middle of a management-labor rhubarb. Since this was in early 1937, it must be remembered that many of the laws and practices governing management-labor matters might seem somewhat innocuous compared to now. Organized labor was on the march. John L. Lewis and others dissatisfied with labor's gains had started the CIO, presumably as a temporary force known as the Committee for Industrial Organization, but which persisted and was renamed the Congress of Industrial Organizations. Edison drew the assignment of trying to achieve the navy's procurement needs while labor and management battled over terms of the Walsh-Healey Act.

The Walsh-Healey Act, in essence, said that corporate suppliers to the government must pay time-and-a-half for hours worked in excess of forty a week to produce materials or equipment for governmental agencies. The navy's large steel requirements for its shipbuilding program were not being met because the steel companies, unlike many other types of producers, had no way of knowing in advance what portion of its production would end up with the navy, or with some other governmental agency, or determining just which employee should be paid time-and-a-half for overtime. The steel companies headed by the "Big Steel" firms, refused to do this because, compared to total production, the government's requirements amounted only to about five percent.

Under this law, however, the secretary of labor, who was Miss Frances Perkins, better known as Madam Perkins, had the authority to waive premium pay for overtime if, in her judgment, conditions warranted such action. This Miss Perkins was loath to do.

President Roosevelt was highly concerned by the navy's inability to obtain sufficient steel, as indicated by a summary of a conference held February 25, 1937, with Edison and his assistant, Lewis Compton.

Comptom wrote in his confidential summary of the meeting:

> The President seemed somewhat surprised to learn that the Secretary of Labor had expressed a definite unwillingness to accept the suggestions made. [A week earlier, it had been strongly suggested to her that she waive the premium-pay requirement.]
>
> The President then said that the original passage of the Walsh-Healey Act was a "pious gesture on the part of Congress." He further stated that he was "wise enough in his generation" to realize then as he does now that the "tail cannot be made to wag the dog." He indicated that business cannot be expected to adjust 95% of their effort to conform to the requirements of 5%, which represents the Government business.
>
> He further indicated that this present situation was another illustration of the necessity for the Government to have the power to regulate and control wages and hours of labor and also the power to definitely settle industrial and labor disputes. He said until this power is established in the hands of the Government that any efforts to attain the desired objectives, such as the Walsh-Healey Act, would be futile in their effectiveness.

Shortly thereafter, Miss Perkins informed Edison that she would issue the waiver, provided he obtained advance consent from most or all of the top unionists. When Edison explained the navy's dilemma to

128

William Green, head of the old-line American Federation of Labor, Green readily agreed to go along in the interest of national defense, but it was a different story when Edison sat down with John L. Lewis.

Lewis, president of the upstart CIO, listened intently, scowled through his junglelike eyebrows, and then replied, "Mr. Edison, you have a God-given opportunity to serve your nation. This is your chance to make the greedy steel barons knuckle under."

Needless to say, Charles did not knuckle under to Lewis.

At the time most steel mills, including those of the "Big Three" companies, were unorganized. They shortly thereafter capitulated to the union's organizing efforts and entered into formal labor contracts. This made the waiver issue academic because the contracts called for time-and-a-half for all overtime, whether or not government business was involved.

"My office phone rang this day," Edison recalled, "and it was Miss Perkins on the other end. She told me, as I remember her words, 'Mr. Edison, I was halfway through putting my signature on the waiver order when I decided not to finish it. Myron Taylor, in case you haven't heard, has just signed up with the union.' "

Myron C. Taylor was chairman of the board and chief executive officer of the United States Steel Corporation, biggest of the "Big Steel" group. When he acted, the other steel companies fell in line.

Thus, Madam Perkins was spared by a split second from performing an administrative act which obviously would have been repugnant from her viewpoint.

Edison initiated a number of changes in the structure of the Navy Department, changes which, per se, involved no greater amount of monies. He was, after all, a businessman by profession. These changes included consolidation of the bureau of Construction and Repair and the Bureau of Engineering into a new Bureau of Ships; upgrading the Naval Research Laboratory and giving it independent status; a shortening of the time between planning a ship and sending it to sea; and providing a more realistic method for treating with contractors serving the Navy. He also made a considerable number of enemies, both within and without the naval establishment. In balance, however, it is safe to say his pluses far outweighed any minuses. These were basic changes, alterations in procedure which proved to be of inestimable value before and during our participation in World War II.

Creation of the Bureau of Ships was triggered by the completion in April of 1939 of the first of a new class of destroyers, the *Anderson*, whose design proved faulty in sea trials prior to commissioning. Not only was the *Anderson* overweight by 150 tons, a fact which in itself was not too serious, but the ship was top-heavy, resulting in instability. To use non-navy words, it tilted too much under test at sea. Investigation by Acting Secretary Edison indicated that divided responsibility among three bureaus—those of Construction and Repair, Engineering and Ordnance—was the root of the problem. Edison's investigation led him to believe that the principal onus fell on the Bureau of Construction and Repair.

The following is quoted from page 218 of *Administration of the Navy Department in World War II*, written by Rear Admiral Julius Augustus Furer, and published in 1959 by the Division of Naval History:

> The Chief of the Bureau of Construction and Repair (Rear Admiral W.C. DuBose) acknowledged this responsibility, but pointed out that the organization and the distribution of duties among the respective Bureaus did not vest in the Bureau of Construction and Repair sufficient authority to carry out this responsibility; that actually, the Bureau of Construction and Repair had to depend on the *bona fides* of the other Bureaus not to exceed the estimated weights and heights of center of gravity originally submitted by them for the parts of the ship coming under their congizance; that the Bureau of Construction and Repair had no authority to enforce compliance with these originally agreed on figures.

It was as though three or four different persons, each not communicating properly with one another, were trying to produce one good automobile. The motor was good, the wheels and brakes were good, and the instrumentation was good; but when assembled, they just did not fit together properly.

Edison had inherited this basic deficiency in the method of ship construction, but nonetheless he had to share in the blame in the furor that followed, even though it was not of his doing.

Personality clashes among top personnel of the various bureaus may have contributed in small measure to the foul-up, but Edison realized that faulty organization was the real culprit. Within the limits of his existing authority, he initiated directives which effected a temporary consolidation of bureaus and led, a year later, to the congressional action necessary to formalize creation of the Bureau of Ships. Edison and others, including the powerful Congressman Carl Vinson, chairman of the House Naval Affairs Committee, originally wanted the Bureau of Ordnance embraced in the consolidation; but in the face of determined opposition, they decided to drop that feature rather than risk possible defeat of the entire consolidation measure.

With customary stubbornness, however, the secretary tried to accomplish by executive order at least a portion of what had failed by legislation. He directed that that portion of the Bureau of Ordnance dealing with armor be placed under the new Bureau of Ships. Again quoting from Admiral Furer's book:

> Secretary Edison believed so strongly in including armor that he transferred its congnizance to the new Bureau of Ships when it was created. After the Chief of Naval Operations (Admiral Stark) and Mr. Vinson objected, President Roosevelt overrode the directive of the Secretary on 24 June 1940, thus leaving armor in the Bureau of Ordnance.

Even without the inclusion of armor, the consolidation brought a new cohesiveness to the Navy Department's diverse and, occasionally, competing bureaus.

If the office of assistant secretary of the navy held a special spot in the hearts of the Roosevelt family, then the same may be said of naval research in relationship to the Edisons—father Thomas and son Charles. Thomas, the scientist-inventor, according to the Navy's official version, not only headed the Navy's World War I research arm, the Naval Consulting Board, but he implanted the idea of such a centralized board in the mind of President Wilson's secretary of the navy, Josephus Daniels. Prior thereto, naval research was fragmented almost to the point of ineffectiveness.

On this subject, Admiral Furer wrote:

> World War I may be said to mark the beginning of a new era in the employment of scientists on naval warfare problems. At the outbreak of the war, the British Navy was confronted with the problem of countering the German submarine. A substitute for the sense of sight had to be found to detect submerged submarines, and a weapon had to be invented to destroy it after detection. During the war, many other problems arose, requiring a scientific approach to their solution.
>
> Scientists from the universities were called in by the armed services in Great Britain and later in the United States to work on these problems. Submarine detection was approached by substituting the sense of hearing for the sense of sight; by listening to sounds made by the submerged submarine. Listening devices did not prove highly successful and were during the following period of peace replaced by devices employing the echo phenomenon of underwater sound waves, nevertheless, they demonstrated the versatility and originality of scientists attacking the

problem. In the United States this led to the establishment of the Naval Research Laboratory.

Thomas A. Edison, more than any one other individual, deserves the credit for starting such a laboratory. When the war broke out in Europe, he became intensely interested in anti-submarine warfare and urged Secretary of the Navy Josephus Daniels to set up a Naval Consulting Board to advise him on this and other problems that were certain to arise if the United States became involved in the War. Such a Board was established in 1915 with Edison as its Chairman, and with two members from each of eleven national engineering societies as members. One of the tasks performed by the Naval Consulting Board was to screen some 40,000 ideas and inventions that during the war were sent by the public to the Navy Department for consideration.

The principal contribution of the Board was, however, in backing Edison's idea of a government laboratory devoted exclusively to naval research. The need for such a laboratory to handle work of interest to more than one bureau in such fields, for example, as electronics and metallurgy, had long been recognized by forward-looking naval officers. An even more important consideration was that such a laboratory would be free from the production problems of the bureaus and could, therefore, concentrate more effectively on research. Authorization for the laboratory was contained in the Naval Appropriations Act for 1917 but the project languished for one reason or another for several years.

Thus it was that on July 2, 1923, the Naval Research Laboratory was commissioned at the Navy's Bellevue Magazine at the southern edge of the District of Columbia. Rear Admiral Strother Smith, its first director, reported directly to the secretary of the navy. The appropriation for the laboratory's operation for 1924 was only $100,000, but it was a beginning.

When Thomas's son Charles became assistant secretary in January of 1937, the laboratory had accomplished some fine work, but its place in the scheme of Navy Department planning had been downgraded. The laboratory's director no longer reported directly to the secretary; he was subservient to the chief of the Bureau of Engineering. Further, appropriations allocated to the laboratory had been held to a virtual minimum. It wasn't until 1939 that they exceeded $1 million for any one fiscal year.

By General Order No. 124, dated September 14, 1939, Edison, then acting secretary, placed the laboratory directly under control of his office. The laboratory was once again a full-fledged member of the navy team. Hundreds of worthwhile ideas and devices emanated from the laboratory during this war period, the most exciting to the general public being radar. That the first experimental radar for shipboard installations was developed and built at the NRL is just one of the navy's proud claims. Sonar, proximity fuses, and a host of other devices had their beginnings in the laboratory.

Edison's choice to head the upgraded Naval Research Laboratory was not, at least at the outset, a particularly popular selection among a number of the reigning admirals. He appointed Rear Admiral Harold G. Bowen, formerly chief of the Bureau of Engineering, which was to be superseded by its consolidation into the new Bureau of Ships. Bowen, though an alumnus of Annapolis, had ruffled too many feathers to be ranked among the academy's most congenial graduates. But Bowen was a fighter, had positive and progressive ideas, and was just what Secretary Edison and the nation needed during such a period of stress.

"Infighting within naval ranks could get pretty rough at times," Edison later recalled. "A fitness report on Bowen reached my desk when I was secretary. I learned for the first time that my controversial choice to direct the Naval Research Laboratory was suffering from 'acute alopecia.' My consternation abated quickly, and my ignorance of this medical term was dissipated when thirty seconds of research in the dictionary let me in on the secret that alopecia is nothing more than baldness. The compiler of that portion of his fitness report certainly was not one of Admiral Bowen's better friends."

When the nation's international commitments against unrestricted building of fighting ships were scuttled at the start of 1937, the navy went all out within the limitations of congressional appropriations to quickly increase the power of its fleet. Past practice dictated that appropriations must be approved and the funds available before the Navy Department could issue specifications, receive bids, and award contracts. To Edison, this was a waste of precious months; so he instituted a program under which specifications were issued and bids were received in anticipation of funds being appropriated by Congress. Under this system, contracts could be awarded immediately upon the availability of funds.

Edison commented in his reminiscences:

This procedural change had the effect of shortening by as much as six months the time between requesting bids and awarding contracts, with the result that completed ships joined the fleet six months earlier. But as the war in Europe flared, even stronger measures were required. Com-

133

petitive bidding, as required by law, had to be abandoned, as had also been the case back in World War I days. During the First World War, however, competitive bidding on large ships was replaced by a system of cost-plus arrangements. A cost-plus arrangement tends to discourage economy, while a fixed fee frequently is unacceptable to ship builders. Therefore, we decided to move in the direction of negotiated contracts, which offered a number of advantages. Legislation to accomplish this was introduced during my tenure in office and became law four days after I left office. I'm certain that my successor, Frank Knox, was delighted to be pre-armed with this broadened authority.

Accomplishment by indirection can sometimes be as beneficial, or more so, than accomplishment by direct action. In connection with what became known as the Hepburn Report, Edison practiced a bit of duplicity, albeit legal duplicity, to accomplish the navy's goals.

For the uninitiated to understand the importance of the Hepburn Report, it must be explained that for a nation to achieve a strong navy, it must have much more than sheer quantity and quality in ships, planes, ordnance, and manpower; it must have superior and far-flung shore installations for the harboring, maintenance, and repair of its ships, of whatever nature. The Hepburn Report dealt with these facets of preparedness.

In the spring of 1938, by authority of an act of Congress, Secretary of the Navy Swanson appointed a special board to study the needs for additional or improved submarine, destroyer, mine, and naval air bases on the coasts of the United States, its territories, and its possessions. Admiral A. J. Hepburn chaired the board; and its findings, submitted in January of 1939, quite properly became known as the Hepburn Report.

As a starter, the Hepburn Report became an important blueprint in the navy's preparedness efforts, at least until they had to be greatly expanded after our involvement in the war. But reconciling the Hepburn Report's recommendations with the viewpoint of an important isolationist segment of the population posed certain major problems.

"In periods of peace," Edison recalled, "the military is accused of warmongering if they plead for preparedness. But after war arrives they are accused of ineptitude, or worse, if preparedness has lagged."

Unfortunately, preparedness among nations of high technological advancement is not as simple or as fast as among primitive countries. When Mussolini's armies invaded Ethiopia in 1935, Emperor Haile

134

Selassie's mobilization order could merely read: "When this order is received, all men and boys able to carry a spear will go to Addis Ababa [the capital]. Every married man will bring his wife to cook and wash for him. Women with babies, the blind, and those too aged to carry a spear are excused. Anyone found at home after this order will be hanged."[*]

In Haile Selassie's case, the spirit was willing but the armament was weak. Here at home, the necessary sophisticated armament was months, even years, behind complete readiness.

Time was of the essence. Edison decided that in partial implementation of the Hepburn Report he could advance farther, faster, if he chose indirection over direction. For example, opponents of fortifying Guam, a key military bastion in the Pacific, took the position that any militarization of that seemingly remote outpost would be like "pointing a dagger at the heart of the Japanese empire." Many said that to militarize Guam would precipitate a war in the Far East.

Edison said:

This was such a state of mind that even one of my New Jersey friends in Congress, Representative William H. Sutphen, backslid on me at the last moment. Bill Sutphen had agreed to carry the ball in pressing for the needed appropriations to implement certain of the Hepburn Report recommendations. He even spoke on behalf of the specific bill, but when the roll was called he voted no.

As quickly as I could get to him after the vote, I asked, "Bill, what are you trying to do to me and the navy? We were depending on your vote."

"Charlie," Bill replied, "I didn't realize it was so important. I'm running for reelection this year, and because my district has been recently gerrymandered, I'll need every vote I can get. On this particular bill, I've already received forty letters from Quakers opposing it."

Representative Sutphen's political nickname was "Barnacle Bill," but it must have been in reference to his deep bass voice, rather than to his support of the navy, at least in this instance.

Rebuffed from many quarters, Edison decided to proceed by indirection. Under the guise of promoting worldwide air travel, just then coming into vogue, the harbors and airfields of Guam and other Pacific atolls were improved and enlarged. True, this promoted civilian air travel, but it also constituted a big step forward in preparedness. *The*

---

[*]From: "Projects of the Bureau of Yards and Docks," an address by Capt. L. B. Coombs (C. E. C.), USN, Assistant Chief, BuDocks, November 5, 1941.

United States Navy, a semiofficial accounting written by Merle Armitage under a 1940 copyright, has this to say:

> Practically all of the Trans Pacific and Caribbean air bases of the Pan American Airways' system may well be considered as supplementary, secondary, strategical, or auxiliary air bases for the United States, especially in time of war. In the Pacific, the United States Navy is in the process of building substantial bases more or less in cooperation with Pan American Airways on most or all of their small island locations. Pan American's value to the United States Navy is obviously much greater than can be described here.

Juan Trippe, who spearheaded Pan American's expansion, later was to enjoy being the target of one of Edison's quips: "When the nation finally was drawn into the war, I knew for the first time that this Trippe really was necessary."

Soon after Edison became the assistant secretary, it grew increasingly apparent that, primarily because of Secretary Swanson's illness, full responsibility for the office of the secretary of the navy was to fall on his shoulders, whether by default or by formal direction. There had been no assistant secretary of aviation in the navy for something like eight years, even though existing law provided for such; and the office of under secretary did not come into being until mid-1940 as a result of urging on Edison's part. Indicative of this situation was a memorandum which Edison sent to President Roosevelt on April 1, 1938, which said in part:

> Yesterday, Secretary Swanson placed the responsibility for coordinating all phases of the Shipbuilding Program squarely on me and announced this to the Bureaus. It may be said that I already had this obligation but it was all rather vague to the Bureaus and many times I did not get a chance to get in on some decision or lack of it until I stumbled over a situation.
>
> Now with everybody aware of the fact that there is one point of focus, it is my hope that some improvement may be effected in our building schedules.

A few months later, on October 15, 1938, Drew Pearson and Robert S. Allen, in their syndicated column "Washington Merry-Go-Round," called public attention to Edison's anomalous position:

> You don't hear much about the Navy during these days of European crises, but probably it is in better shape than at any time since the World War.
>
> Also you don't hear much about the men responsible for putting it in

that condition. There are two of them, one being Franklin D. Roosevelt, once Assistant Secretary of the Navy, who, as President, has kept his finger on the Navy as on no other Government department.

The other is Charles Edison, who has the title of Assistant Secretary of the Navy, but because his chief (Secretary Swanson) is old and ailing actually is Secretary of the Navy in everything but name.

"I never should have taken this job," says Edison. "I don't know the bow of a ship from the stern."

In peacetime, however, the backbone of the Navy is not so much the officers and enlisted men of the line, but the 50,000 civilian employees, most of them workmen in navy yards. They are under the supervision of the Assistant Secretary. He must be an industrial executive, an employer of labor, a coordinator of supplies. Most of all he must understand labor, for no amount of gold braid on the shoulder of an admiral will help build battleships if unionized naval employees go out on strike.

A situation within the Navy that greatly bothered Edison was the seeming impossibility of introducing new techniques of construction and design into the shipbuilding program. Fogeyism was partly to blame, but the system itself was mainly responsible for the fact that new ships were being turned out much as though there had been no technological advances since World War I.

Under the "system," private shipyards and navy-owned shipyards shared in the allocation of construction awards. The so-called Big Three among the privately owned companies—the Bethlehem Shipbuilding Corporation, the Newport News Shipbuilding and Drydock Company, and the New York Shipbuilding Company—and the navy were large enough to support their own internal design departments; but the so-called Little Three—the Bath Iron Works Corporation, the Federal Shipbuilding Company, and the United Drydock Company—could not afford this luxury. The Little Three employed the New York firm of Gibbs and Cox, Inc., as their design agent. Bids on new types of ships also called for competitive bidding on design plans; but lumped with construction, the Big Three or the navy yards always seemed to come in low on the combination costs. Under the "system," the winner of the design contract became the "lead yard"; and other yards, designated as "following yards," might build additional ships of the same type, but they had to adhere strictly to the design of the lead yard. Edison became increasingly convinced that a number of innovations proposed by Gibbs and Cox were highly desirable, the most important of which was substitution of high-pressure steam boilers and propulsion systems as against continued use of traditional low-pressure construction, which the Big Three and the navy itself supported. Even though the Gibbs firm already had achieved world fame in marine circles, primarily for its nonmilitary contributions, its ideas and designs were being rebuffed within the U.S. Navy.

Detractors of high-pressure steam maintained its use would create grave hazards to the ships and to personnel. To Edison, this simply did not make sense, as high-pressure steam was widely accepted in private industry for nonnaval applications. But finding a way to beat the system wasn't easy.

Finally, with the advice and guidance (called "connivance" by some opponents) of a civilian lawyer within the navy's Judge Advocate General's Department—Warren McLaine—Edison came up with a scheme that did the trick. Under the guise of "a change under the contract" he directed that the Bath Company, a "following yard," substitute the ideas of Gibbs and Cox for the design of the "lead yard," in this case, Bethlehem.

"This change," Edison wrote in an official memorandum dated May 9, 1938, "will assure to the Navy the most advanced engineering in the 1939 destroyers, and will produce additional military characteristics, such as, approximately three knots faster speed and twenty-five per cent increase in fuel economy, which will produce a twenty-five per cent saving in cruising radius when the ships built under the Gibbs design are compared with any other design that has been produced up to date, without sacrificing reliability."

Every advantage predicted by Edison turned out to be true, and ultimately high-pressure steam was universally adopted for the navy's big ships. But it had been a rough fight while it lasted—so rough, in fact, that its bare-knuckle aspects crept into the public press.

"Assistant Secretary of the Navy Charles Edison is tired of admirals who haven't learned anything since Farragut fought at Mobile Bay," said an April 1, 1939, article in the *Senator,* a Washington publication, adding:

The March fifteenth shake-up of the naval bigwigs astonished the admirals, especially when the usually mild-mannered, whimsical Mr. Edison pounded on the table and told them, godamit, to do what they were told. The row, of course, was precipitated by the high-pressure temperature installations of the new ships. Edison, smart enough to take the advice and suggestions of young naval engineers, proved that these new installations revolutionized American Naval engineering "as much as the shift from paddle wheels to screw propellers"; that the trouble encountered so far was purely mechanical and not a question of design.

138

Edison found out which men were blackballing him behind his back, had them shifted to "Siberia" posts—and rammed his own proven idea down the throats of reactionary leftovers.

Once the dust of battle had settled and high-pressure steam had proved itself, a number of admirals, including one or two who had opposed Edison, proudly referred to the improved capabilities of the new ships as "our secret weapon."

Gibbs' fame as a designer of ships continued to grow and, with few dissents, he became recognized as the greatest authority in his field. Anyone who has ever crossed the Atlantic aboard the superliner *United States* can readily appreciate that his talents were not restricted to designing fighting ships.

"There are a number of things I take comfort in recalling when I think of my days in the Navy Department," Edison commented. "Such things as the PT boat, the crucial role the overage destroyers played in Lend-Lease; the upgrading of the Naval Research Laboratory, administrative reorganization, and the speeding up of the shipbuilding program, to mention just a few. But if I had done nothing more than to entrench Vernie Gibbs' methods into the navy, I still would be content. He was one of the few true geniuses I ever met."

William Francis Gibbs was just that to most persons. To others, he was Mr. Gibbs, Francis, and, rarely, Willie. But only to Charles Edison was he Vernie. Vernie was Edison's unique way of linking him to Jules Verne.

Another of Edison's executive decisions was to play a dramatic part in the war. Shortly after becoming the assistant secretary, he was astonished to learn that hundreds of naval craft, mostly small but including many of the 162 remaining destroyers of World War I vintage, were to be disposed of as being valueless; also, that scrap metal at the navy's many installations was being sold somewhat willy-nilly, without regard to ultimate destination, which all too frequently turned out to be Japan or some other nation we later had to fight. Edison issued directives halting both practices.

Thanks mainly to this foresight, the United States had a reserve of overage but still seaworthy destroyers when, in the summer of 1940, France fell, and the British navy was sorely wounded in the evacuation of Dunkirk. Fifty of these so-called overage destroyers formed the basis for our highly successful Lend-Lease arrangment with England.

Again quoting from Admiral Furer's *Administration of the Navy Department in World War II*:

While the destroyer discussions were going on, negotiations were actutally in progress for the acquisition by the United States of sites for bases in British territory along the Atlantic Coast and in the Caribbean. Off-shore bases were highly important for the protection of the Atlantic approaches to the United States and to prevent further Nazi economic penetration of Latin America. The trade agreed upon was to transfer 50 destroyers for the right to establish naval and air bases in Newfoundland, Bermuda, the Bahamas, Jamaica, St. Lucia, Trinidad, Antigua, and British Guiana.

Lend-Lease, a name applied to the program by President Roosevelt, did not come into formal existence until a few months after Frank Knox succeeded Edison as secretary of the navy, but the fifty overage destroyers were available mainly because of his foresightedness in halting their destruction. The destroyers, incidentally, performed yeoman service in protecting British convoys from Nazi U-boats.

In a memorandum to Admiral Harold R. Stark, who had succeeded Admiral William D. Leahy as Chief of Operations on August 1, 1939, Edison wrote, in part:

A year, or even maybe two years ago, I was asked to approve the sale of destroyers and auxiliary vessels. It seemed to me at the time that it was not the part of wisdom to dispose of anything, during these rather un-settled times, so long as it would float. Among the above, for example, were some of our decommissioned destroyers. Even if their final use would be merely to fill them up with concrete and tow them to a strategic point and sink them [to block off channels or harbors], it would seem to me that this would be better than to sell them as hulks for scrap to be sent to Japan to be shot at China or possibly at ourselves.

Questioning the sale of these ships precipitated a review of the policy on the sale of scrap generally. However, I put a stop to the sale of ships and also to the sale of scrap. Two or three weeks later the president, himself, wrote a memorandum stating that he thought it would be very bad policy to sell ships as hulks and I was glad to be able to report that the practice had been stopped. Much pressure was brought on me by the ship yards, the Bureau of Supplies and Accounts, and others pointing out the hardships of the policy of saving hulks and general scrap. I, however, stuck fast to the policy.

This memo went to Admiral Stark, a man whom Edison held in high esteem, less than a month after Stark had become chief of naval operations. Apparently, it was to serve as an updated reminder of policy because, generally speaking, it was not a popular set of rules at the time. "From what I can gather," Edison's memo to Stark said, "the policy was considered somewhat silly."

Reorganization, administrative maneuvering, and similar techniques can encourage efficiency and produce economy, but in the final analysis a stronger navy was dependent upon greater spending. Edison knew it, and most members of Congress knew it; but apathy, real or imagined, attributed to the general citizenry, coupled with a highly vocal minority that continued to scream that real preparedness constituted a threat to peace, produced cautiousness among departments in their requests for appropriations and also among members of Congress in voting upon appropriation requests.

Navy Department expenditures had risen in gradual steps from $333,201,000 in 1933, Roosevelt's first year in office, to $672,968,000 in 1939, the year war broke out in Europe. War Department spending between 1933 and 1939 rose from $450,766,000 to $695,750,000. This was progress, albeit inadequate progress under the circumstances of a world headed hell-bent for the worst of all wars. The total federal budget was $4,325,150,000 in 1933; $9,268,335,000 in 1939.

Edison's term in office was nearing an end in the spring of 1940. Roosevelt's decision to replace the secretary of the navy and the secretary of war, both Democrats, with two Republicans to promote the nation's unity image already had been made, if not publicly announced, and Edison had run for and won the Democratic nomination for governor of New Jersey. But Edison decided to make one more strong pitch for a dramatic stepping up of the war effort.

In a confidential memorandum to President Roosevelt dated May 14, 1940 he wrote:

My dear Mr. President:

In this time of international chaos and with the entire population of the country in a state of nervous jitters, it seems to me that the time is opportune to obtain from the Congress a blanket authority to contract for five billion dollars worth of national defense, the funds to be distributed to the various activities of the Army and Navy as the President may direct.

The cash necessary to finance this program would be spread out over several years so that the burden on any one year would not be oppressive. If the situation takes a turn for the better the program could be reduced.

The totalitarian mob must be shown that democracies can act in emergencies—can cut through the delays and ineffectiveness of legislative processes when the need comes.

We must have flexibility if we are to do a job. We cannot be frozen into a meticulously subdivided legislative program when that program to be realistic should be one of constant adjustment to meet changing conditions. The people are alive to the fact that this is no 10-cent limit game we are in. They are ready to play with blue chips, and they will have

141

to if they are to preserve what they have. Five billion is a lot of money and the blank check is a bold idea, but to my way of thinking it is imperative.

I should like to recall to you that I made a similar proposal after Munich (September 29, 1938).

In first-draft form the dollar amount suggested was ten billion instead of five billion. The change was made because a number of admirals and other top naval men said flatly, "Congress would never go for that much money," or words to that effect. Admiral Moreell, chief of the Bureau of Yards and Docks, was not among that number. He is the authority for the statement that at the last moment, just before dispatching the memo to the White House, Edison added this longhand postscript: "I would go along with ten billion."

Having experienced dilatory consideration of earlier communications, Edison and Moreell engaged in a bit of minor conspiracy to prevent a recurrence. To insure that other matters demanding the president's attention did not take priority, they arranged to have the presidential secretary, Brigadier General Edwin M. ("Pa") Watson, to hand the memorandum personally to Mr. Roosevelt with a comment such as "Mr. President, this is from the secretary of the navy, who says it demands your immediate attention."

Edison's suggestions, as such, were not adopted, but their timeliness, accompanied as they were by growing public apprehension as the war in Europe grew hotter, added strength to the forces urging greater preparedness.

Certain episodes during Edison's Navy Department service, some frivolous and some serious, held spots of special affection in his recollections. On the serious side, he regarded his role in connection with the introduction of PT boats into the U.S. Navy as being of particular import. Here is his story of the PT boats, as reassembled from conversations and records.

The generation gap separating Edison and John F. Kennedy was bridged by their mutual involvement in PT (patrol torpedo) boat warfare—Edison as their introducer into the United States Navy, Kennedy as the youthful PT commander whose heroic feats in the Solomon Islands of the Southwest Pacific added luster to his budding career. Edison's successful efforts to gain acceptance of PT boats alienated some admirals, who by tradition were wedded to big ships heavily armored, and so enraged some American shipbuilders that he was threatened with impeachment proceedings. Their rage was induced mainly by the fact that a British-designed craft was imported as the prototype for hundreds of PT boats produced for World War II action.

In 1938, Assistant Secretary Edison foresaw the need for a "mosquito fleet" as an adjunct to the navy's larger fighting ships and its air arm. With support from President Roosevelt, Edison obtained from the Congress an appropriation to promote a design competition among American boat builders. A number of companies responded, and the competition was in progress. Late in the same year, 1938, Edison was contacted by Henry R. Sutphen, head of the Elco Naval Division of the Electric Boat Company, who had exciting news to report. Sutphen had just returned from England, where he had learned, somewhat *sub rosa,* of the existence of a craft that met all the specifications sought by the Navy Department—speeds up to fifty knots, seaworthiness in heavy seas, unprecedented maneuverability, and extraordinary striking power. Hubert Scott-Paine, an established designer, had created and built this unique MTB (motor torpedo boat), but his efforts to interest the British navy in his craft were rebuffed by Admiralty bigwigs.

In the eyes of Edison, the availability of Scott-Paine's boat was like a heaven-sent answer to one of the navy's problems. Not that he doubted the ability of American designers to come up with something equally good; rather, he saw in Scott-Paine's work the opportunity to save months, or even years, in providing the navy with a proven craft.

Consequently, and with some winking at legalities, he arranged for Sutphen to return to England to negotiate a deal with Scott-Paine for his MTB and a royalty on all such craft produced in the United States, in return for which he would serve as consultant. Scott-Paine's MTB was loaded aboard an America-bound liner and arrived in New York on September 4, 1939. From there it was lightered to Elco's plant at Groton, Connecticut.

The British boat, redesignated PT-9, was put through strenuous heavy-seas tests, the results of which overcame even the objections of the reluctant traditionalists in the navy.

A thirty-two-point Navy Department memorandum submitted by Commander Robert B. Carney, dated December 21, 1939, said in part:

Point 23—On 1 November PT-9 was operated under rough water conditions in the presence of Commander Carney of the Navy Department and Mr. Loring Swasey [later a navy captain], both of whom reported favorably on the general performance of the boat. Immediately after receiving these reports, Acting Secretary of the Navy [Edison] directed that negotiations be expedited toward awarding a contract for 11 additional M.T.B.-type Scott-Paine boats and 12 additional sub-chaser type Scott-Paine boats. The boat was again run in rough water for the Trial Board, and although the report of the Trial Board was less favorable than the first report, there was nothing in the Trial Board's report that indicated unsuitability of the type for tactical purposes. . . .

Point 32—Immediately after the award was made (contracts with Elco for $5,000,000 for the construction of 11 motor torpedo boats and 12 sub-chaser types), the Department's decision was attacked by various representatives of the motorboat industry through the medium of letters and telegrams to the Navy Department and the White House, and by means of press dispatches. The Department replied in each case, and pointed out that it would be late spring before the American boats would be operating and additional time beyond that before their merits and demerits could be properly evaluated; furthermore, it would be the latter part of 1940 at the very earliest before any satisfactory American prototype could be produced in quantity, and this estimate is extremely optimistic. In ordinary times a slow and deliberate comparison of American and British types would be in order, but these are not ordinary times and it was felt that obtaining a satisfactory training type at the earliest possible moment was vital in order to develop the potentialities and the tactical uses of the type; the Scott-Paine type is reasonably well-developed and satisfactory, and met those requirements. Therefore, the Acting Secretary felt that although he had faith in the ability of American designers, the interests of national defense demanded that we get to the all-important tactical and operational training without delay and that could be done by using a proven type, even though that type was British rather than American.

Earlier in his memorandum, under Point 20, Commander Carney had said:

On October 3rd (1939) the Acting Secretary of the Navy informed the President by letter that he wished to go ahead with a project of acquiring additional M.T.B.s of the Scott-Paine design, using unexpended funds of the Experimental Appropriation made available by the Second Deficiency Appropriation Act in 1938, and negotiating the best possible bargain with Elco—Scott-Paine's licensee in the United States.

Up to then, Acting Secretary Edison was in disgrace in certain quarters only because he favored an immediately available British-designed craft over an American design still very much in the future. But now he really was in hot water. He was using unexpended funds of the "experimental appropriation"—another name for the design competition monies—to build Scott-Paine boats.

Technically, Acting Secretary Edison was over a barrel, because the funds he tapped were earmarked to reward American designers of craft

144

unbuilt and untested. One southern member of the House of Representatives threatened impeachment proceedings against Edison. His fervor to push the issue died suddenly, however, when a southern-based boat builder demonstrated his entry in the navy competition on the placid waters of Lake Pontchartrain, near New Orleans, only to see it ship water in waves hardly larger than those of a tugboat's wake. Nothing came of the threatened impeachment move.

With all the technicalities surmounted, the navy fell in love with its newest weapon, and the PT boat went on to fame as the service's hardest hitting midget.

The earliest of the American-built PT boats were, in the interest of speed and production, virtually Chinese copies of Scott-Paine's design. They were seventy feet long and carried, in addition to two torpedoes, antiaircraft machine guns and antisubmarine depth charges. Their normal personnel complement was a commander and six men. Later models, refined and improved on the basis of experience and Navy Department know-how, were slightly larger—about eighty feet long—and carried more and larger striking missiles. But they lost none of their speed and maneuverability.

Secretary Edison's refusal to let red tape and technicalities slow the PT boat program proved him right in many ways. No one was to appreciate this more than did General Douglas MacArthur. When MacArthur, his wife, their infant son, and a handful of others were ordered by President Roosevelt to leave the Philippines, a PT boat was their ark of refuge and escape. General MacArthur's "I shall return" pledge later became a prophecy turned truism.

The keel for the feats of Lieutenant Commander John D. Bulkeley, a Medal of Honor winner, Lieutenant (junior grade) John F. Kennedy, and a host of other PT boat heroes was laid when Edison refused to let traditionalists rule the navy.

Shortly after the war, Kennedy, later to become a martyred president of the United States, took cognizance of Edison's contributions. In Boston, on September 4, 1948, Kennedy, as a member of the Executive Committee of the PT Veterans Association, paid tribute to Charles as "The Father of the PT Boat Service." Kennedy was a U.S. Representative at the time.

As an ironic postscript, it should also be reported that when the British government, whose Admiralty bosses had downgraded Scott-Paine's craft, entered into its Lend-Lease arrangement with the United States, PT boats were high on its list of priorities.

"We 'stole' the PTs from England," Edison once remarked, with a twinkle in his eyes, "but Winston Churchill 'stole' them back under Lend-Lease."

Again on the serious side are Edison's recollections involving an agency known as the National Defense Power Committee. His reconstructed recollections follow.

Presidents of the United States, irrespective of party or political savvy, are so overloaded by demands on their time that reliance on assistants, official reports, and presumably other good sources of fact and counsel, becomes a must. One such report, doubtfully by inadvertence, almost trapped President Roosevelt into urging an unwarranted and unnecessary expansion of TVA's generation and transmission facilities so as to serve the Pittsburgh area, nerve center of the steel industry.

This "Report on Present and Future Needs of Electric Utilities," which was prepared in 1939 by staff members of the National Defense Power Committee, gave the impression that unless quick remedial steps were taken the Pittsburgh area would be so short of electric power that the nation's preparedness program would be crippled. The report cited statistics to prove the point and then recommended extension of TVA's high-voltage transmission lines to interconnect with nongovernment owned utilities serving Pittsburgh.

As a member of the National Defense Power Committee, Acting Secretary Edison received a copy of the report from the White House, with instructions from the president to take up the matter with Louis Johnson, assistant secretary of war, and to formulate a policy of action.

If the report's findings were true, then the steel industry did indeed face a crisis. But Edison smelled a rat after studying the report. Before acting on his own, however, he asked Rear Admiral Moreell, chief of the Bureau of Yards and Docks, a man whose judgment Edison trusted implicitly, to review the report. Admiral Moreell reported back: "It's a fraud."

Both men had spotted the fatal flaw in the document's statistics. Only by comprehending an inconspicuous footnote could a reader learn that the statistics on the Pittsburgh area's existing power capabilities had been calculated on an eight-hour day instead of a twenty-four-hour basis. In other words, Pittsburgh actually had three times the power potential indicated in the report.

"I sorely suspected," Edison commented later, "that supporters of public power, as opposed to investor-owned utilities, had been behind this deception. I was also convinced that FDR, even though he had backed creation of Tennessee Valley Authority and a limited number of other federal power projects, was not a party to the deception, because

146

he appeared to be genuinely upset when informed of the misleading statistics."

No one who ever knew Edison well could ever accuse him of not having a sense of humor. Take, for instance, his stories of the so-called Little Cabinet, of which he was a member until Secretary Swanson's death.

A meeting at the home of Sumner Welles, under secretary of state, of the Little Cabinet, an informally defined group of assistant secretaries from the various offices of full Cabinet status, plus three or four presidential assistants, was honored by a visit from President Roosevelt. FDR was relaxed and at his charming best. He made himself the butt of the following joke:

> One day I was out swimming and started to drown. Three young men, at great personal risk to themselves, saved my life. To show my gratitude, I asked each what I could do for him.
> The first young fellow wanted an appointment to Annapolis. I told him he could count on it.
> The second wanted an appointment to West Point. "You can count on it," I said.
> But the third requested a military funeral.
> "Why in the world would a young fellow like you ask for that?" I asked.
> "Because," he replied, "when I get home and tell my old man I saved your life, I'm going to need a free funeral."

The Little Cabinet also recalls to mind one of Edison's stories involving Sumner Welles. Polished and suave, a career diplomat out of Harvard, and an outstanding public servant, Mr. Welles, nonetheless, resembled the prototype of an English lord when it came to grasping jokes. Compared to the more earthy Edison and Louis Johnson, the assistant secretary of war, Sumner was a paragon of prudery.

"Sumner," Charles once said to him as an aside at a Little Cabinet meeting, "a visiting dignitary from the Middle East came to my office yesterday about a problem his rather obscure country is having with ours. I told him the matter properly belonged in the State Department and that he should arrange a meeting with you. Here's his card."

```
Vyisder Zomenimor
Orzizzazzis

Zanzeris, Orziz
```

Mr. Welles studied the card, pondered momentarily, and then replied in all seriousness:

"Charles, neither the name nor his country rings a bell with me, but I'll be glad to look into the matter when he contacts me."

Sumner's reply almost fractured Louis Johnson, who had no trouble deciphering the gag.

Carolyn, Charles' wife, also was not without a sense of humor, but the following may not have been one of her happier moments.

Official Washington, then as now, carried on business, sometimes business mixed with pleasure, well beyond normal office hours. The Edisons, Charles and Carolyn, wealthy and socially grade A, one handsome and the other vivacious, petite, and pretty, were popular members of the evening set. Their after-hours functions, whether semiofficial soirees or less formal gatherings at the homes of reigning hostesses, frequently involved a delicately mixed guest list designed to provide a cross-spectrum of prestige, wit, and, occasionally, political intrigue.

At one such affair at which the hostess was Mrs. Evalyn Walsh McLean, owner of the fabulous and reputedly ill-omened Hope diamond, Mrs. Edison drew as her late supper companion a man whose conversation and courtesy struck her as unusual and provocative. Unfortunately, she had not caught his name when originally introduced; so at the conclusion of the meal she turned to him and said, "I'm Carolyn Edison. Forgive me, but I didn't catch your name."

"I'm Drew Pearson," came the reply.

"Oh, you just can't be," she blurted. "You're much to nice to be that horrible man."

Pearson's reaction to this involuntary slip of the tongue unfortunately went unrecorded. Later, Mrs. Edison suggested that perhaps a small part of the Hope diamond curse had rubbed off on her that night. Even back in those days, the wife of a prominent public official was not supposed to aggravate the Drew Pearson of the Washington scene. In fairness to Mr. Pearson who died in 1969, it should be added that he never made Charles Edison a strong target of attack; in fact, on several occasions Pearson strongly praised Edison in his column.

One of Edison's pet stories involving FDR began during his term as navy secretary, but he had to wait a few years for its denouement.

Lawrence Wood ("Chip") Robert, Jr., headed an Atlanta, Georgia, firm that excelled in engineering and architecture. His firm not only performed well for the Navy Department, but Chip also had the

listinction of being secretary and treasurer of the Democratic National
Committee (1936-41) and for a while (1933-36) had served as the
assistant secretary of the treasury for public works. With such cre-
dentials—professional excellence plus political expertise—one might
conclude that Chip would have had FDR's complete blessing. So it
came as a sharp surprise to Edison, as secretary of the navy, when he was
told by the president, in so many words, "Get rid of Chip Robert. We
can't have his firm designing navy installations when he is so intimately
tied in with the administration and Democratic party."

These words had something of a false ring because, without imputing
any lack of ethics to the president, Edison was not so naive but that he
could sense an ulterior motive in FDR's dictum. Just what that real
motive was did not reveal itself until a year or two later.

For at least two reasons Edison did not want to carry out the
president's instructions. One, Robert's firm was among the best in the
nation, and the Navy Department needed its services. Two, Chip was a
personal friend. Consequently, Edison resolved his dilemma by doing
nothing, in the hope that whatever was provoking the president would
evaporate with time. Edison heard nothing more on the subject; but his
successor as secretary of the navy, Frank Knox, was to get a loud earful.

Knox, like Edison, was upset when, without warning, he was told by
the president to get rid of Mr. Robert. Knox confessed his astonishment
to Admiral Moreell, chief of the Bureau of Yards and Docks, who
shared with Edison and Knox an appreciation of the good work being
performed by Robert and his firm. The admiral, however, had the
solution. He prevailed upon Robert to resign from his positions with the
Democratic National Committee, a move that vitiated FDR's professed
reason for wanting to withhold navy contracts from Robert's firm.

Shortly thereafter it became "known" in Washington circles that
Chip's delightful wife, Evie, was, unsuspectingly, the real *bête noire* of
the episode. An excellent mimic, she had a repertoire that included an
impersonation of the president. With cigaret held atilt in an overly long
holder, and in grave Harvardian tones, her impromptu dissertations,
beginning with "Mah friends," were hilarity producers at a number of
Washington inner-circle get-togethers. Word of her talent kept getting
back to FDR. He did not appreciate her mimicry.

Robert's firm continued to perform well for the navy because the
president, obviously, could not admit that Mrs. Robert's im-
personations were really what was behind his instructions to Edison and
Knox.

149

The heat of a Washington summer has been likened to wearing a parka in the Black Hole of Calcutta. As temperatures rose during August of 1939, official Washington fled to more comfortable places and less arduous chores so that for one week Edison was the unofficial president.

"The extent to which members of that august body [the Cabinet] have forsaken their air-conditioned offices is revealed by the fact that Charles Edison, Acting Secretary of the Navy, was the top-ranking United States official in Washington during the week," reported the *New York Times* on August 20. "President Roosevelt was cruising in the North Atlantic and Vice-President Garner was in Texas. Secretaries Hull, Morgenthau, and Woodring, and Attorney General Murphy and Postmaster General Farley, the five ranking members of the Cabinet, also were vacationing in less torrid climes.

"Secretary Ickes, Wallace, and Perkins all were here, but all of them ranked below Mr. Edison, as did Secretary Hopkins, who was away. If occasion had arisen to require someone in Washington to assume authority over all governmental affairs, Mr. Edison would have been 'it.' "

"I was aware of the situation a few days earlier," Edison recalled, adding with a smile, "I was tempted to move out of the Hay Adams House into the White House, but I was afraid Eleanor might be home and object."

Edison was a man of multiple facets. An engineer by training, an executive of proven talents, a dabbler in poetry, prose, and songwriting—these were just a few of his many sides. Not infrequently, when the problems at hand seemed perplexing, he would sit alone, usually late at night, and put down his thoughts on paper in his highly legible handwriting, which emulated that of his famous father. Typical of such memos-to-self was one dated March 29, 1938, fourteen months after becoming assistant secretary of the navy for a nation once again threatened with involvement in war. He wrote:

The United States Navy is made up of material and men. Whether the material be a battleship, lathe, wheelbarrow, building or an airport, and whether the men wear overalls, gold braid, or bell-bottom trousers or civilian clothes, makes no difference, they are all part and parcel of the national defense.

We live in a world of semibarbarism. A world in which conflict and war are still the dominant perquisites of existence. Order and peace are unnatural. Nowhere in nature do we see it, and unfortunately nowhere among men can it survive for long. Order and peace are a blessing superimposed on nature by a superior intelligence which we call "civilization" and which is hereditary of the ages.

We look out on a cornfield, or an orchard planted in orderly rows and growing true wealth. But except for the eternal vigilance of the farmer, how long would the corn or orchard grow in rows of reproduction. Plants, like all life, including men, are in eternal conflict with their environment and their enemies. Untended, the corn would soon grow in disorderly confusion, each stalk fighting for the means of sustenance from the soil against its neighbor and against the weeds that would choke the corn. Each tree in the orchard would wage perpetual warfare against the curse of blight and scourges, and in the end the unrelenting struggle for mere existence would parch the corn and wreck the orchard's productivity.

Force rules the world and always will. The plow, the chemical spray, vaccine, money, and a host of other things are merely the symbols of war. They are the tools by which man's superior intelligence conquers his environment.

Man has usurped the earth. He has done so by the force of his intelligence. Are we to be criticized if we wage war on the beasts of the jungle, cockroaches, malaria, boll weevils, Dutch elm disease, and thousands of other pests that tend to ruin our comforts and happiness? I think not.

Like the rabbits in Australia, human beings are on a fair way to dominate and overrun the world to their own detriment. In 1927, it was estimated that there were some two billion people in the world, and that the world's population increases at the rate of thirty million a year, which means that in sixty-six years there will be some four billion people in the world. In another sixty-six years there will be eight billion people. Figure it out for yourself. Of course something will have to be done about it; and something, of course, will be done about it. But in the meantime we have to live in the world as we find it with the number of people that we find in it, and we have to organize to meet the situation.

Whether they be yellow, red, black, white, or brown, *Homo sapiens* says, they set out to dominate the world and to dominate its vines. One would think that the leaders on whom the teeming thousands of the world's population depend for guidance and leadership would consider this ever-increasing population on a planet which remains constant in size as one of the primary considerations in fixing policies as to what shall be done with mankind. But unfortunately none will, because sex relationship is a sacred subject—or more soldiers are needed to fight for their country.

Man's inhumanity to man—it is as widespread as it is stupid. The law of the jungle has perpetuated itself not only in our fight with our common enemy but in our fight with each other. Mankind has erected artificial barriers dividing mankind against mankind wholly without regard to the destiny of civilization.

Shortly before stepping down as secretary of the navy to run for the governorship of New Jersey, Edison reviewed fleet maneuvers in the Pacific from aboard the battleship *Pennsylvania*. This was in the spring of 1940; and as his guest he took with him Arthur Walsh, later a United States senator. Walsh was a longtime friend and business associate. Much of the responsibility for directing the Thomas A. Edison Industries during Edison's absences in public office had fallen on Walsh's shoulders.

One day as the pair relaxed topside, Walsh slapped Edison across the back in the spirit of camaraderie and, as a commentary on whatever they were discussing, remarked, "Why you old son of a bitch, you." Between Walsh and Edison these were smiling, not fighting, words. But to Secretary Edison's naval aide, Captain (later Admiral) Mort Deyo, who was standing nearby, as is the wont of naval aides, such words were sacrilege. Drawing himself to stiff attention and addressing himself to Walsh, Captain Deyo remonstrated in crisp tones: "Sir, aboard a United States battleship one does not refer to the secretary of the navy as an old son of a bitch."

Simultaneously with his becoming full secretary of the navy, Edison by an act of his own doing found himself embroiled in a controversy that raged through both the House and the Senate, and emblazoned his name in caustic editorials from coast to coast. In a letter to Speaker of the House William B. Bankhead, Edison proposed that the president be given peacetime emergency authority, along with certain other powers, to commandeer factories for naval construction. Such powers already were invested by law in the presidency, in event of war, under a World War I statute dating back to 1917. But we were not at war, even though the United States was operating under a presidential declaration of national emergency and had been since September of 1939, when Germany invaded Poland.

The legislation proposed by Edison would not have directed the president to take drastic steps, but it would have permitted him to do so if, in his judgment, during a period of national emergency short of war, he thought it wise. Under the proposed act, the president could requisition plants and facilities for naval use, on payment of just compensation; compel the filling of naval orders over all civilian orders, regardless of the existence of prior contracts; take possession of plants and facilities if owners failed to comply; set aside labor contracts; fix 'reasonable'' prices, and thereby exercise authority over wages; and modify or cancel previous government contracts.

Screams of "dictatorship" and "another step toward war" rang through Congress and were echoed in the press. In less than a week, on January 8, 1940, in response to a request by Representative Melvin J. Maas, of the House Naval Affairs Committee, Edison found it incumbent upon himself to make a reply. His statement to Representative Maas was more a retreat than a defense. It follows:

> I was taken completely by surprise by all the commotion stirred up by what I thought was only a recommendation that Congress give consideration to bringing up to date an old World War Act of 1917 which is still on the books.
>
> Various congressmen and the press have seen in the proposal implications that I am free to confess I must have missed.
>
> If they are right and there really are possibilities inimicable to our democratic systems in this proposal, I just made a mistake in making it. It is as simple as that.
>
> National defense exists to defend our liberties, not to nullify them.
>
> I am glad our system of checks and balances is working and that a free press exists to make it articulate.
>
> The matter came to me first more as a correction of a piece of old legislation than as something new.
>
> We, here in the navy, thought we would be derelict in our duty if we did not call it to the attention of Congress in view of the fact that it does not concern peacetime or normal operation but operation under a grave national emergency. One was in prospect at the time the subject was being considered last fall. Many other problems of handling a national emergency were also being considered at the same time. We hoped that through looking ahead and planning we might avoid the chaos and confusion that attended our entrance into the World War should the United States ever be forced into another one. It is our job to be ready.
>
> So, I ask the country not to jump to the conclusion that I am so intrigued with the idea of national defense that I would sell democracy short to get it.

The furor was a seven-day wonder and quickly became obscured by other headlines of the times. Needless to say, the controversial legislation died aborning.

As May of 1940 drew to an end, Edison's career in the Navy Department entered its final weeks. So, preparatory to leaving Washington to run for the New Jersey governorship, he addressed himself to an official *au revoir* to President Roosevelt. On May 28, Edison wrote to the President:

153

As you already know, on May 20, 1940, I issued the following statement:

"When I announced my candidacy for the governorship of New Jersey, I told the President that I felt I should not remain as Secretary of the Navy for more than thirty days after the Primary. I believed then and I believe now that a Secretary of the Navy—the head of our first line of defense—should not also be a candidate for a political office. During these trying times there must not be the slightest suspicion that decisions of a Secretary of the Navy are influenced by political expediency.

Accordingly, I am tendering you my resignation as Secretary of the Navy effective at your convenience.

The plans that you and I have discussed, anticipating my withdrawal, are well in hand, and I leave with the full assurance that this action, at this time, will cause no disturbance in the normal routine of the department.

In general, the objective we have strived for over the past three and a half years have in great part been realized or will be when the Congress passes the current legislative program. The shipbuilding program and plans for its expansion are in good condition as is the Fleet. The affairs of the Navy are in the hands of an exceptionally able group of men at this time from Assistant Secretary of the Navy, Mr. Lewis Compton; the Chief of Naval Operations, Admiral Harold Stark; the bureau chiefs and department heads on.

May I thank you from the bottom of my heart for the fine relations that have existed between us and for the opportunity you gave me to serve my country.

The president's "convenience" turned out to be June 24. From that date through the general election in November, 1940, Edison waged an aggressive and successful campaign for the governorship of New Jersey. President Roosevelt's letter of response, dated June 4, 1940, read:

Dear Charlie:
First of all let me congratulate you on your nomination without opposition for the New Jersey Governorship. I hope you will be elected—and I say this because you have a deep-seated feeling of responsibility to good government and efficient government, which I hope will be recognized by the people of your State.

I am sorry to lose you as the head of the Navy Department because you have had exprience there, because you understand the multifarious problems of the Navy and because you have greatly contributed to the present efficiency of the Service.

In regard to the date of your resignation taking effect, I apply the old rule laid down by former Presidents when Members of the Cabinet or their Assistants have been nominated for elective office. I realize that the active part of your campaign for Governor will not begin for a month or two, but I know also that you will want to visit various parts of the State at an earlier period in order to familiarize yourself with all the sections and all the problems of New Jersey, even though, because of your previous experience, you are conversant with every section.

I know also that in your present position it will take you several weeks to wind up various matters to the progress of which you are essential.

May I suggest, therefore, that this acceptance of your resignation take place on June twenty-fourth? This will give you enough time I think to finish the immediate tasks at hand.

Also, I want you to know that I will continue to count on your advice in many matters which relate to the defense development now underway, and I hope you will find time during the next few months to come to Washington frequently in order that I may talk things over with you.

I need not tell you of the affectionate personal regard in which I hold you, and of the real admiration I have had for your understanding of naval affairs. I congratulate you on the splendid record you have made.

Among the many bright spots in Charles' record were his advocacy of the use of helicopters or gyroplanes for military purposes, a viewpoint not generally shared at the time; and his sense of the value of continuing the use of blimps within the navy. Many were advocating discontinuance of the blimp service, but these lighter-than-air craft performed yeoman duties as submarine spotters during World War II.

A rewarding postscript to his service as secretary of the navy was to reach Mr. Edison from James V. Forrestal, who served as secretary of the navy from May 19, 1944, until September 17, 1947, when he became the nation's first secretary of defense, a new Cabinet post with supervision over the army, the navy, and the air force: "If I can leave the job with the same approval that you did, I shall be happy," Mr. Forrestal wrote three days after his promotion from his position as under secretary of the navy to the new full secretaryship.

"I can testify that you rendered great service—and, as you know, some of the things you initiated I was able to capitalize on when the war began. Without one of them—the consolidation of the BuEng [Bureau of Engineering] with BCSR [Bureau of Contruction and Repairs]—I don't believe we could ever have achieved the rate of building we have."

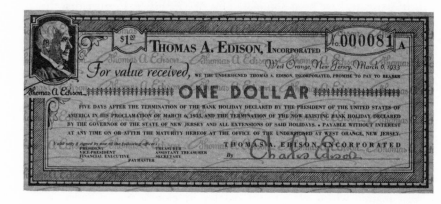

Thomas A. Edison, Incorporated, at Charles' direction, issued its own scrip money (*above*) to employees during the bank holiday declared by President Roosevelt. Local merchants readily accepted it for later redemption. Also, to combat the depression, the company gave $5 checks (*below*) to its several thousand employees, with the admonition, "Buy anthing, but buy something."

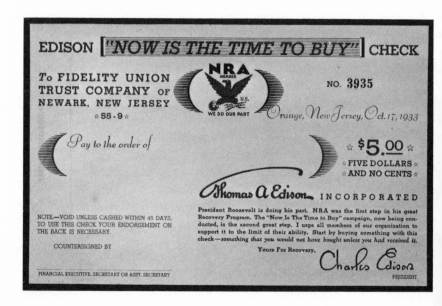

President Roosevelt and Edison share dais at meeting in Newark of National Emergency Council. Charles was head of the council's New Jersey operations (1936).

Acting Navy Secretary Edison explains a point of concern to President Roosevelt and Admiral Harold R. Stark (1939).

Secretary of War Harry Woodring (*from left*), Acting Navy Secretary Edison, Assistant War Secretary Louis Johnson, Admiral Harold R. Stark, and General George C. Marshall gather for a meeting with President Roosevelt (1939).

Hectic days. Secretary of State Cordell Hull (*from left*), Admiral
John H. Towers, chief of the Naval Bureau of Aeronautics; Assistant
War Secretary Louis Johnson, and Assistant Navy Secretary Edison
confer on plans for evacuating United States citizens following
declaration of war by Great Britain and France against Hitler's
Germany (September 3, 1939).

The Washington scene. Carolyn and Charles
leave for an embassy party.

Sweet charity. Carolyn Edison, Eleanor Roosevelt, and Charles share a table at a benefit affair.

Reviewing the Pacific Fleet. Charles (*left*), old friend Arthur Walsh, and a sailor observe maneuvers from aboard the flagship, U.S.S. *Pennsylvania* (April 10, 1940).

Carolyn Edison prepares to christen with champagne the U.S.S. *New Jersey*, at the time the nation's mightiest battleship. Charles laid the keel during his period as civilian head of the navy. The christening in Philadelphia was later during his governorship. At left of Mrs. Edison is Charles' sister, Mrs. John Eyre Sloane.

Like visitors to a zoo fascinating the animals, Navy Secretary Edison and an entourage of admirals and other dignitaries attracted as much attention from the reigning motion picture stars as the stars did from them. The occasion was in the spring of 1940 when Edison, on the west coast to review Pacific Fleet maneuvers, was the guest of Louis B. Mayer, head of Metro-Goldwyn-Mayer. The visit recalled his earlier connection with the movies at the Edison studio in the Bronx before Hollywood became the film capital.

Louis B. Mayer is host at a studio luncheon for Navy Secretary Edison. Mickey Rooney, who starred in the title role in the movie "Young Tom Edison," chats with Charles as Judy Garland joins in.

Clark Gable and Claudette Colbert flank Navy Secretary Edison on an M-G-M set. At left is Admiral Ernest J. King, one of the heroes of World War II. At far right is Captain (later Admiral) Mort Deyo, aide to the secretary of the navy. Peering between Gable and Edison is Arthur Walsh, executive vice-president of Thomas A. Edison, Incorporated.

Joan Crawford and Frederic March exchange pleasantries with Charles.

Still Hollywood-related, but at a later date and another location, Mary Pickford talks over plans for establishing the Thomas Alva Edison Foundation with Charles and Harvey Firestone, Jr. All three became trustees of the organization.

10

Campaigning *

BY A QUIRK OF political circumstance, prominent individuals within one wing of the Republican party in New Jersey were urging me to run for the Democratic nomination for governor at the same time Democratic leaders were advancing my name for the same position. This peculiar interest of Republicans in a Democratic candidacy arose out of an intraparty schism within New Jersey's G.O.P.

In mid-November of 1939 a delegation of New Jersey Republicans representing their party's "Clean Government" faction visited me in my assistant-secretary-of-the-navy office in the nation's capital. Their spokesman, Russell Watson, a prominent New Brunswick attorney, asked me to run for the Democratic nomination. Far be it from me to impugn the motives of Mr. Watson and his entourage, but I must concede they weren't spurred by pure and simple love for Charles Edison or any political aspirations he harbored. At that point in time I wasn't even "aspiring." In fact, my becoming full secretary of the navy was still two months in the offing; and my decision to become a candidate was not to become firm until mid-March of the following year.

Mr. Watson and his group represented New Jersey Republicans genuinely opposed to the state's Democratic chieftain, Frank Hague. Their visit to me was prompted by the fact that former Governor Harold G. Hoffman was again an avowed candidate for the Republican nomination; and Harold had a record of being all too chummy with Hague and his henchmen.

---

*This chapter is a first-person account by Charles Edison in collaboration with Prof. Dayton McKean.

In so many words, Mr. Watson (*et al.*) said that if Hoffman won the Republican primary election in May, Clean Government Republicans would back me in the general election in November. However, if their as-yet-unchosen hopeful won the nomination over Hoffman, then they would oppose me. Somehow it didn't seem like too good a bargain. It was like advertising a fire sale before the alarm rang. No commitments were made.

As things turned out, Senator Robert C. Hendrickson, who became the Clean Government designee, defeated Hoffman in the primary and became my opponent in the November election.

One of the first important New Jersey Democrats to urge my running for governor was Senator Crawford Jamieson, of Trenton. Crawf not only was a fine lawyer; he was handsome, urbane, schooled in the intricacies of politics, and, above all, unbeholden to Frank Hague. In the immediate years to follow I came to know him extremely well and to rely upon his political advice as much as upon that of any one in my home state. Other Democratic leaders from counties other than Hague's Hudson County echoed Jamieson's request. They were tired of being tied to Hague's apron strings.

William R. Clark, editorializing in the *Newark Evening News,* said that local leaders "believe the party needs something more substantial in the way of a gubernatorial candidate than an escaped assemblyman from Hudson."

I was unopposed in the May primary; so, obviously, winning was no problem, even though Hague was lukewarm, at best, to my candidacy. Unfortunately, from his point of view, Harry Moore,* the Hague wheelhorse, was constitutionally unavailable as a candidate; so Hague went through the motions of supporting me.

In the editorial words of the strongly Republican *New York Herald-Tribune,* "Mr. Edison would not be Mayor Hague's ideal of a candidate for the governorship. He [Edison] would not place partisan politics above all other considerations. But Mayor Hague is realistic and practical."

Also in my favor was having President Roosevelt's blessing. Even Frank Hague had to take that into strong account.

It is apropos to mention at this juncture, I believe, that whereas the

---

*Democrat A. Harry Moore was governor of New Jersey for the three years preceding Edison's three-year term. Republican Harold G. Hoffman preceded Moore. Republican Walter E. Edge succeeded Edison.

president had urged me to make the race for the governorship and had promised to make Hague restrict his influence to his own county of Hudson and not try to be the power behind the gubernatorial throne, after the election FDR gave lip service my reform efforts while heeding directly or indirectly most of Hague's wishes.

My campaign tactics were slightly unusual, to say the least. My old friend and business associate, Arthur Walsh, who served as my campaign manager, and I mutually agreed to set up our own state headquarters. The regular state headquarters of the Democratic party was dominated by the Hague organization, which strove mightily to take charge of my campaign. I would have none of this.

Walsh and I engaged Francis A. Jamieson as publicity manager. As a statehouse reporter for the Associated Press—he was a Pulitzer Prize winner in 1933—Francis thoroughly understood New Jersey politics, and especially he knew the crooks and the fakers.

Francis Jamieson was Frank to most persons, but to me he was "Scum," a term of deep affection despite the misleading connotation. Scum was the brother of Senator Crawford Jamieson.

Since we took little advice from Hague and Jersey City, we took no money. My campaign was financed entirely by contributions from a few friends and relatives and from my own funds. To have gone to Hague for campaign funds would have obligated me to him.

I knew I was sincere in saying that, if elected, I would not be another Hague stooge; but widespread cynicism among voters made many persons doubt me. I wanted the people and Hague to understand that I would not be subservient to him. So, to state my independence under conditions carrying maximum impact, I chose to speak out at a giant Democratic rally in Sea Girt, on August 25, 1940, with Hague present.

Whatever his ethical weaknesses, Mayor Hague was a master organizer. In sixty special trains and thousands of private cars and buses, he and his committee got thousands of Democrats from all over the state to Sea Girt. There were present 100,000, 150,000 or 200,000 people, depending upon whether the newspaper reporting was Republican, Democratic, or Independent.

When it was my turn to speak, I said in part: "It is my happy privilege to be able to stand here and tell you that if you elect me you will have elected a governor who has made no promises of preferment to any man or group. I want to make this perfectly clear: you can be sure that I will never be a yes-man except to my own conscience."

I suppose Hague thought this was the usual political hokum. At any rate, he said nothing about it, though I thought his face, always sour, seemed afterward a little sourer than usual. Republicans, of course, professed to disbelieve me.

As the campaign progressed toward the November 5 election day, I toured all areas of the state and developed a series of points which, to me, were the most vital issues. Of first importance, to my way of thinking, was a new constitution to replace New Jersey's archaic ninety-seven-year-old document. To get it, I urged "a constitutional convention, to be elected on a nonpartisan basis, to bring our fundamental law up to date. Democracy cannot work through obsolete machinery. Our society cannot progress while our constitution stands still."

Other major issues raised by me included the appalling election laws, a morass of inconsistencies strung together by different legislatures over many years; reorganization of the state's patchwork administration setup; avoidance of additional taxes and the need for a tax system to encourage industries to locate in the state; the desirability of labor-law reforms that would extend rights guaranteed to workers in interstate commerce to those employed in intrastate commerce; judicial and civil service reforms; and an antilobbying law.

In October, in the very midst of the campaign, a terrific uproar was precipitated by the revelation that Hudson County poll books relating to the election of the Democratic governor A. Harry Moore three years earlier had been burned. There had long been suspicions that that election had been won for Moore by fraudulent registrations and votes in Hudson County. After that election Hague had dared the Republican-controlled legislature to investigate; but when they did send a committee to do so, the poll books were first locked up and then burned. The actual burning took place when it seemed likely that a subcommittee of the U.S. Senate Committee on Elections would demand access to them.

The deputy mayor of Jersey City, John Malone, called Arthur Walsh and first demanded, then begged, and finally threatened me not to say anything about the destruction of the poll books. He offered the "easy out" that they were three-year-old records, destroyed as the law allowed old records to be. His explanation was too thin, because whether they were obsolete records or not, they were in demand in an official investigation.

The burning of the poll books was too much for me, win or lose. I could not face my friends or keep peace with myself if I did not denounce the action. On October 1, speaking in Princeton, I said, "I would rather be respected than elected," and added, "The destruction of election records, no matter what legal technicalities support it, cannot be condoned. I condemn it."

My Republican opponent, Bob Hendrickson, also professed to disbelieve my independence. Employing such slogans as "A vote for Edison is a vote for Hague" and "Edison is the handpicked candidate of Hague," Hendrickson largely based his campaign on the issue of bossism. But since he was being actively supported by Republican bosses, such as Tom Mathis, of Ocean County, and Atlantic County's Enoch ("Nocky") Johnson—who was later sent to a federal penitentiary for income tax evasion—neither the voters nor the newspapers took his charges very seriously. Somewhat parenthetically, I should add that except for being opponents, Hendrickson and I rather liked and respected one another.

On November 4, as required by the New Jersey election law, all candidates filed with the secretary of state in Trenton a statement of their receipts and expenditures. My opponent reported having received $44,232, of which he had spent $40,180. I, whom Hendrickson erroneously charged with possessing a "great international fortune," had received $37,095 and spent $34,440. I had put in $22,000; my mother, $4,000; and my brother Theodore, $1,000. The rest had been from friends.

The election returns were very mixed. President Roosevelt carried New Jersey by a plurality of 71,528; I carried it by 63,895. But the Democratic candidate for the United States Senate, James H.R. Cromwell, the then husband of tobacco heiress Doris Duke, was defeated by 205,438. The Republicans elected a majority in each house of the legislature. The senate of 1941 was Republican, 16 to 5, and the assembly also was Republican, 41 to 19. To obtain this great majority in the legislature, the Republican party produced 26,209 more votes for their Assembly candidates than they did for their candidate for governor. Probably many Hoffman Republicans would not vote for Hendrickson, and either did not vote for governor at all or voted for me. In Hudson County, almost always Democratic, I had a plurality of 107,571, which was 21,766 fewer than Hudson's native son, A. Harry Moore, had received in 1937. I suppose, however, that a candidate usually does better in his own county. Moore had lost Essex County, where I lived, by 13,850 in 1937; I had lost it by 943.

It was gratifying to win, but the prospect of being Governor with a hostile legislature was not promising, because, even before the inauguration, the legislators showed what could be expected of them. Meanwhile, I spent much of the months of November and December nursing a very bad cold or the flu. My wife got it, too; and while I recovered in time for the inauguration, her cold turned into pneumonia, and she could not go to Trenton to the ceremony on January 21, 1941.

11

Ungovernable Governor[*]

JACK ALEXANDER, writing about me in the *Saturday Evening Post* of January 20, 1943, two years after the start of my three-year term, titled his article "Ungovernable Governor." By then, even the most skeptical New Jerseyans understood that it was not a powder-puff war between me and Frank Hague—we were using highly explosive powder worthy of the Du Pont label. A subtitle to Alexander's article read: "Charles Edison, first New Jersey chief executive since Wilson to buck the mercenaries, has Hague and his Hessians groggy in the Second Battle of Trenton."

An Alexander paragraph deeper into his article also said: "It is not yet clear whether the end of his [Edison's] three-year term, which has one year to go, will see Hague dethroned or whether the triennium will limp into history as a footnote captioned Edison's Rebellion."

History will write its own answer to the question Alexander posed. I humbly suggest, however, that Hague's ultimate demise as a political leader with national influence was hastened by me. I hope it was.

Almost from the day of my inauguration, the normal tribulations of exercising competent gubernatorial authority were aggravated both from within and from without my own party. Hague and the powerful Democratic organization he controlled leveled vicious attacks on me almost daily; and the Republicans, emboldened by lopsided majorities in both houses of the legislature and, no doubt, by my relative naivete as a practicing politician, set out to defy me on many, if not most, major issues.

---

[*]This chapter is a first-person account by Charles Edison in collaboration with Prof. Dayton McKean.

Hague wasted no time in showing his true colors. Within my first week in office he privately, over the telephone, excoriated me over a pending appointment to the state's supreme court in four-letter words familiar along the Jersey City waterfront. A vacancy had occurred, and it was my responsibility to fill it. Hague, refusing to believe that a new order existed in Trenton, thought this right still rested in him, as it had during recent Democratic administrations.

Three days after my term began, Justice Thomas W. Trenchard, thirty-seven years on the high court and in failing health at age seventy-seven, submitted his resignation. Since Justice Trenchard was a Republican, I was morally obligated by custom to appoint a Republican as his successor to maintain the political balance of the court. I was determined to select as strong a nominee as I could find.

The day after Justice Trenchard's retirement was announced, Mayor Hague called my trusted advisor, Arthur Walsh, from Florida to urge that I appoint Vice-Chancellor Wilfred H. Jayne, who had come up through the politics of Ocean County under Republican boss Tom Mathis. Regardless of whether or not I nominated Jayne, Hague told Walsh that it was important "to have a man in there whose vote you can get when you want it." Because of an earlier incident, I knew Hague was speaking from experience.

The following incident occurred before my becoming governor, but it serves to illustrate what Hague meant when he emphasized to Walsh the importance of having a judge "whose vote you can get when you want it." Thomas J. Brogan's career was spawned in Hague's backyard and flourished on Hague's approbation, plus his own abilities, which were many. After he had reached the pinnacle of becoming chief justice of the New Jersey Supreme Court, Brogan was called on to hear, sitting as a single justice because the full court was in seasonal recess, a case involving the right of the Hudson County superintendent of elections (a Republican) to open Jersey City ballot boxes in a disputed election won by one of Mayor Hague's candidates. Brogan listened attentively to the opposing views of counsel. Then, with a display of great dignity, he issued a verbal decision (not recorded) which went something like this: "I really can't understand what this dispute is all about. The law is very clear. It specifically gives the county superintendent of elections the right to open the ballot boxes." At this point in the proceedings, the lawyer for the anti-Hague forces tendered a smile, one quickly withdrawn as Chief Justice Brogan continued in this vein: "But nowhere does the law say the superintendent of elections can examine the contents of the ballot boxes. Therefore, I authorize him to open the boxes but forbid him to look inside."

Brogan was highly capable. Some of his decisions in non-political cases were classics of rectitude and wisdom. But in a pinch, when the pinch was against Hague, he could be counted on by Hague.

Despite continuing pressure from Hague sources, I was attracted to a man named Frederic R. Colie, an independent Republican highly respected by the best members of the bar for his vigorous integrity. I learned that a year earlier it had been revealed that the late Merritt Lane, a well-known New Jersey lawyer, had paid off most of a note of $100,000 for Vice-Chancellor Maja Leon Berry, and there was some question whether or not Berry should resign. When a resolution to urge Berry to remain on the bench had been offered to the Essex County Bar Association, Fred Colie stood on his feet and said: "The problem is whether by this resolution we endorse the act of a judicial officer allowing himself to become indebted to a lawyer practicing before him. If that meets the approval of the association, whatever canons of ethics we believe in should be thrown overboard."

Colie also had opposed the appointment by Governor Moore of Frank Hague, Jr., as a lay judge to the court of errors and appeals, New Jersey's then highest court. Young Hague was a lawyer, but he had never been graduated from a college or a law school and he had never tried a case. Governor Moore explained publicly that young Hague's appointment would "make his daddy happy."

I was aware that for me to nominate Colie would precipitate a fight with Hague, but I knew, too, that Hague and Edison could not both be governor. The people had elected me, not Hague; and I was determined to be the governor. A fight was sure to come sooner or later. I decided it might as well be sooner.

Not knowing Fred Colie personally, I asked him to come to see me. He did, and we got along well. We seemed to have the same ideas about the state of Jersey justice. He appeared to be the best man available. I decided to nominate him.

Meanwhile, the wires were hot from Miami and from Jersey City. Arthur Walsh suggested that I break the news to Hague rather than let him read of the nomination in the papers. I called him, and he nearly had a stroke at the news. He called me an ingrate, a Benedict Arnold, and other less favorable names. He said he would ruin me if it was the last thing he did. I must say that he tried his best.

On January 27, I sent to the senate the nomination of Frederic Colie to succeed Justice Trenchard. The newspapers of the state approved the nomination wholeheartedly. Senator Hendrickson, my erstwhile gubernatorial foe, said that it was a splendid appointment. To publicly attack me for a quality appointment to the supreme court obviously was not to Hague's liking. The word from Jersey City was not to fight on this line but to wait for a more salable issue. Even Hague's senator, Edward J. O'Mara, chimed in on the chorus of approval. Notwithstanding the unanimous (if some of it hypocritical) praise, the senate held a public hearing on Colie—something it had refused to do on Frank Hague, Jr. But they confirmed Colie; and so far as I know, he has been a fine justice. I have never seen or heard anything to make me doubt that he retained the integrity he had had before he became a judge.

Other issues were soon to arise—both with the Republican-controlled senate and with Hague—but the arena in which Hague chose to do public battle was my espousal of revising New Jersey's antiquated method of taxing railroads. It was, at least to him, a made-to-order issue in which I could be cast as the "heavy" for public consumption.

With one principal exception—the Pennsylvania Railroad—the many lines serving New Jersey were in dire straits. Making ends meet off their New Jersey operations was virtually impossible for them because of the state's laws. *

I was not the first governor to recognize the plight of the railroads. Two of my predecessors—Republican Hoffman and Democrat Moore— had recommended legislation to compromise railroad taxation. Since 1932 seven railroads, on which 63 percent of New Jersey's taxes had been imposed, had refused to pay their whole tax bills. Litigation costing the state and the railroad hundreds of thousands of dollars dragged on interminably, threatening to outdo the Dickensian lament that disputes in chancery may never end.

Even as late as 1939 the state senate passed legislation that would

---

*Railroads on December 1, 1940, owed New Jersey more than $34 million in unpaid taxes, plus another $24 million in interest and penalties, not counting the annual current levy of $18 million. The railroads, two of them already bankrupt and others facing bankruptcy, simply could not pay up. For 1940, the Interstate Commerce Commission said in its annually published national figures on the taxation of railroads that the average tax accrual per mile of track in the United States was $1,809. But the tax in New Jersey was $10,395. Some other eastern states and their comparable railroad taxes per track mile for 1940 were Pennsylvania, $1,098; New York, $3,276; and Rhode Island, $3,567.

have canceled 25 percent of the back taxes and allowed delinquent rail lines seven years to pay the remaining 75 percent in arrearages. Even if finally enacted into law, however, it would have been stopgap legislation at best because it did nothing to correct the fundamental ills of the existing laws. It would have left the form and the rate of taxation as they were, and ignored the ability of the railroads to pay.

That legislation never reached a vote in the lower house because Hague objected to the proposed remedy since it did not give preferential treatment to his very own Hudson County. Hague, at taxpayers' expense, ran full-page ads in many of New Jersey's daily newspapers denouncing the proposed "steal" by the "railroad lobby" and threatening reprisals on assemblymen who might vote for the bill.

His success led Hague to believe he had found another method of blocking legislation he did not like: the use of huge false advertisements.

I was to be victimized by Hague, employing the same technique, only on a stepped-up scale, a few years later when I proposed an overhaul of the basic method of taxing rail lines serving New Jersey.

To find a solution of the whole problem that was just and workable, and, at the same time, no mere stopgap, I asked four citizens of New Jersey as a public service to undertake a study of the matter and to suggest remedies. They were Albert R. Jube, of South Orange, a lawyer; Brigadier General Lewis B. Ballantyne, of Newark, a businessman; Carl Holderman, of Newark, state chairman of Labor's Non-Partisan League; and Dr. John F. Sly, of Princeton, director of the Princeton Surveys. They made an independent study of the whole problem and studiously avoided conferring with anyone connected with any of the railroads up to the time they submitted their report to me, on February 22, 1941.

The principal elements of the legislation, drafted in accordance with the proposals of the citizens' committee, were these:

(1) The total principal of back taxes must be paid in full, but railroads were given from two to twenty years to complete their payments, depending upon their ability to pay, as determined by a formula in the law. From December 1, 1940, they were required to pay 3 percent interest on unpaid taxes. The penalties, which had accumulated since 1932 at 12 percent annually, were canceled, but only if and when the railroads completed payment of the back taxes.

(2) An annual tax was imposed upon all property used for railroad purposes at the rate of 3 percent of its true value.

(3) A franchise tax of 3 percent was imposed upon each railroad's net

174

operating income or, as in the case of interstate railroads, upon that part of the income allocable to New Jersey on the basis of their respective intrastate trackage.

The state chamber of commerce, the New Jersey Taxpayers Association, and other organizations voiced their approval.

The senate and assembly appointed a joint committee which held public hearings, examined witnesses, and considered various alternative proposals.

In a letter of transmittal to the legislature, the majority of the joint committee said:

> The four specific bills presented to the Legislature herewith are the same bills, with some minor changes, prepared for the governor's special committee by the Princeton Group and submitted to your Joint Legislative Committee by Governor Edison, with his approval and recommendation.
>
> It is the opinion of your Joint Committee that this program is equitable, sound, and meritorious and is in the public interest.

For weeks thereafter everyone connected with the tax proposals was subjected to every imaginable vilification in newspaper statements and in several series of full-page advertisements, written by Hague (he boasted in them of his authorship) but paid for by the taxpayers of Jersey City. Members of the legislature, members of the citizens' committee, and I were described in libelous terms, indicating that we were being paid bribes for stealing for the railroads the fantastic sum of $121 million.

Over and over again Hague and his henchmen used this figure of $121 million. It was a startling sum, calculated to jar the newspaper reader—it was used on Hitler's principle that the bigger the lie the more readily it will be believed. In the years that followed, a radio speech by one of Hague's men was a speech wasted if it did not mention a "$121 million tax steal" or a "121 million gift to the railroads." Anyone interested in the mental processes of a political boss might be curious about how Hague arrived at this magic number. First, he assumed that the 3 percent franchise tax would never bring in any money, although, as will be shown, it actually brought in millions; and on this assumption he asserted that the loss of revenue would be $5 million a year. This figure he multiplied by 20, because one of the railroads was allowed twenty years to pay up its back taxes! He could, of course, just as well have picked 25 or 1,000 instead of 20; one figure was as irrelevant as another. But by multiplying $5 million by 20 he got $100 million. To this he added $21 million, which he thought represented the interest penalties. And he arrived at $121 million. It was that simple—and that absurd.

Day after day, in full-page advertisements, Hague published attacks upon the legislature and upon me. "The Gravy Train is Pulling into Trenton" was a headline on one of them. "Governor Edison Should Never Have Injected Himself into This Controversy" was another. Something of the mayor's English style may be seen in this nonstop sentence from the advertisement of June 19:

> It must be very evident that the railroads are exercising undue influence in the Legislature, in view of the fact they have come to the Legislature for the purpose of avoiding delinquent payments which have been passed upon by the courts and also for the purpose of changing the method of taxation of railroad property, which has been approved by over 110 state court decisions, and which has also been approved by every federal court, including the United States Supreme Court, even as late as April 28th of this year.

Newspapers published the advertisements, though some of them deleted, as the Passaic *Herald News* said editorially, "the more palpably libelous statements of Hague." On one occasion the *Trenton Times* began an editorial by saying "On another page Mayor Hague published another lying advertisement," and then went on to deflate the arguments in the advertisement.

The heat was put on all Democratic legislators by Jersey City City Hall. They were threatened with everything the boss could think of if they voted for the bills. Most of them wilted, but three Mercer County assemblymen and Senators Crawford Jamieson and James I. Bowers stood firm. When the bills were before the senate, Senator Bowers, who was minority leader, after reviewing the abuse that had poured out of Jersey City, said:

> Apparently it is up to me to choose between Governor Edison and Mayor Hague. That task is not a difficult one, and I declare right here that I stand with Governor Edison, who has demonstrated capacity, honesty, courage, and unusual leadership. The people of the state of New Jersey . . . will not be misled by bombast and hot air from Mayor Hague.

Early in the morning of July 22, after an all-night session in which the Republican leaders joined me in stiffening the backbones of legislators terrified by Hague's blasts, the bills passed the assembly 33 to 22, the senate by 12 to 3. That was a slim majority in each house. Both houses were overwhelmingly Republican, but the bills could not have passed either chamber without the votes of the few Democrats who refused to be intimidated. No jobs, no favors, no promises were given to any legislator; the persuasion was strictly on the merits of the legislation.

I was staying then at the governor's summer home at Sea Girt. I had hardly got to bed at dawn when I was called to the telephone to be notified that Hague had issued his most vicious attack yet. He charged that I had bought legislative votes with judgeships "to perpetrate this steal for the benefit of the railroad lobby and to put over these graft bills." He asserted that I was interested in the legislation because the Edison companies did business with the railroads. He also singled out Senator Bowers for special abuse. There were hundreds of words in the statement, all dripping with lies and half-truths.

Up to that time I had refrained from issuing statements. I wanted the bills considered on their merits, so far as that was possible, and not mixed into any Hague-Edison feud. But now, with the bills passed, I felt free to answer his attack. I reviewed the history of the problem. On the mayor's knowledge of the problem, I said:

> Unfortunately, Hague knows nothing about economics. He believes that Jersey City can go on piling up one of the highest per capita costs in the nation, and if his citizen homeowners lose their properties through tax foreclosures, it must be the railroads' fault. If the Home Owners Loan Corporation denounces the excessive tax burden on Jersey City property, it is the railroads' fault—the great greedy, bankrupt railroads.

I answered each of his charges. On the judgeship business, it is worth mentioning that not one of the senators or assemblymen he charged me with buying was during my term appointed to the bench. As to the business the Edison companies did with the railroads, I pointed out that our largest customer was the Pennsylvania Railroad, which had paid its taxes and had, therefore, no back taxes or penalties to compromise, and another customer was the Hudson and Manhattan, which claimed that the new law would bankrupt it. The Edison companies were then doing around $600,000 of business a year with railroads that had any trackage in New Jersey, but repeatedly Hague asserted that I sold out the state for some $30 million of business. I must say for the men who ran the railroads that they never used their purchases from the Edison companies to bring any pressure on me.

Late in August the attorney general, David T. Wilentz (who first burst upon the national scene as the prosecutor of Bruno Richard Hauptmann in the Lindbergh kidnaping case), announced that he was going to attack the constitutionality of the tax acts in the courts. He was a holdover from A. Harry Moore's term as governor; he was also Democratic leader of Middlesex County and one of Hague's principal lieutenants. He came into my office and said, "Governor, I hate to do this, but you know how it is." He meant that Hague had forced him into it.

I pointed out to him that if he went into court against the constitutionality of an act passed by the legislature and signed by the governor, the state would be deprived of the services of its attorney general, because he could not carry water on both shoulders. The state would have to hire special counsel to defend its legislation against its own attorney general. He proceeded, nevertheless.

Wilentz attacked the constitutionality of the laws chiefly on the ground that in canceling the interest penalties the legislature had made a donation of money to a corporation, in violation of article 1, paragraph 20, of the state constitution. But we felt when the bills were drafted that we had plenty of precedents for the cancelation of penalties. For more than half a century it had been the practice both of the state and its municipalities to cancel tax penalties and even taxes when the full amounts proved to be uncollectible. Moreover, the court of errors and appeals had held in the Dorrance estate case that interest did not inhere in a tax as a legal incident; that it was a penalty, or in the nature of a penalty.

The interest penalties were canceled, but they were not donated to the railroads. They were exchanged for an agreement that was of substantial value to the state. A gift or a donation means a gratuity for which the donor received nothing. The railroads accepted system liability for taxes on operating roads, and they agreed to withdraw pending litigation, covering the years 1938 to 1941, inclusive, in which they claimed that their properties had been overvalued for tax purposes. In these proceedings the railroads claimed they were entitled to reductions in excess of $30 million. Had the railroads been successful in their litigation, the state would have lost this sum, which exceeded the canceled penalties by about $6 million. In waiving their rights to appeal their assessments for 1938 to 1941 they gave the state a very valuable consideration.

The litigation dragged along slowly. A decision was not handed down by the court of errors and appeals until late in June 1944, three years fter Wilentz had begun the proceedings. By a vote of 10 to 4, the ourt, disregarding its finding in the Dorrance case, held that 1 percent er month was not a penalty; and consequently the cancelation of the nterest was unconstitutional as constituting a donation of public nonies to the railroads.

The decision of the court, however, did not in itself affect the new cheme of taxation—it went only to the cancelation of interest. The ailroads in 1944 were in much better financial condition than they had een in 1940, largely because of the war, and, except for those still in he hands of the bankruptcy courts, were able to pay their back taxes nd some of their interest. On their part they lost the consideration they ad given for the new laws, and they might have upset them; but they id not.

It is a curious fact that Jersey City and Hudson County received more rom the new taxes which Hague opposed so violently than they ever ad from the old ones.

But, after all, he was fighting not taxes but me.

12

Constitutional Reform *

THE STATE CONSTITUTION under which I was elected governor in 1940 already was ninety-six years old. For decades, Democrats and Republicans alike had urged constitutional reform; but definitive action was stalled by disagreements over procedures to be followed and by just what should be reformed and how.

The constitution of 1844 had not been in effect thirty years when some of its weaknesses were pointed out by Governor Joel Parker. As the years passed, more and more inadequacies were revealed, and almost every governor after the Civil War urged revision. Governor Robert Green, in 1886, Governor Franklin Murphy, in 1905, and Governor Woodrow Wilson, in 1913, urged complete rewriting. Governors Edward C. Stokes and Franklin Fort attempted, without success, to obtain fundamental reforms. My immediate predecessor in office, A. Harry Moore, had said in 1927, during the first of his three terms as governor, that the constitution was "so archaic and so inadequate to meet the conditions of the present day as to require complete revision." There was no partisanship about the matter; revision was favored by both Democrats and Republicans. In seeking to obtain constitutional reconstruction, I only took up the campaign where others had left off.

In the opinion of Woodrow Wilson, "The powers of corrupt control have an enormous and abiding advantage under our constitutional arrangements as they stand." I certainly agreed with him.

But Wilson went on to Washington, and the movement he had started for constitutional revision languished. It never quite died, however; and as Frank Hague established his power in the state through

---

*This chapter is a first-person account by Charles Edison in collaboration with Prof. Dayton McKean.

180

his control of the multitude of state boards and courts, more Republicans came to see constitutional reform as being necessary before Hague could be shaken. But the Republicans, in their then virtually perpetual control over the state senate, had an effective veto on the state government which they never for one moment proposed to relinquish. They would discuss any other constitutional reform—but not of the senate.

Arthur Walsh once discussed revision with Frank Hague before the Colie appointment. Hague was all for revision by convention, provided "they leave my courts alone." When Walsh suggested that a convention might not in other respects do what was wanted, Hague said not to worry: "I'll buy the bastards!"

So the situation amounted to this: Hague was for revision if his courts were left alone; the Republicans were for revision if their senate was left alone. Only the executive branch remained a place where reform could be attempted without arousing powerful hostility.

In the campaign of 1940 I went over the chief defects of the constitution as I saw them, urging the calling of a constitutional convention to overhaul the entire charter. I favored the overall kind of revision that a convention could produce, rather than the method of revision by amendment, because it seemed to me that each of the three divisions of the government needed considerable improvement, and the three were so interlocked that endless confusion might result if some amendments were adopted and others failed.

In my inaugural address I summarized the principal defects of the constitution as I saw them:

> We have more than four score independent, or semi-independent state agencies, some with their own incomes and budgets, some of which are little governments of their own.
>
> No one, therefore, can say just what the government of New Jersey costs. No one can get a complete picture of what is going on.
>
> The governor should be given effective control over this administrative conglomeration. The eighty agencies should be consolidated into no more than twenty, and a governor's cabinet should be drawn from their executives.
>
> A veto power that amounts to something should be given to the governor. He is the one state official elected by all of the citizens; and he should have power to stop faulty, partisan, or sectional legislation.
>
> The governor's term should be changed from three to four years, and the elections should be held in years other than presidential ones to avoid confusion of national and state issues.
>
> The existing representative inequality that permits a majority of the

senate to be formed from the representatives of 15 percent of the people should be eradicated. If the two-house legislature is to be retained, which is a debatable question, the term of the senators should be lengthened from two to four years. The term of assemblymen should be two years instead of one.

A new constitution should be more amendable.

The needlessly confusing system of courts should be altered to produce an arrangement that would be simple, responsible, and less costly.

Although the titular leader of the Republican party in the state, Senator Hendrickson, and I agreed on the need for a convention, we made no progress with the legislators. The legislature was snarled in a patronage row over who was to get elected to the various jobs filled by joint session. Notwithstanding the obvious desire of the legislators to have me leave the matter of constitutional revision alone, I took every opportunity to address organizations of people throughout the state to urge the necessity of it.

Public response was most encouraging. Statewide organizations such as the Chamber of Commerce, the League of Women Voters, and the Taxpayers Association were for it. So were the AFL and the CIO. Special groups like the New Jersey Committee on Constitutional Convention and, later, the New Jersey Constitution Foundation, were established.

On July 28, 1941, I assembled the two houses of the legislature in joint session and made a personal appeal for nonpartisan support of a constitutional convention. The members listened respectfully, then recessed and went home without acting.

Forces friendly to me were in control of the Democratic state convention when it met two months later in September. A strong constitutional convention plank was adopted for the platform.

The opposition party was split. The Republican state chairman, H. Alexander Smith, proposed constitutional reform through a series of amendments. The party's Clean Government wing favored a complete rewriting of the constitution via the convention approach.

The election of 1941 returned Republican majorities to both houses of the legislature, but the legislators were not disposed to put through the constitutional amendments their platform had promised. That was just as well, because no set of amendments could correct the multitude of defects in the constitution, as the Republicans themselves came to recognize. A majority in the assembly probably would have been favorable to a convention, but the senate was overwhelmingly opposed.

The legislature reconvened in November, and a compromise was proposed—a commission to study the constitution and suggest amendments. The appointment of a commission to investigate and report is a well-known device among politicians for killing a proposal with kindness, and I did not like the scheme. I much preferred a constitutional convention, but that was impossible in view of the attitude of the senate. I was presented with half a loaf, and I took it. On November 18, 1941, I signed the joint resolution creating the commission.

Under the terms of the resolution the president of the senate, the speaker of the assembly and the governor each appointed two members; and these six picked one more. The president of the senate appointed Senator Robert C. Hendrickson and Professor John F. Sly, of Princeton; the speaker appointed Walter J. Freund, a former assemblyman and then freeholder of Bergen County, and Judge Walter D. Van Riper, of the Essex County Court of Common Pleas; I appointed Senator Crawford Jamieson and Arthur T. Vanderbilt, leader of the Clean Government Republicans and former president of the American Bar Association. The whole group then selected as the seventh member James E. Kerney, Jr., editor of the *Trenton Times*.

The commission surprised and doubtless disappointed many legislators by going right to work and by keeping at it. They first tried to draft amendments to correct the defects that everybody agreed upon. I heard unofficially that they had drafted twenty-four amendments when they gave up that plan and rewrote the whole constitution. In the belief that, over nearly a century, there had been sufficient discussion of the shortcomings of the constitution, they did not hold public hearings. Rather, they pushed their work along and reported in May of 1942.

The commission conceded that the constitution they had drafted was "not a model constitution." It represented, however, a vast improvement over the constitution of 1844. Every change except one was, in my judgment, an improvement. That one was a prohibition against a governor's being reelected. The report was a high point in the history of the long campaign to obtain a better government in New Jersey.

For a variety of reasons, the legislature would not pass a bill to submit adoption of the proposed new constitution to a referendum. The assembly might well have passed such a bill, but the senate was adamantly against it. Public demand was so strong, however, that the senators felt they had to take some action. They seized upon the fact that no public hearings had been held and, with the assembly concurring, adopted a resolution creating a joint legislative committee to hold hearings. The president of the senate appointed four senators known to be hostile to revision, and the speaker of the house appointed two who were for revision and two who were not.

Public hearings lasted from July to mid-September. The committee's record and its report comprised a volume of 1,124 pages, a compendium of everything that everybody in the state thought wrong with the constitution. I was one of those who testified. In all the hearings there was not one person who expressed satisfaction with the 1844 constitution.

Notwithstanding the unanimity of the witnesses, the committee, by a vote of 6 to 2, seized upon the war as an excuse for inaction and recommended that "no further action for change in the New Jersey Constitution be taken until after the termination of the present war."

The committee expressed fear that discussion in wartime of a matter of such "highly controversial character" might "cause disunity." This is the kind of patriotism that Dr. Samuel Johnson may have had in mind when he defined patriotism as the last refuge of a scoundrel.

The legislature was quite content to accept the committee's report and allow the whole matter to die quietly. But outside pressures would not let the issue die. The New Jersey Constitution Foundation got speakers on the radio and placed publicity in newspapers and magazines. Editors kept constitutional revision alive by a succession of editorials. Notable among the newspapers that hammered away for revision were the *Newark Evening News,* the *Trenton Times,* and the *Camden Courier-Post.* I did my bit whenever I had a chance.

In my annual message on January 12, 1943, I took the position that constitutional revision was the most important problem before the state, even though the problem was an old one. I reviewed what had been done up to that time and concluded the message by saying:

> Many people deplore the concentration of power in Washington and profess to see in the increasing federal authority a threat to popular government. I do myself. But I realize that the growth of federal power dates back beyond the Civil War, and that it is constantly accelerated by the failures of the states themselves. When they insist upon attempting to operate under constitions that are unequal to present-day needs, and when there is a national government aware of those needs and able to act, power is sure to flow to that government which will exercise it.
>
> When the war ends, the states and the nation will be faced with tremendous and complex problems. If we are honest with ourselves, we

cannot expect that the haphazard, inefficient and irresponsible state government that we have under the constitution of 1844 will be halfway competent to deal with the new problems it will have to face. Washington will once more be compelled to act.

Those who object to having all sovereignty gathered into Washington, those who believe that the states must be the base of representative democracy if it is to be maintained over such vast distances and over so many millions of people as there are in America, and those who fear that the national government has approached the point of growth where sheer size makes it inefficient and dangerous—all these people are under a moral obligation to do something about it.

Name-calling is not enough. Deploring is not enough. Blaming some one man or some group of men, living or dead, is both absurd and ineffectual. The decline in the relative position of the states is due to causes, not to persons. We must remove the causes. Our responsibility here in New Jersey is to produce, under a reformed and modernized constitution, a state government able to meet the needs of our times. When we have done that, then—and only then—can we consistently say that there is no need to go to Washington, that our representative government in New Jersey can solve our problems.

The campaign, now more than fifty years old, to revise and modernize the Constitution of New Jersey was not ended by the failure of the last legislature to act.

I have been much heartened by the expressions of confidence I have received in the last few months. I know that the campaign will continue, will increase in intensity. But I dread the possibility that a sudden crisis may find the government of New Jersey under its 1844 constitution unequal to its tasks before the inevitable reform is accomplished.

In these times when crisis follows crisis, you members of the 167th legislature of New Jersey have a great responsibility. It is in your hands to determine whether our commonwealth is to stand still, or meet the postwar emergencies with a state constitution equal to any emergency.

Among the proposals considered and rejected by the legislative committee that held hearings on the constitution during the summer of 1942 was one to refer to the people the question whether the legislature should act as a constitutional convention to draft a new constitution to be ratified or rejected by the people. Early in the 1943 session Assemblyman Milton A. Feller, of Union County, introduced a bill for such a referendum. He obtained the active support of the Clean Government Republicans, particularly Dominic A. Cavicchia, of Newark. The proposal appealed to most Republicans because it kept the control of constitution-drafting in their hands. The bill eventually passed the assembly, only to be buried in the senate. The senators were still afraid that they might lose some of their powers.

By 1943 the Harold Hoffman faction of the Republican party had lost so much influence that the party was more unified than it had been for many years. The county bosses and leaders agreed before the primary upon Walter E. Edge, who had been governor from 1917 to 1919, as their candidate for governor in the November election. During his first administration Governor Edge had shown little or no interest in constitutional revision; but when his party united behind him as its candidate, he accepted revision as the paramount issue. Perhaps one reason was that Judge Walter Van Riper, who had been on the constitutional commission, was a close friend and advisor. At any rate, Edge got the Republican senators in a private meeting and put such pressure upon them that he produced a political miracle—he got twelve of them to vote for the Feller bill, one more than a majority.

Somewhat reluctantly, I signed the Feller bill into law following its passage on May 10, 1943. I would have preferred an elected convention to the legislature, acting as one; but there was no question that it was this scheme or nothing. I felt that if the legislature, serving as a convention, drafted a poor constitution, I would not be bound to support the result. On the other hand, if the lawmakers wrote a good one, the method would not matter too much.

The immediate task ahead was to obtain a favorable vote on the referendum. During the summer of 1943 each time I was invited to speak on the constitution, I took up a different point. I went through the constitution article by article in a series of speeches, explaining what I thought was wrong and what needed to be done to correct each defect. These talks were incorporated into a pamphlet, several thousands of which were distributed prior to the referendum in November.

All major organizations interested in better government urged their members to vote "yes" on the referendum. Opposition arose from three principal sources. Political bosses in both parties opposed any revision. They had done well enough under the old constitution and had no reason to think they would do as well under a new one. The state bureaucracy had much the same attitude, because the officeholders feared that a revised constitution would surely consolidate the proliferation of boards and bureaus to limit their independence. Some farm groups that had enjoyed considerable control over the senators feared that the senate might lose some of its prerogatives. All of these interests, of course, were correct in their fears and expectations.

Underestimating the sentiment for revision, Mayor Hague hired billboards around the state to display pictures of soldiers, accompanied by variants of the wait-until-the-boys-come-home theme. He and his henchmen even blamed the referendum on his old standby devil—the railroad lobby.

A caprice of circumstance prevented him from blaming the referendum on another of his favorite whipping boys—the Communist party. For reasons not necessarily clear or cogent at this writing, the Communist party in New Jersey endorsed Hague, in July of 1943, presumably because Hague-controlled congressmen supported President Roosevelt. Long an antagonist of Hague, the Communist party, by switching its support to him, performed a startling political flip-flop. As a natural aftermath, I was attacked by the Communists as a reactionary.

This Communist flip-flop was rich fodder for the nation's editorial writers and cartoonists. I like best a poem by H.I. Phillips that appeared in the *New York Sun*. Two stanzas will give its flavor:

> From the steppes of Jersey City—
> From the far off Ural heights—
> Ivan Hague, the old-time Cossack,
> Takes his stand for human rights;
> See him on his Russian pony,
> Leather boots and sheepskin hat;
> Ivan of the rugged Jerseys,
> Asking sternly, "Who threw that?"
>
> Edison? He's just a Czarist—
> He is clearly lacking all
> Of those signal civic virtues
> Found in Jersey City's Hall;
> Vladimir (That is, our Frankie),
> For a righteous world is he;
> Those who fight him are just blocking
> Government by purity.

The bosses were so sure the referendum would be defeated that they spent relatively little money on the campaign. The proponents spent very little because they had little to spend. Reporters just before election day gave the referendum little chance.

The referendum triumphed by a majority of 154, 334; and it carried nineteen of the state's twenty-one counties. It lost only in the two most boss-ridden counties—Hague's Hudson and Mathis' Ocean.

Despite opposition claims that nothing should be done about updating an antiquated constitution until World War II ended, the vote of men and women in the armed services was four to one in favor.

Only about half of all those voting in the election, however, voted on the referendum question, a fact that showed how much work still needed to be done to reach the public in New Jersey.

Immediately following the election and referendum, my successor, Governor-elect Edge, got the Republican-dominated legislature busy drafting a new constitution. The drafting was done by the Republicans alone, although a good many Democrats had had something to do with bringing the matter along over the generations. The whole conduct of the drafting was so high-handed that many resentments never disappeared, and that affected the final result.

However arbitrary the Republicans were, they did follow in most respects the excellent draft prepared by the constitutional commission of 1941.

The draft of the proposed new constitution was rapidly finished. It was introduced in the legislature on February 25, 1944, briefly debated, and passed on March 3, less than two months after my term had ended.

It did not do everything I thought ought to be done, but it was such an immense improvement over the constitution of 1844 that I was glad to support it.

As the proponents of constitutional revision had underestimated their strength in 1943, they overestimated it in 1944. Hague and his allies were not so deluded. In the words of *Time Magazine,* the campaign put on against the proposed constitution was a "Donnybrook of bigotry, lying and slander." For the first time in years, Hague stumped the state in person, charging (as the spirit moved him) either that the proposal was a product of the railroad lobby or that it was a Republican constitution designed to ruin him.

Governor Edge was sincerely favorable to revision, and he worked hard for it, as I had. He got promises of support from local Republican leaders; but as the *Newark News* said, "The state's small-time Republican bosses apparently lacked enthusiasm for Mr. Edge's cause."

A few days before the election a public opinion poll indicated that the proposed constitution would be approved by about 150,000 majority. But at the last minute the hierarchy of the Roman Catholic church in New Jersey brought all its force to bear against the proposed constitution. In 1941 the legislature had passed a bill requiring public school buses to carry parochial school children, but in mid-summer 1944 a taxpayers' suit was decided in Part II of the state supreme court against the constitutionality of the act. Though this was no final determination, because the case had yet to be passed upon by the whole bench of the supreme court and then by the court of errors and appeals, still the decision was seized upon by the opponents of the proposed constitution to make a demagogic appeal for Catholics to vote against it. One priest said that the drafters of the constitution should have anticipated the decision and inserted a clause specifically authorizing public school buses to carry Catholic children to parochial schools.

Some of Hague's men also tried to make it appear that the public officers' clause of the proposed constitution would compel priests to testify to a legislative committee concerning the secrets of the confessional. This allegation was, of course, absurd.

Governor Edge called upon Archbishop Thomas J. Walsh, of Newark, shortly before the election to try to stop the developing opposition from the Catholic church. He got no response. Several hundred leading Catholic laymen in New Jersey signed a public statement that there was nothing in the proposed constitution that would offend Catholics. But this appeal made no impression.

On the weekend before the election, messengers from the Catholic chancellery in Newark took to all the priests in the diocese written instructions that at the Sunday masses they were to advise their parishioners to vote "no" on the proposed constitution, to "remember the bus bill," and not to enter into any controversy or argument on the matter. Apparently this was done all over the state on Sunday, November 5, two days before the election.

The effect upon the vote was devastating. As Monsignor John J. Murphy, of the Sacred Heart Church, Newark, said in an address to the Holy Name Society after the election, it was a perfectly timed move, "the straw that broke the camel's back." He took credit for the church for the defeat of the constitution, saying, "This won't be very comforting to Governor Edge." What Governor Edge had ever done to arouse this animosity toward him on the part of the church, I do not know; nor am I prepared to say why the church took up Hague's cause. I am sincerely convinced that there was nothing in the proposed constitution that would in any way have injured any interest of the Catholic church or any other church.

One Catholic priest in Trenton was not to be intimidated by the order to direct his parishioners to vote "no." He read the chancellery's directive in Latin so that few, if any, in the congregation would get the message.

The constitution was defeated in thirteen of the twenty-one counties by a vote of 761,151 to 602,421. The service vote was approximately four to one in favor of revision. The *Newark News,* in an editorial entitled "A Good Cause Lost," said that the result was due to the failure of the proponents to implant in the state a sufficient "affirmative psychology" and to "the opposition of pressure groups, the Catholic clergy, and Mr. Hague's machine." The editors of the *National Municipal Review,* in concluding a long editorial that reviewed the campaign for constitutional revision in New Jersey, said, "The most disquieting aspect of this contest was the strained injection of religious considerations . . . to reject a forward-looking document and to save the political skin of a notorious spoilsman."

It was a good cause lost—lost in the dirtiest campaign in my experience. I do not now know how many more generations must struggle toward self-government in New Jersey under the archaic constitution of 1844. But I do know that there were more than 600,000 citizens who realized that the old constitution was fatally defective for a modern democracy; if they could persuade the 300,000 who voted for president but did not vote on revision to follow them, there would still be a chance for constitutional reconstruction in New Jersey.

For my own part, I do not regret the work I did and the time I devoted to the cause. I cannot think of any statement I made about the constitution of 1844 or about the proposed constitution that I would recant if I could. All of us who worked to bring a better constitution for our commonwealth have a right to feel that we constributed something to the eduction of the people on the most fundamental problem before them. We can hope that sometimes this work will bear fruit.

[Although Charles Edison was to live almost fifteen more years, he did not get around to writing autobiographically on events of the ensuing three years that led to the adoption of a new constitution for New Jersey in 1947. Highlights of this triennium are filled in by the author as follows:]

The defeat of constitutional revision in the referendum of November 7, 1944, did not stifle proponents of reform. The New Jersey Committee for Constitutional Revision—an instrumentality that Edison helped create—continued to play a key role in focusing attention on deficiencies in the constitution of 1844. Many other organizations also fanned the flames of reform.

Governor Edge was succeeded on January 21, 1947, by another Republican, Alfred E. Driscoll, a supporter of constitutional revision. In his inaugural address to the combined houses of the legislature Governor Driscoll stated that "the people in 1944 did not vote in favor of our present constitution of 1844 as much as they voted against the document submitted to them as a whole to replace it." He asked the legislature to call a constitutional convention.

The Republican-controlled legislature responded promptly. It authorized this two-pronged approach:

(1) to avoid the extra cost and possible delay of a special referendum, the spring primaries were to be used to determine whether the electorate desired the calling of a convention and

(2) if so, to elect simultaneously the delegates to the convention.

The vote was favorable; and delegates to the convention assembled at Rutgers University in New Brunswick on June 12, 1947, to begin deliberations. They were under a mandate to complete their work by September 12 so that the New Jersey electorate could vote for adoption or rejection of their work at the November general election.

The convention had certain built-in restrictions imposed by the legislature. It was proscribed from changing the existing method of apportioning members of the legislature among the state's twenty-one counties. Each county was to continue to have one state senator, irrespective of its population (acres versus people), and each county's assembly strength was to be based on population. * A compromise to be sure, but one aimed at minimizing opposition to whatever final draft the convention came up with.

The eighty-one delegates to the constitutional convention labored diligently, completing their duties well ahead of the September 12 deadline. Despite, or possibly because of, heated criticism by Hague and others during the convention, the finished draft contained sufficient compromise to insure broad support without neutering the document's basic worth.

Edison endorsed the final document and worked for its ratification, as did Arthur T. Vanderbilt, the leader of the Clean Government wing of the Republican party, Governor Driscoll, and former governor Edge. There was little, if any, organized opposition. Even the recalcitrant

---

*Somewhat ironically, the U.S. Supreme Court not too many years later enunciated its one-man, one-vote rule that vitiated New Jersey's practice of allotting one senator to each county.

Frank Hague joined the proponents after certain original proposals pertaining to taxation were modified by the convention.

The new constitution was ratified at the general election on November 4, 1947, by a vote of 653,096 to 184,632. For the most part, the new constitution became effective on January 1, 1948. An exception was article 6, relating to the judiciary, which, for procedural reasons, did not go into effect until September 15 of the same year. Thus ended the state's 103 years under the constitution of 1844.*

Some of the significant changes in the new constitution were those propounded by Edison as early as 1940. They included:

(1) Lengthening the governor's term from three to four years, permitting a governor to serve a second successive term, and scheduling future gubernatorial elections so that they would not coincide with presidential elections.

(2) Strengthening the governor's power by sharply reducing the number of independent state agencies and bureaus, by authorizing a cabinet of top departmental officials to serve the chief executive, and by requiring a two-thirds vote of each legislative house to override a governor's veto. Formerly this could be done by a simple majority.

(3) Extending assembly terms from one to two years and senate terms from two to four years.

(4) Unification of the state's court system under a supreme court, followed by a superior court (including law, chancery and appellate divisions) and substituting county courts for what had been courts of common pleas. These changes eliminated the cumbersome old court of errors and appeals, formerly the court of last resort, and the old chancery court, which was superseded by a chancery division within the new superior court.

(5) Inclusion of the clause that read: "No member of the Senate or General Assembly, during the term for which he shall have been elected, shall be nominated, elected or appointed to any state civil office or position of profit, which shall have been created by law, or the emoluments whereof shall have been increased by law, during such term."

---

*Another constitutional convention was held at Rutgers University in the spring of 1966. This convention was called essentially to make New Jersey conform to the U.S. Supreme Court's one-man, one-vote mandate. Convention delegates proposed that the state senate have forty members instead of twenty-one and that the general assembly have eighty members instead of sixty, with districts no longer necessarily being individual counties. These changes were ratified by the general election on November 8, 1966, by a vote of 890,710 to 506,884.

Retained in the new document, to Edison's regret, was that the president of the senate became the acting governor in event of the elected governor's demise, resignation, removal from office, or inability to serve, including his absence, even through brief, from the state. Edison felt strongly that New Jersey should have a lieutenant governor elected by all the people, rather than reposing this responsibility in a man elected merely by the voters of a senatorial district.

Three governors in succession—Edison, Edge, and Driscoll—worked diligently for constitutional reform. Since success came under Driscoll, he understandably received a lion's share of the public credit.

Privately, during a conversation at an annual dinner of the Legislative Correspondents Club, of which the author was a member, Driscoll confided that without the momentum generated by Edison and continued under Edge he doubted that success could have been achieved by his administration.

13

Government by Investigation *

MANY SINCERE BUT misguided people think that the beginning and the end of good government is the election or appointment of honest and capable men to office. We do not get good government if crooks or incompetents are elected or appointed, to be sure; but the form of the government—its structure and powers—has a lot to do with whether good men can be elected or appointed. A government, moreover, can be set up in such a way that good government is almost impossible under it.

During my term as governor, the state senate was a constant block to attempts to get good men in office. Under the New Jersey Constitution of 1844 there was one senator elected from each county, regardless of population. This provision resulted in such undemocratic representation that in the 1940s the senator from Cape May County spoke for 28,000 people; the senator from Essex, for 837,000. Since more than half of the population of the state is concentrated in four urban counties, the rural senators always had control of the senate. These senators tend to be either county bosses or men acceptable to the county bosses. Aside from the dozen important officials elected by the legislature in joint session, almost all major New Jersey officials are appointed by the governor with the "advice and consent" of the senate. The governor is the only state officer elected by all of the voters of the state. Thus it happens that state senators stand at the gates of patronage, where they may take toll of all who pass.

The rural senators were almost all Republicans. During my term as governor there were never more than four Democrats among the

*This chapter is a first-person account by Charles Edison in collaboration with Prof. Dayton McKean.

194

twenty-one, and most of the time at least two of the Democratic senators were Hague men as eager as the Republicans to frustrate the governor. There was always a bipartisan understanding between the rural Republican senators and the Hague senators. Occasionally the Republicans would desert Hague, as they did at the time the new Hudson County Tax Board was confirmed, but the alliance would re-form.

Probably the motives of these Republicans were mixed—they both wanted Hague and did not want him. They wanted to preserve him as an issue, a talking point, because his notorious suppression of civil liberties, his corrupt city government, and the sky-high taxes in his domain always enabled them to say in effect that bad as conditions might be in some Republican counties, such as Atlantic, they were worse, oh, ever so much worse, in Hudson. For this reason they did not want to do anything that would really put Hague out of business; the cry of Hagueism had been so useful in so many campaigns that they hated the thought of losing it. In addition, many of them really liked Hague and his system—not in public, of course, but on weekends in Atlantic City or at the country home of Senator Arthur F. Foran, a Republican representing rural Hunterdon County, where the machine politicians of both parties got together to make the real decisions. Many of the Republican senators liked Hague and his men because they spoke the same language, the language of practical politics, with no palaver about good government but with clear appreciation of the importance of jobs for themselves, their relatives, and their political adherents.

Some Republican politicians and senators were ambidextrous. They liked Hague up to a point, but they did not want him to elect pro-Hague governors because that would give him a strong voice in patronage. They would divide the melon with him if necessary, but they preferred to divide it only among themselves. And they did not like to have him invade their counties to elect local officials and thus weaken their own machines; they wanted him to stay in his own county—and at keeping him there, while keeping his organization alive, they were very successful.

Typical of the frustrations imposed on me by the senate was its handling of my nomination of J.F.S. Fitzpatrick, an anti-Hague Democrat, to the Civil Service Commission, which was required by statute to be bipartisan. The Republican senate refused either to reject or conform—but simply did nothing month after month, year after year, while courts remained without judges, counties without prosecutors, state departments without heads. It was not that the nominees were unfit—not one was rejected during my term, even after the most careful scrutiny; rather, it was that the senators did nothing.

One of the most important offices to fall vacant during my term was that of commissioner of education. Charles H. Elliott of New Brunswick had been commissioner since 1927. He was in his middle sixties; and his record in the office, so far as I could judge, was undistinguished. I felt that the department needed new life and vigor. I talked with schoolmen from all over the state about the office. They were unanimous in agreeing that the state needed a new commissioner of education, and the best man in the country, if we could get him, would be John W. Studebaker, head of the United States Office of Education. On one of my trips to Washington I talked to Mr. Studebaker. I liked him very much indeed. He was willing to come to New Jersey both because the state was then paying its commissioner a third more salary than he was receiving in Washington and because things in his department were not then moving to his entire satisfaction.

When I nominated him early in 1943, the schoolmen were delighted, and the newspapers generally approved of the selection. Commissioner Elliott, however, trotted to Hague; and the mayor got out a statement in which he said that I had refused reappointment to Elliott because Elliott has been "obstructing the radical elements in the school system of New Jersey in their efforts to get control of the educational system of the state." This, of course, was before the Communists endorsed Hague; but it was pure myth. There was no radical element trying to get control of the school system. Beyond refusing to listen to the grievances of certain Jersey City teachers, I do not know what Elliott had done for Hague. But Hague's statement was enough to show his Republican friends in the senate what he wanted. The majority leader, Republican Senator Howard Eastwood, said that he thought the nomination should have gone to a resident of New Jersey. After the nomination had slumbered in the senate for some weeks, Eastwood added that he had heard that Studebaker had some liberal ideas and so should not be confirmed. Nobody, so far as I know, ever accused the senator of having even one liberal idea. The senate would not invite Studebaker for a hearing. They simply refused to confirm or reject.

After his name had been before the senate for three months, and when it became plain that the senate would never act, Studebaker telegraphed me, asking that the nomination be withdrawn because the situation embarrassed him in Washington. There was nothing I could do but comply with his request.

I then nominated John H. Bosshart, who for sixteen years had been supervising principal of the South Orange-Maplewood School District. Even though he was not born in New Jersey, he had lived in the state so long that the senators could not use the carpetbagger argument they had used against Studebaker. Bosshart was president of the Schoolmasters' Club of New Jersey and had long been an officer of the State Teachers Association. The senate could not refuse to confirm him without offending the teachers. The senators delayed, nevertheless, because, as some of them told reporters, they had heard that Bosshart might appoint Dayton D. McKean as a deputy commissioner of education. McKean, deputy commissioner of finance at the time, was *persona non grata* because he had written a book about the Hague organization which the mayor did not like. No such appointment was ever contemplated, but of course the senators wanted to check every possibility. The schoolmen began writing letters, and after about a month Bosshart was confirmed.

Some senators were willing to desert Hague if they could get me to make a patronage deal with them. "Advice and consent" in their case, I was advised, meant their consent could be had only at a price. The instance of Senator Herbert J. Pascoe, Republican of Union County, will serve to illustrate.

When a vacancy occurred in the office of prosecutor of the pleas for Union County, I nominated John E. Barger, a Democrat, on January 12, 1943. Under the custom of the senate, his nomination would have to be moved by the senator from the county of the nominee's residence. When the nomination went in, Senator Pascoe is reported to have asked, "What's the hurry?" In the words of the *Newark Star-Ledger,* which was a paper not friendly to my administration, "It became known that Pascoe would move the confirmation if he could have the naming of one of the assistants. . . . Pascoe wanted the post for his old friend and adviser, Edward Cohn." There was no criticism of the nomination of Barger. It was simply that the nomination could be approved, not on its merits, but only at a price.

I refused then and always to make such deals, and Barger was not confirmed. After several months he joined the army, and I withdrew his nomination and sent to the senate the name of Francis E. Gordon, of Elizabeth. It was a futile gesture. He was never confirmed. There was no prosecutor for Union County for all of 1943, and there was none when my term ended.

The instances involving Fitzpatrick, Studebaker, and Barger, while just a sampling, are sufficient to demonstrate the extremes to which the senate majority would go in interpreting the constitutional provision that a governor should appoint with the ''advice and consent of the senate.''

Under the guise of senatorial courtesy—frequently a euphemism for senatorial discourtesy—the phrase "advice and consent of the senate" was twisted to mean advice and consent of a single senator.

Even before I became governor I had heard rumors out of Trenton that the most and richest gravy was to be found in the biggest bowl—the New Jersey Highway Department. At that time, its $50-million-a-year budget represented about 50 percent of all state expenditures.

The New Jersey Voter, a nonpartisan magazine, had, for instance, published the charge that a relative of Senator Foran, of Hunterdon County, had sold farmland worth $500-an-acre, at the most, to the highway department for $30,000 an acre. This charge was indignantly denied, and the editor apologized. The real figures were $3,000 an acre for $300-an-acre land.

New Jersey was not unique among states in building roads with a mixture of cement and politics. The Edison Portland Cement Company was still operating, and one of the whispered complaints about its product within the highway department was that Edison Cement didn't have any "give" in it. This version of "give" meant bribery, not elasticity.

The incumbent state highway commissioner, when I took office, was E. Donald Sterner, formerly a state senator from Monmouth County. He was adept in many ways, not the least of which was his ability to placate his former associates in the Upper House.

Sterner's six-year term was to expire on April 29, 1941, just three months after I became governor. Under the law I was empowered to nominate a successor; and, as governor, I wanted a man in whom I had full confidence in this post, which controlled expenditure of half of the state's overall budget. I did not want Sterner. But there was a holdover provision which would keep him in office until a successor was nominated by me and confirmed by the senate.

On February 28 I nominated Democrat William L. Dill, who had had as long and honorable career in public service as any man in New Jersey. Dill was so unswervingly honest that he was not particularly popular with Hague's organization, which had not urged Dill upon me. He was an administrator of proved ability, just the man to clean up the Highway Department.

Since the controlling Republican senate caucus could find nothing substantial to use as criticism against Dill, it took refuge in the do-nothingness of stagnation. Not only would the senate neither reject nor confirm Dill; it wouldn't allow me to withdraw his nomination to permit submission of another name. Months dragged on, and Commissioner Sterner continued to hold office. It became obvious, therefore, that if I was to be governor over the state's biggest department, I would have to govern by investigation. I had no illusions that government by investigation was an adequate substitute for government by administration. I knew that an investigation was bound to upset the department for a year or more; that it would cost money that good administration would not; that it was bound to take up a great deal of my time, which I could better spend on broader problems of the state; and that unless somebody went to jail as a result of the investigation, the public and the newspapers would be sure to regard it as a failure. I knew that my motives would be misinterpreted—that the investigation would be regarded as a mere patronage fight in which I sought to replace a Republican with a Democrat.

Commissioner Sterner issued a statement challenging me to investigate, a familiar political tactic. He followed Hague's method of howling for an investigation and then hounding the investigators with every trick in the political books.

Because the governor of New Jersey had no power to investigate, I had urged in my inaugural address that he be given this power. Fortunately for me, my opponent, Republican Senator Hendrickson, also had urged an investigation act during his campaign. The Republican-controlled legislature enacted a much weaker investigation law than I desired, but at least it was something. While the bill permitted gubernatorial investigations, it allowed no money except as the legislature might appropriate in each case, provided for no subpoena power and punishment whatsoever, and did not authorize the removal of any official whom an investigation might demonstrate to be inefficient or corrupt. But the power to remove the highway commissioner after hearing was, for some unknown reason, in the Highway Department Act itself. So there was legal authority to proceed.

With no funds appropriated, I had to obtain for chief examiner a man who would serve the state for nothing, if necessary; and he had to assemble a staff which would work for nothing, if necessary. I was fortunate, and the state was fortunate, to obtain without promise of remuneration the services of Roger Hinds, of South Orange, as chief examiner. He assembled a staff of accountants, attorneys, engineers, real estate experts, and stenographers. The only people promised any pay were the stenographers. It was felt that they could least afford to work for nothing, and if worse came to worst, they could be paid out of the governor's emergency fund of $10,000, which is appropriated to cover the expense of entertaining distinguished guests of the state, the governor's travel, and so forth.

I asked the legislature for $50,000 as a start; and, of course, the legislators were reluctant to provide any money. But when the investigation was actually underway and it was apparent that their withholding funds would not stop it, they appropriated $25,000. This amount was obviously insufficient to open up all of the practices of a department spending $50 million a year; so in some respects the scope of the investigation had to be narrowed. The public-hearing part of the investigation attracted the most attention, obviously, because it made daily headlines. This mainly consisted of probing into the right-of-way policies of the department. Had more money been available, more could have been done. When the $25,000 ran low toward the end of 1941, a portion of the investigation stopped, the stenographers were paid, and an honorarium was given to each of the lawyers.

At the same time that the legislature allowed $25,000 for the investigation, it appropriated $7,500 to the highway department to fight the investigation, notwithstanding that the department already had its own staff of full-time attorneys and millions of dollars in other appropriations. I am quite sure that in the annals of American legislative appropriations this trick appropriation of $7,500 is hard to match!

Roger Hinds and his fellow investigators bared instance upon instance of gross overpayments for the acquisition of right-of-way properties to owners with ''good'' political connections and owners represented by politically well-connected attorneys.

Some of the more beneficial results of the total investigation, although the least publicized, were the findings and recommendations of a continuing study and investigation of the highway department's diverse operations directed by Sidney Goldmann, a Trenton attorney. One of the lasting fruits and relatively unpublicized portions of the investigation was the publication of a scholarly and definitive 781-page report, *The Organization and Administration of the New Jersey State Highway Department*, prepared by Goldmann with the assistance of Thomas J. Graves, a government research specialist lent for the task by the state chamber of commerce.

Although no evidence was produced to show that Commissioner Sterner had personally profited from the land deals, there was ample

200

evidence to justify his removal on grounds that he was an incompetent administrator when he allowed such shenanigans to go on under his nose. He said privately that he would fight removal proceedings through every court in the state. He offered to resign with the ending of one more year in office after the end of his normal term. Rather than to engage in a long legal battle for which no funds were available, I accepted his resignation when it was submitted on March 2, effective April 29, 1942, one year after his term ended.

His resignation surprised many of his Republican associates who had stood by him faithfully during the investigation. They had expected him to stay, either to the end of my term in office or until some deal or "ripper" legislation could be worked out to keep control of the department in the hands of the politicians.

When the legislature of 1941 ended, my nomination of William L. Dill to succeed Sterner lapsed. Realizing that it would be futile to resubmit his name, I looked around for a logical and competent candidate. He was an old friend, Spencer Miller, Jr., an engineer, an independent Republican whose ideals of government seemed to coincide with mine. He was no stranger to governmental operations at their various levels. At that time he was president of the board of trustees of the village of South Orange, a title equivalent to that of mayor.

Miller agreed to let me nominate him even though he knew that he probably would be kicked around by the senate, and might never be confirmed.

To the surprise of the politicians, I submitted Miller's nomination on March 9. True to predictions, he was kicked around. Senate President I. Grant Scott* pocketed the nomination and didn't release it to the judiciary committee, where it belonged, for three weeks. When he finally released it to Senator George Stanger, chairman of the judiciary committee, Miller's nomination mysteriously became "lost," finally to

---

Tactics such as these were not foreign to Scott. At one point when he, as senate president, was acting governor because Edison was out of state—all the way across the Hudson River in New York City—he rifled the desk of one of Edison's assistants (Sidney Goldmann), withdrew a legislature-approved bill which Edison intended to veto with a strong explanatory message, and signed it into law. This new law benefited clients of a close friend and fellow senator. Edison unsuccessfully questioned the legality of the law in the courts, but he could not establish that he had reentered New Jersey prior to the exact moment that Acting Governor Scott signed the bill into law. This footnote is based on the words of Mr. Goldmann as told to the author on May 6, 1977.

turn up in Stanger's desk. Unfounded allegations of being a "pinko" were leveled at Miller by the *Bergen Evening Record*—an accusation the newspaper withdrew in an editorial of apology.

Finally, in a last-minute capitulation, the senate confirmed Miller the night before Sterner's resignation took effect.

Miller was a successful administrator, and under him the department for the first time functioned without political interference.

The state is indebted to Roger Hinds and the capable and conscientious men and women who assisted him. These assistants included Henri Schwob, Harold Fisher, Sidney Goldmann, Milton Cooper, Elmer Bertman, C. Thomas Schettino,* William Bolan, John Palaschak, Jr., and Joseph Clossick, attorneys, and a battery of auditors and clerical assistants.

At the risk of sounding apologetic, I believe it fair to state that government by investigation, as opposed to government by administration, was forced upon me. My predecessor in office, Democrat A. Harry Moore, the man who explained his appointment of Frank Hague, Jr., to the state's highest court by saying that it would "make his daddy happy," was an adept at compromise; and his predecessor, Republican Harold G. Hoffman (who said, "To me Hague is like Haig and Haig; I can take it or leave it alone"), regarded compromise and exigency as ways of political life. Sometimes I have almost wished I had Harold's glibness of tongue, because I must say that one of the accusations leveled against me from time to time was that I stuck too strongly to a straight-and-narrow path without sufficient willingness to bend even to a small degree.

The Sterner investigation was not alone in demanding attention at the very outset of my three-year term. Things were not good in a variety of areas—perhaps in many areas beyond my perception and that of my staff—but we were determined to try to do what was right within the limitation of the meager funds allocated by the legislature for such purposes. For the second year of my term, for example, no legislative funds for this purpose were forthcoming.

Not that there weren't many areas crying for investigation. What with a century-old state constitution that withheld reasonable powers from the chief executive, coupled with an opposition-controlled legislature and an intraparty foe in Frank Hague, investigation was better than stagnation.

---

*Mr. Schettino later became a justice of the state supreme court.

Details of these investigations—but not the investigations themselves—are relatively unimportant at this point in time.

Sufficient to say, an inquiry directed into the Civil Service Commission showed blatant disregard for the basic principles of civil service—those of rewarding superior talent and avoiding discrimination and political favoritism. An investigation of the Board of Shell Fisheries demonstrated that entrepreneurs in the back roads of New Jersey frequently had the ethics of a Tweed. Other investigations produced widespread evidence of at least misfeasance (to use a kind word) in the New Jersey Banking and Insurance Department and in the County Board of Elections in Frank Hague's own county of Hudson. There were other instances of misdoing and other investigations.

None struck me as so basically corrupt, however, as the Hague-organization-generated charges against Leo Rosenblum, a Jersey City lawyer, then president of the Hudson County Board of Taxation.

Anti-Hague, Leo and his four compatriots on the bipartisan Hudson County Tax Board held their positions as a result of nominations by me which, for reasons sufficient within themselves, members of the Republican majority in the senate confirmed in defiance of Frank Hague.

In addition to Rosenblum, they were Paul Doherty and Michael Donovan, Democrats, and Republicans August Ziegener and John Wilkins, recommended by the Republican state chairman, H. Alexander Smith. They were nominated by me only after my ouster of their predecessors following public hearings.

The five constituting the new Hudson County Tax Board all suffered recrimination from the Hague organization, but the case of Rosenblum was exceptionally iniquitous.

Leo was a young lawyer, about thirty; and the passions of World War II were inflaming the hearts of Americans. Peace was a hoped-for goal, but a goal still many months in the future. And—to make matters worse—Leo was a member of a minority. Although he had a lengthy history of high blood pressure, he found himself accused of evading the draft by inducing a fraudulently high blood pressure reading during local draft-board-directed examinations, through the use of self-administered drugs. This was an accusation which, during the heat of World War II, could have done in most men. Not so Leo Rosenblum.

With assistance from my office, he underwent a controlled examination by doctors untempted and untainted by the factors that might influence local physicians indebted in one way or another to the Hague organization. Jersey City's *Jersey Journal,* a daily newspaper quick to say *"Gesundheit"* whenever Frank Hague sneezed, played up and replayed every small facet of the Rosenblum story.

Since Rosenblum and his fellow tax board members had been put in office by me as governor to replace a Hague-controlled board with an unsavory reputation for using its powers to reward political friends and punish political enemies, it was only natural for Leo to turn to me to try to obtain justice for himself. This was accomplished by my contacting the office of Maj. Gen. Lewis B. Hershey, national director of Selective Service.

Shortly thereafter, an independent and exhaustive physical examination, conducted under controlled conditions, completely exonerated Rosenblum. His indictment as a draft evader was killed. And the *Jersey Journal* suddenly became contrite.

On November 11, 1943, this pro-Hague daily carried the following on its editorial page:

> When Leo Rosenblum, president of the Hudson County Board of Tax Appeals, was exonerated at the time of the quashing of a federal indictment, the Jersey Journal published the news of the quashing on the front page. Mr. Rosenblum's reputation for patriotism and good citizenship had been vindicated. Consequently, the Jersey Journal, in fairness to Mr. Rosenblum, publishes on today's front page a full retraction of all published statements which may have reflected in any way upon his good character.

The *Jersey Journal's* front-page apology and retraction, under a headline reading "Statement Made in Fairness to Leo Rosenblum," ran twenty-nine column inches.

Perhaps I had more experience with investigations than most New Jersey governors and therefore some of my conclusions about them might be worth noting. Investigations are costly, slow, and time-wasting. They upset the routine of the office being examined. They make enemies of people whose acts are questioned. They consume a great deal of the chief executive's time and effort, which in his short time in office might better be devoted to broader problems. The governor of New Jersey, nevertheless, is, like most governors, directed by the state constitution to take care that the laws are faithfully executed. If he has evidence that the laws are being flouted in some state agency, and if he does not have the authority to reorganize the agency, he has no choice, if he is to be true to his oath of office, but to investigate. This he may do in the hope that the legislature will be moved to impeach offenders, that evidence sufficient to convict them in court will appear, or that publicity will cause them to resign.

As I said in my final message to the legislature, "Unless criminality is charged and proved with the finality of a mathematical demonstration, any clever miscreant can concoct some plausible story that is satisfactory to his partisans." So officers investigated and on whom much is proved will not resign; their friends in the legislature for whom they have done favors, some illegal, will defend them against impeachment, and friendly judges and prosecutors will not use the law against them. Unless the power of investigation is accompanied by the power to remove, it is largely a futile authority. Men whom my investigations showed to be very poor officials indeed are still in office.

Hard as it is to prove criminality, it is even harder to prove laziness, inefficiency, negligence, or the operation of an office in a partisan way. A governor of New Jersey has always enough evidence at hand of fraud or corruption so that he can investigate agencies where actual illegal behavior is charged and let the merely inefficient alone.

There was never in my experience enough money for a thorough investigation of any big department. To examine what has been done by any agency that employs hundreds or thousands of people and that spends millions a year is a big job. The records of the agency are bound to be voluminous. It costs a great deal to hire the necessary accountants, auditors, detectives, handwriting experts, lawyers, and stenographers to work on them—not to mention the rent, postage, telephone expenses, and traveling expenses. Sometimes the work of accountants and lawyers may be obtained as a public service, but the services of others cannot. When people work for nothing, moreover, they are likely to go off the job when private matters arise, and they are also less susceptible to direction than when they are paid.

The New Jersey legislature not only would not appropriate enough money for executive investigations, but it appropriated money to agencies to fight them. The legislature of 1942 refused to appropriate any money for investigations in spite of my appeals for funds.

I have observed that there is something in the timing of investigations. All of mine inevitably suffered from the fact that revelation of their misdeeds was overshadowed by the news of war, but also there was always the criticism that compelling officials, such as Highway Commissioner Sterner, to respond took them away from their duties during the emergency. Hollow as the criticism was, it was something that could be said by legislators who did not want their friends investigated anyhow. But sometimes important witnesses were in the army or navy, or otherwise unavailable. Another element of timing is that the public hearings should, if possible, not be conducted during an election campaign; to do so permits the charge, however false, that the whole investigation is political, partisan. Private hearings and the research or preliminary work can be done then, and the public hearings conducted after the election. Timing is important in relation to a governor's term—the later the investigation comes in the governor's term the harder it is to conduct, because officials will try by legal tactics, such as court actions, or by merely stalling, as by inflating the record of hearings with endless talk and innumerable character witnesses, to filibuster for the end of the chief executive's term.

I have observed that it is a general tactic on the part of an official about to be investigated to issue a statement to the effect that he has nothing to hide, that except for the waste of taxpayers' money he would welcome an investigation, and that in any event he will cooperate 100 percent with the governor's investigators. Of course, he hates the very idea of an investigation, and the governor for making it; and he will do everything that he or his lawyers can think of and dare to do to frustrate the proceeding, from concealing witnesses to destroying records. But if considerable preliminary work has been done, the moment he issues the cooperation statement is the moment to present him with a list of key questions and to ask for various documents. He cannot at that moment refuse to answer or decline to yield the papers, as he will do a month later.

I have also noticed that there is an almost invariable counterattack from the official being investigated. Commissioner Sterner, for example, tried unsuccessfully to show that the Edison Cement Company sold a disproportionate amount of cement to the state. Actually, the company sold very little, because it would never be party to a rake-off. A similar device is to investigate the governor's investigators—to try to find, if possible, one with a police record so as to imply in statements that an honest official is being investigated by a lot of crooks. My investigators were thus harassed, but I think none was ever shown to have robbed his son's piggy bank or done any other heinous thing. But it is easy for an official—say he is a Protestant—to look over the governor's men and claim that the Catholics are after him, or the Jews, or the Masons. Such a claim of persecution can always be issued on the same day that a particularly damaging bit of evidence comes out. A chief executive is well advised, therefore, to pick his staff as carefully as he possibly can, both to see that not one of them has any record that can be used against him and also to see that all racial and religious groups are represented on the staff. It is a good thing, also, to have both Democrats and Republicans among the investigators.

New York City has a permanent department of investigation attached to the Mayor's office. It seems to me that a populous state like New Jersey should have a similar office, responsible to the governor. Most investigations save money for the taxpayers; I am certain that the investigation of the highway department literally saved millions of dollars in revealing and stopping unsound or corrupt practices. Just the existence of such an office would give many officials pause, would strengthen their consciences. There is enough work, year in and year out, to keep a staff very busy; and they would, furthermore, develop an acquaintance with state law and bureau routine which each temporary investigator has to develop for himself.

All in all, I believe my investigations were worthwhile. Nobody went to jail, in spite of the evidence; but some officials lost out and some others stopped undesirable actions. That, I suppose, is as much as could have been expected.

14

End of the Term *

JUST A FEW DAYS after the election of 1943, when my term as governor had less than three months to run, W. Warren Barbour, United States senator from New Jersey, a Republican, died suddenly in Washington. The very next day the New Jersey newspapers had me picking his successor from lists which contained the names of some people who were extremely objectionable to me.

I was not in a hurry to name a senator. He would serve only eleven months. I wanted someone who would not follow the White House line blindly and who, on the other hand, would not be so anxious for election to fill the remainder of the unexpired term that he would do Hague's bidding as the price of the nomination. My friends, Secretary of State Joseph Brophy and Senator Crawford Jamieson, were both suggested, but both were in state positions of importance that lasted for longer terms. I would have liked a man with enough leadership already established in the Democratic party so that he could have made a fight against Hague, using such control as a senator has over federal patronage as a start; but there was no such person on the political scene.

Early in December I appointed Arthur Walsh, who was executive vice-president of Thomas A. Edison, Incorporated. He was a native of New Jersey and a lifelong Democrat. He had long been a close friend. He had been my campaign manager in 1940. Besides, he had served in various public positions, most of which were unpaid, and had, I thought, earned the honor.

[Arthur Walsh was an unusual individual. His background hardly foretokened a distinguished career as a business executive. As a child

---

*This chapter is a first-person account by Charles Edison in collaboration with Prof. Dayton McKean.

prodigy on the violin, Arthur, at about the age of ten, began his career in the Edison organization as a solo performer on phonograph records. As he grew older his other talents pushed his musical ability into the background, but he never lost his love for the violin. Harry S Truman was one of his contemporaries in the U.S. Senate. Harry on the piano and Arthur on the violin frequently performed at get-togethers with their colleagues.]

The Republicans said that I should have appointed a Republican to succeed a Republican, but I have not observed that Republican governors have appointed Democrats when Democratic vacancies occurred. The Hague adherents thought that I should have appointed someone acceptable to them, such as William Smathers or Elmer Wene, but I certainly did not owe them anything, and I was sure I did not want Hague in the United States Senate, even by proxy. There was some muttering in Democratic beards that Walsh had not served the party long enough, but I think that on the whole the appointment was well received.

As a temporary senator, so to speak, Walsh was independent. Sometimes he followed FDR; sometimes not. Sometime he voted as I would have; often he did not. But he was certainly entitled to vote as seemed to him best—he was the senator, not I, not FDR. Incidentally, he was very popular with other senators and soon made friendships which lasted long after his short term was over.

The other United States senator from New Jersey was Albert W. Hawkes, a Republican. Under the usual practice of senatorial courtesy, when there was a Democratic senator and a Democratic president, the president did not send to the senate the names of nominees unless and until the senator from the nominee's state had been consulted. But where Hague was interested, and with the fourth-term election coming up, the tradition of senatorial courtesy went by the board as far as Roosevelt and Walsh were concerned. Hague could get to see the president at any time; Walsh could not.

A vacancy occurred in the office of postmaster in Trenton. The Mercer County Democratic Committee held a meeting and endorsed Charles J. Trier for the position—the normal, democratic process. Walsh duly submitted his name to the White House, but the president followed the advice of Hague rather than the advice of the senator from the state of the nominee's residence. FDR sent in the name of a Mercer County Hagueite instead, a man who had been four times repudiated at the polls by the voters of Mercer County.

Franklin Roosevelt was undoubtedly a great man. He had great gifts of national leadership. But the picture of him as the knight in spotless armor that some of his friends now seem to be trying to paint seems to me overdrawn. Mixed with his idealism were the traits of a ruthless and ambitious politician who, to attain a third and then a fourth term, would treacherously surrender his friends to a vicious political machine such as Hague's. Instead of building up the party at the grass roots by taking the recommendations of local committees, he would kill off these local organizations by taking Hague's recommendations. I could not get myself very much interested in campaigning for Roosevelt in 1944, and I did not.

Toward the end of my term, when I looked back over the three years, some things which earlier had seemed of great importance had somehow diminished in size. Such a matter was the Roscoe McClave bill to dissipate the state surplus by handing it over to localities. The bill was a nine-day wonder when it passed, but the uproar it caused was so great that my veto was sustained.

Events showed that two vetoes which were overridden by the legislature and received little public attention at the time should have been sustained. The incredible, not to say unspeakable, State Senator I. Grant Scott got a bill through the legislature in 1941 to allow the state prison officers to withdraw from the state employees' pension fund. I vetoed this bill as a bad example for employee groups, but it was passed over the veto, and the prison officers took out of the state fund some $170,000, which was distributed among them.

Then another law sponsored by Scott was passed over my veto, setting up, on what I thought were unsound lines, a special pension system for prison officers. I was interested to notice during Governor Edge's administration that a New York actuary named George B. Buck reported to Governor Edge that this special pension fund was already insolvent, with liabilities of $4,582,615 and assets of $154,666.

Looking over the hundreds of appointments I made during my term, I must say that some turned out badly, even though the great majority was all right. A governor is bound to rely somewhat upon advice from others in making appointments because he cannot personally know all the possible candidates. By and large, the appointments that went sour were the practical politicians or men who were recommended by practical politicians. It seems to me now that the protestations of reform by candidates for appointment, who promised never to do Hague's dirty work again, were no more dependable than the protestations of a drunkard that he will never touch another drop. No sooner had some of hese appointees got their feet under the desk than they were doing Hague's bidding again. Two outstanding examples were William Gilfert, whom I appointed as Hudson County clerk, and Thelma Parkinson Sharp, whom I reappointed to the New Jersey Board of Tax Appeals. She was subsequently removed on charges by Governor Edge.

But on that same board I appointed a man who turned out to be a stand-up fellow, a man of personality, intelligence, and integrity, Donald M. Waesche, of Teaneck. I am proud of that appointment.

A group of appointees who turned out to be absolutely reliable were the five members of the Hudson County Tax Board. Frank Walsh did a good job as finance commissioner and budget commissioner. Sidney Goldmann made a fine state librarian and later became an outstanding judge. Crawford Jamieson was excellent as a public utility commissioner and Joseph Brophy as secretary of state.

When, in January 1944, I came to write my final message to the legislature, I found, as I find now, that some controversies, such as those over soldiers' voting and civilian defense, had lost their interest. Others, like the fight for constitutional revision, had then and still have importance. All in all, the progress made toward constitutional revision was, I thought, the most important achievement of my administration.

Some progresss, but not enough, was made toward the establishment of justice in taxation.

When I took office, the state debt was $140,791,000; when I left, it was $87,720,000 and there was a surplus in the state treasury. I seek no undeserved credit for leaving the state in sound financial condition. The measures to reduce the debt were already in effect; and every year I presented the legislature with a balanced budget and every year managed to lapse some funds into the treasury, so that the debt never increased.

I could never get the legislature interested in planning. It has always seemed to me that, unless the states plan against the next depression and do a better job of it than they did before the last depression, there will be renewed demands for Washington to handle everything. Annually, I urged the legislature to provide adequate funds for the state planning board, and annually I set up in the budget more money for the agency. Just as regularly, however, the legislature ignored the recommendation and, not willing to kill the board, still kept it on starvation rations. The legislature of 1943 set up its own postwar planning committee, which amounted to nothing.

Throughout my term as governor I had the support of most of the newspapers, Republican, Democratic, and independent. I am particularly grateful to the *Newark Evening News*. When I came to turn over to the new governor the hot seat on which I had sat for three years, the newspapers generally said kind things about my attempts to improve the processes of democracy in my native state. The *Trenton Times* said:

> During the three years of Governor Edison's administration, a Republican legislature, numerically strong and under arrogant leadership, felt that it was in a position to treat an independent Democratic governor contemptuously, and it took full advantage of the power it held. It was inevitable, under the circumstances, that Governor Edison's term of office should fail to be marked by the achievements which he hoped would distinguish his administration [but] even if there was nothing else on the affirmative side of the record, which is not the case, the governor's achievement in advancing [constitutional] reform so far along the road to success would make his administration memorable.

A Republican newspaper, the *Elizabeth Daily Journal*, said of me:

> Governor Edison . . . has given of his best to improve the political conditions in his own party and to lift government in the state to a higher level. . . . Few states have been so cursed with political gangsters as New Jersey. Edison, or any other who might try it, would naturally find it difficult to do a good job of political reformation in a state where a partisan dictator gangs up with renegades of the opposite party to manage the state's affairs. . . . What is needed is a coalition of men of the Edison type and purpose in both parties to clean up conditions created by scheming and trading between bosses and renegades of both parties, who are in politics simply for purposes of power and self-advantage.

As my term was coming to an end, Bruce Bliven, then editor of the *New Republic*, asked me to set down the ideas I had acquired about democracy and public life from my experience in New Jersey politics. He published my observations in the issue of March 20, 1944. I want to draw upon some of them here.

I have been impressed by the hold the idea of democracy has upon Americans. They want it, and they want it sincerely. They also know when they are not getting it. They hate dictatorship, whether in Rome, Berlin, Madrid, Moscow, or Jersey City. When I was governor I used to get hundreds of letters from ordinary citizens, letters often written with a pencil, telling me that the writers had followed what I had been trying to do and wanted me to keep it up. The faith of the mass of the people

212

in democracy is not waning. On the contrary, it seems to me that it is stronger today than it has ever been.

But the two-party system as it has operated in New Jersey tends to frustrate the voters. The party bosses on both sides engage in a battle with each other only for show. Regardless of their nominal party allegiance, they get together to protect each other from some "threatening" reform or reformer. So that what the bosses want and what people want are often diametrically opposite, and to speak of the people versus the bosses is no mere catch phrase of editorial writing or political speaking; often it describes accurately enough the line-up of interests in our state's politics.

I do not pretend to know all the answers to this problem of providing adequate leadership for the mass of the people against the party bosses. If I did, Mayor Hague's retirement would have taken place six years earlier than it did. But part of the answer, I am convinced, lies in drafting state constitutions that will place political power where it should be—in the hands of the governor elected by the people. Power is going to concentrate somewhere, as by a law of nature; and if a constitution will not permit it in the hands of the men responsible to the people, then power will grow up outside the official government in some boss or combination of bosses not responsible to the people.

Perhaps another part of the answer is that we must continually urge upon young men and women the desirability of careers in fighting the battles of democracy. In our educational systems we tend to overemphasize the perfection of democracy; what we need to emphasize, rather, is its perfectability and the opportunities that are offered thereby to young people who want to do something to make names for themselves.

The two-party system, with all of its advantages, is frustrating to voters in another way. Either or both parties may ignore issues, especially state issues, and view with alarm or point with pride to what is going on in Washington. I would like to see vigorous state parties, comparable to some of the city parties, which would draw their chief interest from state affairs. I tried, without success, to get such an organization going in New Jersey. Perhaps the time was not ripe; it was during World War II, and people were not interested in state and local affairs.

The inconsistencies within each national party should lead citizens who want to improve their state and local democracies to break away, if possible, from the forcing of national parties upon the states. During

213

my day the Republican party contained such strange bedfellows as Hamilton Fish and Fiorello LaGuardia, Herbert Hoover and Wayne Morse; and the Democratic party, such strange combinations as Harry Byrd and Robert Wagner, James Farley and Henry Wallace—not to mention Hague and Edison. The ordinary citizen does not long struggle to understand such curiosities; he has other affairs to tend to, and he is likely to give it all up as a hopeless job.

He is further inclined to throw up his hands when he sees a party stand for different—even for opposite—things in different places, for instance, when it can fight a dictator in Berlin and honor and protect one in Jersey City. It can advance the most exacting standards of national and international ethics at one level and pursue the most sordid ones at another.

Notwithstanding all the dangers and difficulties of the democratic process, I am neither cynical nor pessimistic about the future. I think we must encourage and cherish the states, not because I am attached to some half-mythical concept of states' rights, but because I cannot see how democracy can filter from the top down. Rather, it has to work its way up. The experience of self-government needs to be attained in the 3,000 counties, the 35,000 cities, and in the [then] forty-eight states. The states must progress; they must experiment; they must be willing to spend their own money or borrow on their own credit. They must be laboratories where statesmen can learn the business of government.

It is because I have held these ideas for years that my struggle with Hague seemed to me no mere contest for party leadership. Bosses like him are a grave danger to American democracy. They instill in their followers the same blind and unquestioning obedience that Hitler and Mussolini demanded: "Okay, boss" and "Heil Hitler" are equally fatal to the critical judgment necessary for popular self-government. Furthermore, I cannot see how a national democracy can be established on a foundation of local dictatorship.

I have been less worried than some of my friends about the danger of Communism to American democracy. Our history does not point toward a revolution by a group of ideological fanatics. A more real danger, and one more in line with American experience, is that some powerful state boss might sometime build up alliances with other bosses until he or they could control the whole nation. Bosses like Hague and Huey Long have not hesitated to use force, have indeed shown no scruples of any sort about the methods they used. If we should get a dictator, I should look for him to arise, not through some Brownshirt or

214

Blackshirt organization, not through some army clique, but through a political machine. I should not expect him to win with some collection of foreign ideas, some economic theory such as Marxism, but rather to win, if he does, with the kind of demagogic, opportunistic all-things-for-all-men appeals used by such homegrown dictators as Hague and Long. If in my term as governor I hastened one boss toward his retirement, if I promoted structural improvements in our state government to make the rise of future bosses less easy, I accomplished something for my fellow citizens, born and unborn. And as long as I have health and strength, I propose to continue the effort.

[Friend and foe alike have commented many times on Edison's impact on New Jersey as its governor. Although they used different words and may have stressed different aspects of his accomplishments, there was general agreement, even by enemies, that he restored public confidence in the state's government by attracting and encouraging men and women, with deep feelings of civic responsibility, to seek election or accept appointment to public offices.

Perhaps the former governor, Robert B. Meyner, whose term followed Edison's by a decade, said it most succinctly. Speaking at the dedication of the Charles Edison Memorial Room in the Seton Hall University Law Center in Newark on December 14, 1976, Governor Meyner commented:

"There was no doubt that Charles Edison was controversial. But he established integrity in government and made it clear he wanted only able people in government.

"He was also unpopular because he made it clear he would run the government, and not the state's political bosses."]

President Roosevelt gave a boost to Charles' campaign for governor by touring the shipyards in Camden with the candidate.

Before the storm. Democratic Boss Frank Hague (*at right*) and Charles were still on-the-surface allies in this rare campaign photo of the two together. Others (*from left*) are Governor A. Harry Moore; Edison; Mrs. Moore; James H. R. Cromwell, Democratic nominee for the U.S. Senate and husband of "the world's richest woman," Doris Duke; and Mrs. Edison.

Under arrest. Mayor Frank Hague's woes did not begin with his battles with Edison. This 1928 photograph shows the immaculately dressed, stern-visaged "boss" when he was placed under arrest by a sergeant-at-arms of the state senate, charged with contempt by a senate investigating committee for refusing to testify. He was immediately released on $1,000 bond. A court ruled in favor of Hague, and he did not have to appear as a witness.

Hague, as vice-president of the Democratic National Committee, sounds off at a 1940 meeting of the committee in Washington, D.C.

Backfiring strategy. In the twilight of his career in 1948, Hague and Attorney General David T. Wilentz drew up a resolution to draft Eisenhower as the Democratic presidential candidate to supplant incumbent Harry Truman.

The oath of office is administered to Edison by Chief Justice Thomas J. Brogan, of the New Jersey Supreme Court (January 21, 1941).

Paperwork absorbs Charles as he acclimates to his surroundings in the governor's office.

State Senator Crawford Jamieson, who was among the first important Democrats to urge Edison to run and who became one of the governor's most trusted advisors, talks things over with Charles.

Commuting. Charles says good-bye to Carolyn at front door of their Llewellyn Park home preparatory to driving to Trenton. State Trooper George Hays was assigned to accompany the governor.

Official. If there was an official photograph of Charles during the campaign and during his three-year term, this was it.

15

Experiments in Small Business

There were occasions when I thought Charles spent too much time with things not associated with the Edison Industries. And I'm not talking about his periods of being assistant secretary of the navy, secretary of the navy, or governor.

Those indeed were separate and distinct jobs. He did fine work in many of them and particularly, I thought, in his days in the NRA.

However, Charles tended to be something of a dilettante. He touched on so many, many things such as sideline businesses not directly related to the Edison Industries.

THESE WERE THE views of Theodore Edison when interviewed by the author in August of 1976.

Although Theodore's commentary on certain of his brother's diverse activities may have been somewhat overstated, his words, nonetheless, contain grains of truth. Throughout his lifetime, Charles launched a succession of sideline enterprises, ranging from a country inn to small manufacturing units. Simultaneously, as president of Thomas A. Edison, Incorporated, he was the head of industries doing business at an annual rate of as much as $50 million and, later, as chairman of the board of McGraw-Edison Company, with an annual gross at the time of approximately half a billion dollars. The McGraw-Edison Company came into being on January 2, 1957, with the merger of Thomas A. Edison, Incorporated, with the McGraw Electric Company.

Capital for Charles Edison's sideline businesses was provided mainly from his personal fortune. On occasions, some portion of the costs came from the Edison Industries, usually in the form of technical or legal services, rather than money or materials. Also, there were instances of joint ventures in which a third party invested time and/or funds.

With some exceptions, Charles viewed these ventures as holding forth prospects of enhancing the Edison Industries, just as in his Greenwich Village days he had thought of the Thimble Theatre as a "talent search" operation for the Edison phonograph business.

One of his side ventures which accrued to the benefit of the Edison Industries was the manufacture and distribution of medical and industrial gases and allied products and equipment. A Mrs. Gladys Knight, widow of a Boston railroad executive, was attempting to refurbish her finances through her knowledge of gases, more particularly oxygen. Lacking both financial backing and adequate expertise, she interested Charles Edison, through his wife, Carolyn, in her project.

Her rather unprofessional setup was physically moved from Boston to be near Charles' headquarters at the Edison Industries. This was in the late 1920s.

Starting as the E-K (E for Edison, K for Knight) Medical Gas Company, this venture, after a number of lean years, grew into one of the leading producers of medical and industrial gases in the Northeast. Additional plants were established at Stuyvesant Falls, New York, and North Grafton, Massachusetts. E-K Gas was absorbed into Thomas A. Edison, Incorporated. Several years after the merger that created McGraw-Edison Company, the operation was sold to National Cylinder Gas Company at a comfortable profit.

Among the "strictly for kicks" ventures initiated by Charles was the Beverwyck Inn in Troy Hills, New Jersey, about a dozen miles northwest of the Edison Industries. It was a club-type operation, limited to members and their guests who, for a price, could catch their own trout in a meandering stream on the property and have them prepared and served by the inn's personnel.

In addition to providing kicks, Beverwyck Inn directed the spotlight of personal publicity on Charles.

An Associated Press dispatch, dated March 30, 1935, and widely used by newspapers across the nation, told this story:

Charles Edison, who heads fifteen corporations associated with the enterprises founded by his father, the late Thomas A. Edison, inventor, became an innkeeper today.

Edison, youthful and genial, said he thought he might get a kick out of playing host to "folks who are interested, as I am, in trout fishing, hunting, and riding."

He bought the old Howell homestead because he was intrigued, he said, by its quaint setting, spacious grounds and fine trout brook. Edison said the venture is partly social, partly commercial, but expressed hope that it would succeed financially.

"I thought I might get a kick out of it," he said. "It may prove a relaxation—something different from the things I've been doing."

Some of the things he's been doing include a year as vice-chairman of the State Recovery Administration and several months as state chairman of the federal housing drive. At the present, he is New Jersey director of the National Emergency Council.

A not-so-memorable event occurred at Beverwyck Inn in September of its opening year. Arthur J. Neu, a national champion at manipulating wet and dry flies, demonstrated his dexterity to the membership, but not a single trout rose to his enticements.

In October of the same year, skeet shooting was added to the list of activities available to Beverwyck Inn's well-to-do patrons.

The inn closed its doors in early 1937 when the Edisons moved to Washington, D.C., and Charles took over as assistant secretary of the navy. Financially, Beverwyck Inn was a flop.

Another restaurant figured prominently in one of Charles' more ambitious extracurricular entrepreneurships. For simplicity's sake, this undertaking and its ramifications were called the Sag Harbor Experiment.

Sag Harbor is a quaint village about forty miles from Montauk Point, the eastern tip of Long Island. This vintage village was best known as a whaling center up until the mid-1880s, when the industry began to abandon sailing ships for steam and moved its bases to new locations. In the postwar 1940s, Sag Harbor was in need of historical restoration and industrial revitalization.

Even though it is next door to Easthampton, Southampton, and other wealthy, society-minded South Shore resorts, Sag Harbor is on the "wrong side of the tracks," figuratively speaking. Its roots go back to whalers and artisans, rather than to creators and inheritors of metropolitan fortunes. Thus it was when Charles first became interested in Sag Harbor.

During visits to the homes of socialite friends on Long Island's South Shore, he became enamored with a fine, albeit rundown, mansion in Sag Harbor, the Hannibal French house. Although portions of the home dated back to the late 1700s, it drew its name from a later owner, Captain Hannibal French, operator of a whaling fleet. Charles bought it in September 1947. Necessary repairs and renovations were kept in harmony with the basic characteristics of the home.

The Hannibal French House was no ordinary edifice. Nancy Boyd Willey, in the 1948 revised edition of her pamphlet, "A Tour of Historic Sag Harbor," described the house in these words:

> Because of its association with the French family and because of its distinction and beauty, it seems to stand for the final period of whaling enterprise, even though part of it was built early in the century.* It came into the French family in the 1860s with its veranda and stoop of twisted columns and its beautiful white drawing room, the latter an example of the genius of Minard Lafever, to whom, more than to any one man, is due the clear inviting quality of the interiors of Greek Revival houses and the crisp, imaginative detail of the wood and plaster detail that so frequently accents and beautifies them.
>
> It has been said that a society is at its best *after* its wealth has been accumulated. Hannibal and a brother, Stephen French, were the last of the great whaling firms. The first of the steamships were theirs, and the very last of the whaling vessels, the *Myra*, in 1871.**

Contemporaneously with his acquisition of the home, two major but dissimilar ideas were aborning. Charles, himself, had been seeking a place to experiment with his ideas that small manufacturing units, decentralized both as to physical location and management, could be made more productive and lead to less labor strife than large, centralized plants with hundreds, perhaps thousands, of employees. Also, he had an active interest in historic preservation.

Entirely apart from Charles and his embryonic plans, many residents of Sag Harbor already had launched a movement to save the Old Custom House, among the village's most historic landmarks. The Custom House of 1790 and the first post office were located in the Henry Packer Dering home. Mr. Dering served the fledgling federal government both as collector of the port of Sag Harbor and as postmaster. Sag Harbor claims to be the nation's first official port of entry, a claim based on its having led off the initial list of ports of entry authorized by the first Congress of the United States.

Sag Harbor's campaign to preserve its old Custom House had its origin in a church's need for an expanded school playground. By 1947,

---

*Subsequent research lent credence to the claim that a small part of the structure antedated 1800.

**Talbot Hamlin, *Greek Revival Architecture in America*, Oxford University Press, 1944.

227

ownership of the Custom House and the land it rested on had become vested in St. Andrews Roman Catholic Church which sorely needed additional school grounds.

Enter Charles Edison. He "bought" the Custom House, paying $1 to the Reverend Mr. Julian Zebrowski to formalize the transaction. Charles then donated a portion of the spacious grounds surrounding the Hannibal French house as a new site for the Custom House, paid to have a new foundation constructed there, and then underwrote the physical movement of the old building over the tortuous three-block-long route to its new resting place. Just for starters, this ran about $10,000. The year was 1948.

Through the efforts of its own membership, plus continued support from Charles, the Old Sagg Harbour Committee, headed by Mrs. William Lloyd Bassett, Jr., transformed the Custom House into an authentically furnished museum. After the project proved viable, Mr. Edison gave the Custom House, plus additional land area, to the old Sagg Harbour Committee. The Custom House continues (1978) to attract large numbers of visitors and, since 1966, has been owned and operated by the Society for the Preservation of Long Island Antiquities.

The adjacent Hannibal French House, starting in 1947 when Edison bought it, became the focal point of the multiple operations he launched in and around Sag Harbor. He maintained a suite of rooms on the second floor of the stately mansion for his own accommodation, but elsewhere in the home many activities sprang up.

Mr. Edison operated mainly through a corporation, wholly owned by himself, called Argonaut Enterprises, Incorporated. In jest, he said he named it after the Argonauts of mythology, who, under Jason, sailed the good ship Argo in quest of the Golden Fleece, because "We, too, are out for gold and we don't care whom we fleece."

One extensive first-floor room and an abutting porch became a summertime restaurant called the Captain's Table in memory of Hannibal French. Good food and good drinks were served.

This same area was made available to Sag Harbor civic organizations and also accommodated meetings of the Sag Harbor Forum series, inaugurated by Mr. Edison.

Another portion of the ground floor was devoted to the display and sale of fine antiques under the direction of Walker Heimburg, an antiquarian who transferred his operations from Connecticut to Long Island on invitation from Mr. and Mrs. Edison.

A key element of the Sag Harbor Experiment was the creation of a second corporation, in 1948, called Sag Harbor Industries. A young engineer named Alfred Colabella was placed in charge. The new company's product line consisted of small electrical coils which were sold to various industrial firms for incorporation in finished products, such as automobile clocks and electrical appliances. A sizable quantity of the coils was purchased by the Voicewriter Division of Thomas A. Edison, Incorporated, for use in office dictation equipment.

Under Edison's guidance, Colabella developed a profit-sharing plan to encourage the twenty or so original employees of the Sag Harbor Industries. Another element of experimentation was in the area of communication with employees. A variety of methods of communication was used over a period of time, including halting all production for the final half hour of work on Fridays. These half hours were devoted to reports on sales and profits by management and to receiving suggestions from employees. A committee of employees reviewed suggestions for their practicality and, in fairly frequent instances, adopted them for use in the plant or office.

After almost two years of experience with several methods of profit sharing, Sag Harbor Industries decided to look into the merits of a bonus plan espoused by Joseph Scanlon, a former union leader turned instructor at the Massachusetts Institute of Technology.

As part of its evaluation of the so-called Scanlon Plan, Sag Harbor Industries sent its president, production manager, secretary-treasurer, chief accountant, personnel consultant, and two women production employees selected by their co-workers to M.I.T. to study the plan under the personal tutelage of Mr. Scanlon. They were intrigued by it and, after explaining it to the other employees, a vote was taken. Eighty-six percent of the employees favored the Scanlon Plan over profit sharing, and the plan was officially introduced on July 1, 1951.

Under the plan, employees shared in a bonus fund based on meeting production and cost bogeys. They also were represented on management-labor committees established to evaluate suggestions for improving operations.

The small Sag Harbor Industries plant on Bay Street had been acquired from a former owner. A year later, in 1949, the operation had grown to the point where an extensive addition, larger than the entire original plant, became necessary.

Thirty years later, Sag Harbor Industries was still going strong, and small and miniaturized coils remained as the principal components of its product lines. A second Sag Harbor plant was acquired. The number of employees passed the 100 mark by a comfortable margin.

With the death of Mr. Edison in 1969, ownership of Sag Harbor

Industries became vested in Paul R. Scheerer, Jr., a godson, and Stuart A. Miller, a first cousin of Charles, with a minority interest being held by the Charles Edison Fund, the philanthropic foundation created by Mr. Edison during his lifetime.*

For most of the years subsequent to Colabella's short reign, Scheerer and Miller, each approximately thirty-five years younger than Charles, have headed Sag Harbor Industries.

Contemporaneously with the early years of Sag Harbor Industries, Charles' activities in and around Sag Harbor mushroomed. Argonaut Enterprises, in addition to its activities within the Hannibal French House, embarked on a wide variety of other ventures.

It acquired the rights to manufacture small electric motors for sale into the toy market. A hat, resembling a pith helmet, also was manufactured for the toy market. Concealed within the helmet was a miniature radio employing an earphone. A youngster wearing it resembled something from another world because of an external loop antenna and two protruding vacuum tubes. They were called Man from Mars hats.

The postwar boom in bowling, triggered by the introduction of automatic pin-setting equipment, led Argonaut Enterprises into the manufacture of Bowl-O machines, a shuffleboard-sized automated bowling game.

John Tye, a young man who turned his talents to the sedentary job of glassblowing because of lameness, was set up as a one-man operation. His delicate creations—graceful swans, penguins and other animals, plus crystal highball stirrers—were sold into the gift market.

The products of Johnny Tye's glassblowing expertise and other gift and specialty items developed by Argonaut Enterprises were marketed under the name of CarOtti. These items included silk and woolen materials handwoven in their home by two Sag Harbor sisters, Dorothy and Helen Hubbard, who also fashioned their materials into stylish skirts, jackets, and cocktail aprons; a unique line of aluminum giftware, which included candlesticks, salad bowls with mixing implements, and dishes, all of which were individually cast in sand molds; and canasta sets.

CarOtti canasta sets constituted the most ambitious sales venture undertaken by Argonaut Enterprises. They consisted of two decks of playing cards especially designed for CarOtti, a clear plastic tray, score

*Originally incorporated as The Brook Foundation, the name was changed to the Charles Edison Fund following Mr. Edison's death.

ads, and a book of rules written by Oswald Jacoby, the world-renowned card expert.

An import from South America, the game of canasta swept across the nation during the late 1940s and early 1950s. CarOtti was the first to offer specially designed, complete canasta sets. Its original order for cards, designed to its own specifications, ran to 80,000 decks.

Long addicted to playing bridge, Charles and Carolyn were among the early converts to canasta. It was their strong interest in cardplaying, at which each was adept, that led Argonaut Enterprises to enter the canasta field.

A third wholly-owned corporation established on Long Island by Charles was Phoenix Minerals, Incorporated. Its plant, a former schoolhouse, was in Southampton, near Sag Harbor.

Phoenix Minerals employed a remarkable piece of machinery created in the minds of brothers Peter and Paul Tyhala, trained in their native Hungary and seeking to capitalize on their talents here in their adopted country. Their basic piece of equipment, which cost about $25,000 of Charles Edison's funds to build, was a multiheaded lapidary machine capable of automatically faceting up to 100 man-made gems at the same time.

The man-made raw material—called boule before splitting and polishing—ranged from amethysts to zircons, including garnets, emeralds, and even rubies, second only to diamonds on the Mohs hardness scale.

Industrial diamond dust, called bort, was used for faceting and polishing the synthetic gems. These man-made gems possess every characteristic of their natural counterparts. Their flaw is that they are flawless. Natural diamonds and other precious stones have infinitesimal defects that set them apart.

During its relatively short life, Phoenix Minerals produced and sold thousands of its beautifully faceted stones into the jewelry trade. But in the end, the Tyhala machine could not compete costwise with imported synthetic stones hand-faceted in India and other countries where wages were a mere pittance compared to those in the United States.

In the end, Phoenix Minerals disposed of its specialized equipment to a group planning to operate in Puerto Rico to take advantage of the island's low labor costs.

Synthetic gems, so beautiful and perfect that only experts can tell them apart from nature's own, sell for a mere fraction of the price of real gemstones.

Needless to say, Phoenix Minerals was not a money-maker.

231

A joint venture entered into by Charles was Sag Harbor's Whaler's Point Boatyard, owned by young Lou Dorschel, who needed extra financial support to keep his head—and business—above water. Situated on Peconic Bay, hard by the Sag Harbor Industries plant, Whaler's Point Boatyard catered to small craft owners and, occasionally, the larger craft of commercial fishermen. It was a feast or famine operation, with more famine than feast.

Dorschel serviced yachtsmen in the summer and stored their craft in the winter. A good year was one in which a sufficient number of the stored craft required expensive repairs and renovations during the winter doldrums.

There was a local saying applicable to most Long Island boatyards that "there's nothing wrong with the business that a good September hurricane can't cure." Hurricanes wrought damage to boats and brought business to the boatyards.

The half-dozen years or so that Charles Edison dedicated to the Sag Harbor Experiment are well remembered by residents of the village. As an individual, he is recalled with affection.

Argonaut Enterprises and Phoenix Minerals no longer exist. Sag Harbor Industries, under Scheerer and Miller, continues as an important economic factor within the area. The Whaler's Point Boatyard operates under a different name. The Hannibal French House was donated by Charles during his lifetime to the Servants for the Relief of Incurable Cancer, of Hawthorne, New York, as a summer rest home for the nuns of the order. It subsequently reverted to individaul ownership as a private home. The Old Custom House is a popular museum, with a beautiful memorial rose garden dedicated to Charles. *

Some of the lessons learned from the Sag Harbor Experiment proved beneficial and were introduced by Charles into aspects of Thomas A. Edison, Incorporated.

Charles never ceased being intrigued by the unusual—whether in a product, a method, or an individual. Edward Converse was a direct case in point. He qualified as unusual in all three categories.

A chemist, Converse realized that anyone who could come up with a formula for producing an inexpensive but effective substitute for carnauba wax would be tapping a gold mine. Carnauba wax is a prized

*During the late 1940s and early 1950s, the author served as president of Argonaut Enterprises, Sag Harbor Industries, Phoenix Minerals, and Whaler's Point Boatyard, in addition to his principal function as executive assistant to Charles Edison in his capacity as president of Thomas A. Edison, Incorporated.

232

ingredient used in fine polishes. It is a secretion from insects found only on the underside of the fronds of the carnauba palm in South America. It is expensive and in limited supply.

Like so many persons, Converse was short of capital. He had his shop in a rat-infested loft in an old broken-down building underneath the Manhattan approach to the Brooklyn Bridge. When not working on formulas, Converse liked to spend hours on end in Greenwich Village bistros, consuming cup after cup of coffee and chatting with the "natives."

Converse, in some manner not overly clear at this writing, came in touch with Charles Edison. The potential of Converse's efforts to produce a substitute for carnauba wax appealed to Charles, who agreed to become a part owner in the Longyear Company, until then totally owned by Converse. The operation was moved from New York City to West Orange, New Jersey, to a small but neat plant.

Converse did produce a substitute for carnauba wax that was acceptable to some polish manufacturers, but his product never quite reached perfection. In the denouement of their association, Converse used a valuable coin collection to buy back the stock held by Charles, with a two-year period—insisted on by Charles—in which Converse could reclaim his collection at no personal loss. Converse never reclaimed them, and the coins ended up in Charles' estate and became an asset of the Charles Edison Fund.

Charles was involved in other business ventures, but those mentioned in this chapter were the most interesting and extensive.

16

Postwar Activities

AT THE CONCLUSION of his three years as governor, in January of 1944, Charles resumed active direction of the Edison Industries. World War II was still going strong, and the Industries were heavily engaged in war production.

In August of that year he would turn fifty-four. Maturity and exposure to national attention, both as an important figure in the first two of President Roosevelt's more than three terms in office and as governor, unquestionably guided him into new attitudes and ambitions.

Planning for the postwar conversion of the Edison Industries to peacetime business received increasing attention as the war entered its final months. Such was the case in most segments of American industry, but it was particularly important in the Edison instance. Charles owned more than 50 percent of all voting stock of Thomas A. Edison, Incorporated. Much of the rest of the voting shares, plus the nonvoting preferred shares, was tightly held by Thomas Edison's widow, Mina, and other members of the Edison family. That so much of the wealth of Charles and his aging mother was invested in Edison stock, for which there was no ready public market, placed them in precarious positions. It was a case of too many eggs in one basket. If the Industries failed to prosper, both could be disastrously affected; and if either died suddenly, lack of a broad, ready market might force the sale of assets at distress prices to meet inheritance taxes.

Consequently, after months of study, members of the board of directors of Thomas A. Edison, Incorporated, at Charles' behest, took steps to permit the general public to invest in the company. When couched in Wall Street legalese, the financial maneuvers necessary to accomplish the desired ends assumed ominously complex proportions.

234

In simplified language, however, they added up to this: The existing 15,000 shares of common stock, with a par value of $100 per share, became 150,000 shares of Class A common stock of $3.33⅓ par value, and 300,000 shares of Class B common stock, similar in all respects to the Class A stock but without voting rights.

"In August 1946," to quote from the corporation's annual report for that year, "110,000 shares of the Class B common stock were publicly sold by the holders thereof (members of the Edison family). This sale, the proceeds of which went to the selling stockholders as individuals, did not change the capital-stock structure of the company. It did, however, serve greatly to broaden the public interest in the company, increasing the number of holders of common stock from three to a present total of approximately 1,100 in thirty-two states and the District of Columbia."

These public shares were traded over the counter since the company was not eligible for either the New York Stock Exchange or the American Exchange because of their rules banning the listing of concerns with common stock carrying no voting rights. *

For somewhat similar reasons, Charles also began to think about the possibility of an advantageous merger. Such a merger was not to materialize until a dozen years later, when, with the joining of Thomas A. Edison, Incorporated, with the larger McGraw Electric Company, the McGraw-Edison Company came into being.

Other elements in Charles' new set of attitudes and ambitions included expansion of his participation in civic, philanthropic, and political affairs without again seeking elective office, and in honoring the memory of his father.

Somewhat in reverse order, helping to perpetuate his father's memory was an abiding desire held deep within his heart almost since childhood. That his father's achievements were such as to be self-perpetuating did not lessen the earnestness of his efforts. "I sincerely hope," Charles was known to say in so many words, "that nothing I do, or can keep from being done, will reflect adversely on the regard in which he was held."

The year 1947—February 11 to be precise—was to mark the centennial of Thomas Edison's birth. For years in advance, Charles knew that recognition of the occasion would be accorded national and in-

---

* "Going public" was a fortuitous move for the estate of Mina Edison, as she died the following year at age 82.

ternational attention. Among his concerns, however, was the thought that the occasion might prove to be something of a one-day wonder, with no permanent impact.

Two major developments associated with Charles' ambitions for preservation of his father's memory peaked in 1947, the centennial year. In each, he played an important but subdued role.

Major American industries virtually as a whole joined in forming the Thomas A. Edison Centennial Committee. The great Charles Franklin Kettering, head of General Motors research and a lifetime admirer of Thomas Edison, served as chairman of the committee. Henry Ford was its honorary chairman. This was the impermanent aspect of the centennial observance.

At small risk of contradiction, it can be said that the Thomas A. Edison Centennial observance was among the most successful such events in the history of American industry. The president of the United States and all but a handful of the then forty-eight governors proclaimed his greatness. The United States Postal Department issued a special commemorative stamp. Newspapers and major magazines devoted not just inches but yards of space to Edison. Radio was bountiful in its treatment of the event; and the infant television industry followed suit.

Serving on this committee under Boss Ket, as the chairman was affectionately known, were the heads of virtually every major industrial and business organization, plus many public figures. Among the members of the committee were men such as Alfred P. Sloan, chairman of General Motors; Philip D. Reed and Charles Wilson, chairman and president, respectively, of General Electric; David Sarnoff, chairman of RCA; Thomas J. Watson, president of IBM; Joseph Egan, Western Union's chairman and president; George H. Bucher, president of Westinghouse Electric; Walter S. Gifford, president of AT&T; Harvey S. Firestone, Jr., president of Firestone Rubber; David J. Goodrich, chairman of B.F. Goodrich; Dr. Harold W. Dodds, president of Princeton University; Dr. Karl T. Compton, president of M.I.T.; Henry R. Luce, editor-in-chief for *Time-Life-Fortune;* and Arthur H. Sulzberger, publisher of the *New York Times.*

John C.F. Coakley, on leave as the public relations director of the Edison Industries, directed the committee's small working staff.

Events of the centennial observance spanned the whole year of 1947. One of its offshoots continues today to have a strong impact nationally and internationally on the power and light industry and related enerprises. It is the Thomas Alva Edison Foundation, now headquartered in Detroit. Its first president was Mr. Kettering, who was succeeded by Walker L. Cisler, then head of the Detroit Edison Power and Light Company. Mr. Cisler is now chairman of the Edison Foundation, and ames G. Cook is president.

After the passing of Thomas Edison in 1931, his original laboratory in West Orange was preserved virtually unaltered as a museum by Thomas A. Edison, Incorporated. Likewise, the company acquired and preserved nearby Glenmont, the Edison home, after the passing of Mina Edison in 1947. The annual cost of their preservation, considering their relatively small use for corporate functions or by the public, represented a severe drain on the company. Charles recognized that this could not continue indefinitely, particularly after the Edison stock went public. He was instrumental in interesting the Department of the Interior's Nation Park Service in their preservation.

The laboratory grouping of buildings was given to the federal government on July 14, 1956, by Thomas A. Edison, Incorporated. The gift of Glenmont, which occurred three years later, was made by the McGraw-Edison Company. Together, they constitute the Edison National Historic Site and annually attract in the neighborhood of 75,000 visitors.

An additional honor was heaped upon Thomas Edison's memory when he was elected to the Hall of Fame for Great Americans in 1960, the first year in which he was eligible for consideration under Hall of Fame rules. His bust was installed at the Hall of Fame on June 4, 1961, with General Sarnoff, guiding genius behind the Radio Corporation of America, delivering the principal address in which he recalled his inspirational contacts with Edison.

Charles was to make at least one more dramatic move to express the love and admiration in which he held his parents. From her death in 1947 until 1963, the remains of Mina and Thomas rested in side-by-side graves in Orange's Rosedale Cemetery. In the interim, Glenmont, the Edison home in Llewellyn Park, and the nearby Edison laboratory had become National Historic Sites under National Park Service control. Through Charles' efforts, his parents' remains were exhumed and reinterred on the grounds of Glenmont, adjacent to the home they loved so well.

Subtly but effectively, Charles lent guidance and support to the manifold events memorializing his father. He was achieving one of his major ambitions.

Shortly after he resumed day-to-day direction of the Edison Industries, Charles' business career began to take on new proportions. The legendary Sosthenes Behn, head of the International Telegraph and Telephone Corporation, invited Charles to serve on IT&T's board of directors. Similar invitations were received and accepted by Charles from the United States Life Insurance Company and the Jones and Laughlin Steel Corporation.

Charles served effectively on each of the boards, but for more than one reason his favorite was Jones and Laughlin. Joining its board reunited him with Admiral Ben Moreell, who, following retirement from the navy, was elected to head up J & L. The Pittsburgh-based firm selected Moreell to prosecute a much-needed modernization and expansion program.

Admiral Moreell, who was chief of the Bureau of Yards and Docks when Charles was assistant secretary and secretary of the navy, directed J&L's fortunes with the same forcefulness and success that marked his career in the navy. Charles considered him to be one of America's true greats.

Another reason Charles enjoyed being a J&L director was that it was a business he readily understood. Contrariwise, there were many aspects of IT&T's operations and those of U.S. Life which were short of appealing to him.

It was not that he did not enjoy his duties and associates at IT&T and U.S. Life. But, in his words, "I guess I wasn't cut out for juggling with international currencies, as was constantly the case at IT&T, or in deciphering actuarial tables at U.S. Life."

It was at Jones and Laughlin that Charles met and became friendly with one of the company's rising young executives, Harold Geneen, who later was to be a successor to Sosthenes Behn at IT&T.

Some years after Geneen left J&L, Charles and the author met him for luncheon in Boston. The brilliant and ebullient Geneen bubbled with his plans for shaping important events in the world of business.

At the conclusion of the luncheon and after Geneen's departure, Charles commented: "There goes a young man in a hurry. For his own sake, I hope he isn't in too much of a hurry."

There are latter-day contemporaries in the world of business who think that Geneen went too fast and cut too many corners on a number of occasions.

As Charles devoted more time to outside activities, he began to think seriously about reducing the demands on his time required by Thomas

A. Edison, Incorporated. He had been president of the company since 1926, and it had functioned without a board chairman since Thomas Edison's death in 1931. Charles began to cast around, both inside and outside the company, for a person to succeed him as president. His intentions were to become chairman of the board and to retain his designation as chief executive officer.

One obvious candidate for the corporate presidency was Arthur Walsh, who, as executive vice-president, had served as operating head of the industries during Charles' protracted absences in Washington and Trenton. Walsh, too, had managed Charles' successful gubernatorial campaign and, under appointment by Edison as governor, had filled an unexpired term in the United States Senate. Their extremely close friendship of old, however, had cooled somewhat after World War II. Rightly or wrongly, Charles thought Walsh had let service in the Senate swell his head. "In appointing a good United States senator, I'm afraid I ruined a good business executive," Charles once commented.

The question of whether or not Charles would have selected Walsh as his successor soon became academic. Walsh died suddenly on December 13, 1947.

Virtually without exception, top executives of the Edison Industries were more closely attuned to production and selling rather than to high finance. This fact pointed Charles in the direction of seeking a successor from the outside business world.

Among his acquaintances was Henry G. Riter 3rd, president of Riter and Company, with a seat on the New York Stock Exchange. Riter was one of those who recommended to Charles that Thomas A. Edison, Incorporated, "go public." The Riter firm handled the issuance of Edison shares to the open market in 1946. Shortly thereafter, Riter joined the board of directors of Thomas A. Edison, Incorporated. Two years later Riter was made chairman of the board's executive committee, a new position.

In May of 1950 Charles became chairman of the board, and Riter moved up to the presidency. Riter was instrumental in arranging several relatively small acquisitions for the Edison Company, but when the big deal came along—the merger with McGraw Electric—happenstance played the key role.

Contrary to the myth that major corporate mergers and acquisitions are products of machinations within smoke-filled rooms, the wedding of the McGraw and Edison Companies grew out of a shot-in-the-dark letter.

That letter to Charles, dated July 18, 1956, was from Max McGraw, founder and president of the Midwest-based McGraw Electric Company. It read:

Dear Governor Edison:

A couple of days ago I received a very interesting telephone call from the president of one of Chicago's largest banks. He had been reading our first quarter report, and wanted to compliment us on our showing. Then he added: "Why don't you talk to Governor Edison about a consolidation with McGraw Electric Company, and have the Edison name applied to some of your important products?"

I told him that we had not initiated any of our past consolidations—that the merging companies always sought us out. But, as I thought it over, this unexpected suggestion appealed to me so strongly that I am going to change the rules in this instance.

It is not that we need your products to round out our already varied lines. But I feel that there would be a natural affinity—that the great name borne by your company and the high reputation enjoyed by your products would be congenially associated, to our mutual advantage, particularly with our own "Toastmaster" brand, which has been identified with quality in its field for three decades.

Accordingly, I am enclosing our Annual Reports for 1954 and 1955, and I believe that a study of our growth, profit performance, and dividend record will give you an assuring picture of financial soundness and progressive policy. Our sales for the first six months of this year are up over one-third, and our net after tax up over one-half, compared with 1955.

You will see, too, how our constituent companies retain their individual identities. In that connection I would like to quote a paragraph from our 1954 report: "It may be of interest to point out here, as we have in the past, that all of our divisions are autonomous. Each conducts its own research, purchasing, manufacturing, and selling, though finance, accounting, pension plans, and division results gauged by returns on invested capital are concerns of the central management. We believe that our divisions are best qualified to formulate their internal policies, and we find that many large companies are adopting this principle. At the same time, we encourage fullest cooperation between divisions and the free exchange of ideas, in engineering and production or in sales and merchandising."

You may be sure that I shall be greatly interested in learning whether this suggestion appeals to you and your associates as meriting further study. If it does, I shall be very glad to come to West Orange to talk things over.

I should like to retire shortly, and perhaps you have a good man who would like my job as president.

When Charles finished reading McGraw's letter, he turned to his executive assistant (the author) and inquired: "Who is this man McGraw with a Jewish first name and an Irish last name?"

A hasty inspection of *Who's Who* revealed that McGraw was quite a personage. Seven years older than Charles, he had headed the McGraw Electric Company since its founding more than three decades earlier. Toastmaster appliances constituted the company's best-known consumer product line. McGraw was in his sixties when he stepped up his entrepreneurship to build his company into another major force among electrical manufacturers. Apart from the McGraw Electric Company, he headed a combine of independent domestic telephone companies exceeded in size only by AT&T and General Telephone. He also was nationally known as a sportsman and wildlife conservationist.

Five days later, Charles sent his reply:

Dear Mr. McGraw:

Your letter of July 18 and the two annual reports have just been received. Your suggestion is certainly an interesting one, but coming as sort of a bolt out of the blue it catches me a little off balance.

Our company has been going along quite contentedly for a good many years, producing a pretty good living for all concerned, and has always been a little coy when it comes to merging with some other group. But Father Time is catching up with me and it may well be that I need to look at things through new glasses.

I admit freely that your suggestion opens up intriguing vistas.

Are you coming to New York in the near future? I would be delighted to talk things over in an exploratory way with you at my apartment in the Waldorf Towers in New York.

In the meantime, I will find out how a select few of my associates feel about the matter. Let's keep it confidential for the time being.

McGraw and Charles met for the first time two months later. The Edisons and friends were en route by train for a September vacation in Colorado Springs. Charles and Max chatted during a brief layover in Chicago. It was apparent that the dynamic McGraw was eager to effect a merger that would link his name with that of Thomas Edison, his idol of idols since boyhood.

By the time the train carrying the Edisons west departed Chicago, it was agreed that McGraw would follow by plane two days later. Following two to three days of *entre nous* discussion at the spacious and gracious Broadmoor Hotel, McGraw and Edison reached a meeting of the minds. A handshake sealed the deal.

Mere handshakes in matters such as major mergers do not a final agreement make. Much work remained to be done; many bases had to be touched. Directors and officers, stockholders, the Internal Revenue Service, the Securities Exchange Commission, and other agencies and entities had to be informed and their approvals received. Preliminary requirements were expeditiously achieved by both companies so that a month later, on October 10, 1956, a formal agreement was signed by the parties after a two-day meeting at the Homestead Hotel in Hot Springs, Virginia.

Selection of the Homestead as a meeting place sheds light on one of Max McGraw's characteristics. He liked to work and he also liked relaxation, but business always came first. When he informed his key assistant in corporate financial matters—Raymond H. Giesecke, later to become president of McGraw-Edison—that the merger meeting was scheduled for October 10 in Chicago, Giesecke remonstrated that he and his wife, Marie, had long planned to take their first vacation in several years by going to the Homestead, a decision Giesecke had cleared with McGraw sometime earlier. In a sense, it was to have been something of a second honeymoon for the Gieseckes.

"That's no problem," McGraw replied in these approximate words. "We'll still hold our meeting on October 10, but it will be at the Homestead instead of in Chicago."

Needless to say, the demands of the meeting effectively frustrated any "second honeymoon" ideas harbored by the Gieseckes.

This October 10 agreement varied only in minor respects from the terms agreed to by Edison and McGraw with a handshake a month earlier. In essence, the terms were these:

Thomas A. Edison, Incorporated, common shares, whether Class A, with voting rights or Class B, without voting rights, would be treated as equals for exchange with McGraw common stock, all with voting rights; and all preferred stock shares of the Edison Company would be exchanged for three shares of Edison common stock. Then, common stock of McGraw Electric (the only kind outstanding or authorized) would be split two-for-one so that holders of McGraw Electric stock would then own twice as many shares as they held before the split. This split had the approximate effect of reducing the value of McGraw Electric stock by one half, thereby bringing the market price of the two stocks into near parity. With these steps accomplished, there was a one-for-one exchange of Edison stock for McGraw Electric stock.

The merger became *un fait accompli* on January 2, 1957.

Max McGraw continued as president and chief executive officer of the ompany, now officially known as McGraw-Edison, and Charles became hairman of the board, a post he was to hold until his retirement four years later at the age of seventy-one.

Income from sales and other sources to McGraw Electric for 1956 aggregated $211 million. The comparable figure for Thomas A. Edison, Incorporated, for the same year was $37.5 million. McGraw Electric's profit margin was better than that of Edison. While McGraw was the moving party in the acquisition (technically a merger under rules of he Internal Revenue Service), Edison shareholders made out well.

An added plus was that the public market for shares held by former Edison stockholders was greatly widened because McGraw-Edison shares were traded on the "Big Board," the New York Stock Exchange.

The harmony professed by both sides of the merger was outwardly continued, but internally it was short-lived. Charles held Max McGraw and several other of the McGraw directors in high regard, particularly Robert E. Wood, who also headed Sears, Roebuck and Company.

Max McGraw and many of his associates respected Charles for his accomplishments in the federal government and as governor of New Jersey; they liked him as a charming individual; but several of them cared little for his business habits. More attuned to paying strict attention to corporate matters than to civic and public affairs, they considered Charles to be dilettantish in certain aspects of business.

In one or two instances animosities ran high. During a dinner following a meeting of the directors, Charles and another director (who shall remain unnamed) almost came to blows. The unnamed director had questioned the veracity of the Edison financial statements supplied when the merger was pending.

The following comment was once made to Raymond Giesecke by a staff member who had worked closely with both Charles and Max: "In one manner of speaking, I'm sorry I didn't know Max McGraw earlier. I'd certainly have learned more about running a business. On the other hand, Charles could be much more charming and much more interesting, and he really wasn't a poor businessman."

Of all the outside activities in Charles' broadening spectrum of interests following his term as governor, three attracted the lion's share of his attention: conservative politics; support for Chiang Kai-shek and the Republic of China; and the National Municipal League, a leading exponent of honest and efficient government at the local and state levels.

Charles' interest in Sino-American affairs started to crystallize prior to

World War II when he was the civilian head of the U.S. Navy Department. He considered Chiang Kai-shek's forces to be a bulwark against Japanese expansion and a strong deterrent to the spread of Communism in Asia.

These convictions involved him deeply in Asian affairs after his gubernatorial term ended in January of 1944, when the war was still on. While still governor, he had met and admired Mme. Chiang Kai-shek during her visit to the United States in March of 1943. She was a guest of honor at a Madison Square Garden rally sponsored by a citizens' committee chaired by John D. Rockefeller, Jr.

A year later, Charles was elected national chairman of United China Relief, whose efforts, during 1943, had raised $8,683,000 to aid war-ravaged China. Charles succeeded Frederick H. Wood, distinguished New York attorney, who died in December of 1943. In the first year under Charles' leadership, UCR sent $9,523,000 to aid the Chinese people.

At the time of his acceptance of the chairmanship, Charles was quoted in *Time* magazine in these words:

"The Chinese people have purchased time for all their allies with space of their country and blood of their people."

The chairmanship of UCR sent Charles off on another round of public speeches. Major metropolitan centers and relatively obscure cities across the nation began to know him in a new role, that of an effective protagonist for China. Datelines such as New Haven, Connecticut, and Indianapolis, Terre Haute, and Fort Wayne, Indiana, started to be included in clipping service returns.

Although each speech differed, a central theme ran through them. It was that the United States, even if not for humanitarian reasons, should for selfish reasons unstintingly support the China of Chiang Kai-shek.

He took the position in a talk at Yale Divinity School that China could have defeated Japan long ago if the United States had "substituted one pound of munitions for every thousand words of praise and advice."

"The time now was passed," he continued, "for explanations and apologies for the delays and inadequacies in America's assistance to our Chinese allies."*

At that point in time China already was in its seventh year in its war against Japanese aggression. World War II wasn't yet five years old.

---

*From an Associated Press story datelined New Haven, Connecticut, September 1, 1944.

Charles' concern over the wartime and postwar impact in Asia of continental China under Chiang Kai-shek led to his active participation, both timewise and moneywise, in other Orient-related organizations.

He subsequently became vice-president and trustee of the China Institute in America; honorary chairman and a director of United Service to China, Incorporated; and a director of the American Bureau for Medical Aid to China. These new affiliations created many new acquaintances and friends. Two the the dearest of these friends were Henry R. Luce, publisher of the *Time-Life-Fortune* magazine complex, and his brilliant beautiful effervescent wife, Clare Booth Luce, playwright ("The Women"), congresswoman and ambassador. Luce had been born and raised in China, son of American missionaries.

As busy as he was with the Edison Industries, conservative politics, and various other civic and philanthropic activities, Charles squeezed the time to pay a dual tribute to Clare Booth Luce. The occasion was her fiftieth birthday, in 1953, which coincided with her being appointed ambassador to Italy by President Dwight D. Eisenhower.

One of the Waldorf's larger ballrooms was taken over for the occasion. Rose Cummings, a brilliant albeit somewhat irascible interior decorator, was engaged to beautify and individualize the room for the occasion. A high-society orchestra was hired. Phillippe of the Waldorf personally oversaw the menus, both solid and liquid. The guest list of about 150 read like selections from society's blue book liberally sprinkled with other celebrities. Firestones and Fords and Whitneys had a ball along with the Robert Montgomerys and others of stage and screen.

Rose Cummings, grossly overweight and imperious in manner, managed to rub raw the Edisons and many Waldorf employees before the event. But in fairness to her talents, everything turned out excitingly fine and beautiful.

The ballroom was lined with honest-to-goodness cedars of Lebanon, so tall that to be hoisted to the ballroom several stories up, each of the thirty-six trees had to be suspended individually from the bottom of a Waldorf elevator, removed, and painstakingly put in place.

Each of the tables for eight bore a centerpiece, the like of which is difficult to imagine. The centerpieces were either lumps of irridescent Pennsylvania anthracite, roughly a cubic foot in size, or beautifully tinted chunks of rose quartz of comparable dimensions. The quartz chunks were collected by Charles and Carolyn and a friend, Mrs. Gladys Scheerer, while vacationing in Colorado.

Elizabeth Firestone, a concert pianist, performed solo. The orchestra played into the early morning hours. One of the songs included, with words and music written especially for Mrs. Luce, was written by Charles and another by the author.

With the dawn, Charles and Carolyn Edison were left with memories of a magic evening—and bills considerably in excess of $35,000.

Of all his involvements with China, the most time-consuming and probably the one nearest to his heart was the Committee of One Million (against the Admission of Communist China to the United Nations). He was one of the founders and a member of the steering committee of the organization, originally named the Committee *for* One Million. The *for* was changed to *of* after the committee and its thousands of volunteers had collected in excess of a million signatures of men and women opposed to opening the doors of the United Nations to Mao Tse-tung's China.

The more than 100 organizing members of the Committee of a Million constituted a cross section of American thought. They included many conservatives, some liberals, and others considered to be moderates.

As an example, when a small so-called executive group of the committee arranged to present certification of the million-plus signatures to President Eisenhower, it consisted of such disparate individuals as U.S. Senator John J. Sparkman, unsuccessful Democratic candidate for the vice-presidency when he was Adlai Stevenson's running mate in 1952; Joseph Grew, ambassador to Japan at the time of Pearl Harbor; Congressman Walter Judd of Minnesota; U.S. Senator Paul Douglas of Illinois; and, of course, Charles.

In the end, the Committee of One Million's opposition to seating Red China in the United Nations lost out, but this did not occur until after Charles' passing.

His efforts on behalf of the Committee of One Million were extensions of the conservative viewpoints he grew to cherish with increasing conviction during the 1950s and 60s. In the several years immediately following his term as governor, Edison expressed his conservatism by backing particular candidates within the two major parties, mostly Republicans. In 1949, Alfred E. Driscoll, New Jersey's Republican governor, was backed for reelection by Edison in a campaign that crushed Democrat Elmer H. Wene, Frank Hague's handpicked candidate. In 1952 he backed Bob ("Mr. Republican") Taft against Eisenhower for the G.O.P. presidential nomination.

In announcing his support for Taft, Edison referred to himself as an independent Independent." He said in a news release issued March 8, 1952, through the Taft Campaign Committee headquarters in Washington, D.C., that Taft was one of two men "best qualified to serve our country in this critical period, which demands the utmost in leadership." The other man was General of the Army Douglas MacArthur.

Eisenhower's victory over Taft in the cloak-and-dagger atmosphere of the G.O.P. convention in Chicago left Edison with a choice between the Eisenhower-Nixon ticket and the Democratic combination of Stevenson and Sparkman. He opted for Eisenhower-Nixon. About two months later, on September 29, 1952, Edison said in a statement released to the press that a Republican victory in November "will derail the Acheson (Secretary of State Dean Acheson) Too Pinko and Santa Claus Express that has been highballing our nation down greased rails leading toward Socialism."

Earlier in 1943, the last full year of his governorship, Edison had remained aloof from the campaigns of the Hague-backed gubernatorial candidate, Vincent J. Murphy, and Republican Walter E. Edge. That Charles' mother, Mrs. Thomas A. Edison, spoke out on Edge's behalf was considered by political observers to be indicative of Charles' preference. Edge swamped Murphy, who was both mayor of Newark and secretary of the New Jersey Federation of Labor.

Edison also sat on his hands the following year when Dewey made his first run for the presidency against FDR. Charles couldn't bring himself to support—or oppose—the man who had made him secretary of the navy almost a decade earlier.

Ensuing years found Edison more and more supporting ultraconservative parties and principles represented by independent candidates with little or no chance of victory. The lack of success of these candidates did not discourage him or cool his ardor for conservative causes. As he explained in chapter 8, "Apologia," in his judgment the political nostrums prescribed during the Great Depression to cure deflation were still being employed, unwisely, as panaceas for the ills of inflation.

Additionally, Edison believed that postwar attitudes and sympathies within the Congress, the executive branch, and the judiciary were encouraging the spread of Communism domestically and abroad. He felt that in some instances high-placed Americans deliberately were lending aid and comfort to Communist causes, a viewpoint espoused by many.

Edison's postwar political efforts—efforts which entailed financial assistance or active campaigning or both—varied considerably from center to right, depending in some respects on whether candidates and issues were national, statewide, or local.

In 1948, he actively supported the Republican party's national ticket of Tom Dewey and Earl Warren. Two weeks before the election, in an American Broadcasting Company network radio broadcast sponsored jointly by the Dewey-Warren Clubs of America and Edison Democrat for Dewey in New Jersey, he said in part:

> There are those who say that while Harry Truman came up through the (Tom) Pendergast machine (in Kansas City, Missouri), he has lived it down. Unfortunately, he has not. His appearance this month in Jersey City with Frank Hague is a recent example of his machine training. There is no reason to expect that his future behavior will be anything better than his past.

A rough, gruff Harry Truman and his running mate Alben Barkley surprised the overconfident Dewey and Warren. The Truman-Barkley ticket not only won the popular vote by a 24,000,000-22,000,000 plurality over Dewey and Warren, it also captured 303 electoral college votes to 189 for Dewey-Warren. In retrospect, this was not too much of a jolt for Edison. While he continued to admire Dewey, he came to think that Warren, as a chief justice, left much to be desired.

In the following spring of 1949, Edison plumped for John V. Kenny for mayor of Jersey City. A former lieutenant within the Frank Hague organization, Kenny led a successful revolt against Hague's thirty-two years as the Democratic leader in New Jersey. Kenny soundly trounced Hague's nephew, Frank Hague Eggers, for the mayoralty. Hague's star never again was in ascendancy.

The sweetness of this victory in which Edison shared had a bitter aftertaste. A decade later, Kenny went to prison for accepting kickback for political favors.

Although Edison ended up supporting the Eisenhower-Nixon national ticket in 1952, after first trying to help Taft get the Republican nomination, he switched four years later to the independent candidacy of T. Coleman Andrews, a former commissioner of Internal Revenue. A southerner, Andrews campaigned across the nation urging repeal of the graduated income tax as violating constitutional guarantees of due process and equal protection under the law.

The Andrews campaign hardly raised a ripple in the mainstream of politics. New Jersey's results were typical of the national outcome

ndrews attracted 5,317 votes. New Jersey totals were 1,606,842 for
istenhower and Nixon, and 850,337 for Stevenson and Estes Kefauver.

Because of Charles' age and failing health, the presidential election
f 1964 was the last one in which Edison, then seventy-four, par-
icipated actively. That year he was an ardent backer of Republican
larry M. Goldwater in his unsuccessful bid to unseat incumbent
yndon B. Johnson.

Edison maintained a continuing interest in the politics of his native
ate, but his involvements in his later years were principally with
ational and New York affairs after he changed his domicile of record
om West Orange, New Jersey, to the Waldorf-Astoria in New York
ity in 1961.

Although his postwar political activities produced more disap-
ointments than victories, few if anyone, whether friend or foe,
oubted that Edison acted other than in accordance with his conscience
nd in a manner he believed to be in the best interests of the nation. He
as respected as a man of honor.

Other of Edison's postwar actvities proved far more successful and
ewarding.

Always attracted by the stock market, and now freed from any ethical
straints that might have flowed from his succession of federal posts
nd the governorship, he stepped up his program of investments. A
udent of the marketplace in his own right, Edison nonetheless sought
nd paid for the advice of top analysists and counselors. The decade or
wo following the war were good ones for intelligent investment. An
ducated guess is that Edison's holdings in securities (other than those
1 Thomas A. Edison, Incorporated, and, after the merger, the
IcGraw-Edison Company) quadrupled in a few years. His large stock
oldings in the Edison and McGraw-Edison companies also fared well.

Looking ahead, Edison in 1948 created The Brook Foundation as an
istrument through which he would funnel his philanthropic giving.
he name Brook derived from a Sunday School song Charles
emembered from his childhood. Written by Lucy Wheelock, one of
ie pioneers in kindergarten school techniques, the words follow:

> Give, said the little brook,
> Give, Oh, give—give, oh, give.
> Give, said the little brook,
> Oh, give, Oh, give away.
>
> I am little, I know, but wherever I go
> I give, I give, I give.

I am little, I know, but wherever I go
I give, I give away.

Giving, giving all the day,
Give, oh, give, oh, give away.
Giving, giving all the day,
I give, I give away.

Annual gifts to the Brook by its creator were aimed at building a reserve
so that, even during a bad year, the Brook's level of giving to deserving
organizations and institutions need not vary with changes in the
financial climate.

As the residual legatee under Charles Edison's will, the Brook
emerged from being a relatively small personal trust to a relatively large
philanthropic foundation. Its trustees, under president Paul J
Christiansen, changed the name to the Charles Edison Fund, something
the founder would not permit during his lifetime.

One indication of the high regard in which Edison was held was his
service in connection with the National Commission on Organization of
the Executive Branch of the Federal Government, more popularly
referred to as the Hoover commission because it was chaired by the
former president, under appointment by President Eisenhower. Edison
served the Hoover commission in three different capacities—as a
member of its Task Force on Federal-State Relations, as an advisor to the
Task Force on Water Resources and Power, and as a member of the
Citizens Committee for Hoover Commission Reports.

The commission generated many proposals for reform, a number of
which were enacted into law by Congress.

Like many governors, Edison not only tried to surround himself with
a competent staff; he also sought advice and counsel on governmental
matters from private individuals and organizations. One such
organization that rendered invaluable assistance was the National
Municipal League, headquartered in New York City. Still going strong
today, the NML already had a half-century record of prestigious ac
complishment during Edison's terms in office, 1941-1944.

Over the years, the league has served as a developer of and a
clearinghouse for the best in good-government procedures at local
county, and state levels. It proved particularly helpful to Edison in his
long battle to obtain a new constitution for New Jersey.

One of the members of the governor's staff, Executive Assistant
John Bebout, was a college professor whose forte was political science

250

Among his varied duties, Bebout drafted speeches for Edison, particularly those on constitutional revision. Earlier, Bebout had been associated with the NML on other matters. Some years later he became its assistant executive director. In all probability, it was Bebout who introduced Edison to the NML's abilities and benefits. In any event, Edison's introduction to the NML was to exert strong influence on his own future as well as that of the league.

The governorship behind him, Edison was drawn closely into the league's orbit of operations. For the four years starting January 1, 1947, he served with distinction as the NML president.

Outstanding men had preceded him in this capacity—Charles Evans Hughes, former chief justice of the United States, and Harold Dodds, one-time president of Princeton University, as examples—and others equally distinguished were to follow. Among his successors were Alfred E. Driscoll, also a former governor of New Jersey, whom Edison virtually drafted for the league presidency; George Gallup,* renowned pollster; William W. Scranton, former governor of Pennsylvania; and Carl H. Pforzheimer, Jr., New York investment banker and educational leader.

So diligent were Edison's efforts as president of the NML that many of his contemporaries credited his leadership with lifting the league to a new plateau of effectiveness throughout the nation. Sound leadership by a business executive and former public official recognized for his honesty not only attracted outstanding men and women to serve on the league's council; it also helped loosen the purse strings of individuals, companies, and organizations interested in improving government.

In an article titled "Are You a Good Citizen?" Edison set forth what he called the Seven Deadly Sins of Citizenship. First published in the *American Weekly* magazine of February 17, 1952, at which time he had relinquished the presidency of the NML to serve as chairman of its council, the article was hailed as a classic dissertation on citizenship; it attracted widespread favorable editorials in newspapers and has undergone numerous reprintings.

Edison's Seven Deadly Sins, with his commentaries on each, follow:

---

*Mr. Gallup had a distinct sense of humor. As a scheduled speaker at one of the league's annual meetings, he arose from his chair on the dais and, resplendent in a beautifully tailored tuxedo, told a Cincinnati audience in so many words: "As a poller of public opinion, I am supposed to keep my finger on the pulse of public thinking and my ears attuned to public trends. At last year's annual meeting, I was the only head-table occupant in business dress. Tonight, I am the only one in formal clothes. I think I had better start paying greater attention to the fine print in invitations."

1. *Indifference, or apathy.* Do you say "I don't care," or "I'm not interested in politics"? In Germany, the man who said that found himself in a concentration camp. The man who says "I'm not interested in politics" is looking for a free ride from his fellow citizens. I doubt if we can carry 43,000,000 free riders in our American democracy.

2. *Laziness,* or, to use an old-fashioned word, *sloth.* It is often the real reason for an "I don't care" attitude. The schemer, the man who goes into politics for his own good, the tyrant, may grow fat—but he doesn't get what he wants by being lazy.

Many a clean-up campaign has failed simply because not enough people could bring themselves to be as busy in their own interest as the politicians were in theirs.

3. *Cowardice.* We have the cowardice of the little man who will not vote in a party primary because he is afraid to have his neighbors know which party he belongs to. We have the cowardice of nice, well-mannered people who will not denounce corruption, or the evils of stupid and incapable officials, because they don't want to be known as reformers.

And we have the cowardice of the apparently powerful, of men in high places in business, labor, industry, finance, the professions—even in institutions of education and religion dedicated to enlightening the mind and freeing the spirit of man.

How many times have you heard one of these say, "I feel as strongly as you do, but, of course, in my position I can't be quoted," or "I know that the gang in City Hall is ruining the reputation of the city and gambling with its future, but, of course, I don't dare say anything about it because you know what they would do to us."

4. *Greed,* shortsighted selfishness which leads men to seek little personal gains through politics—a parking ticket fixed, an inspection done lightly. However little the favor sought, it immediately puts the one who gets such favors in the power—if not altogether in the class—of those engaged full-time in the business of using democratic government for their strictly private ends.

5. *Twisted or misdirected loyalty.* I believe we should all ally ourselves with one or another of the recognized political parties. But many a crooked machine has been kept in power by the votes of the best people in the city simply because they had neither the imagination nor the sense of higher duty to openly attack such setups, even in their own party, perhaps among members of their own club, social set, or business circle.

6. *False pride.* It expresses itself in many smart-aleck cracks, such as "I never talk politics," "Politics is a dirty business," "I teach children; I don't have any time for politics." In the name of all that is American, how can any one of us feel superior to politics? We achieved our independence by politics; we freed the slaves by politics; we extended the

benefits of modern knowledge of health, of education, and human welfare by politics. Our business may expand or wither by politics.

7. *Cynicism.* The person who says, ''Oh, you can't do anything about it,'' ''It's always been that way and always will be.'' All I can say to the cynic is that there is no hope for him or for any society in which there are many of his kind.

The effectiveness of Edison's participation in National Municipal League affairs, both as president and council chairman, probably was best summed up by John S. Linen, retired vice-president of the Chase Manhattan Bank, whose top-level association with the NML goes back to the early 1930s.

''Governor Edison's experience in government,'' Linen wrote the author from his retirement home in Lake Wales, Florida, ''gave him an excellent background to serve as president of the league. Because of his keen interest in better state and local government, and the respect he commanded nationally, which in turn benefited the league, he rendered a most valuable service in advancing the constructive programs and objectives for which the league has labored through the years.''

Other NML officials contemporary with Edison volunteered equally glowing praise.

The Involved Citizen, a short history of the National Municipal League written in 1969 by NML secretary Alfred Willoughby to coincide with the league's seventy-fifth anniversary, said that the election of Edison as president in 1946 ''was the turning point'' for the league, then threatened with dissolution because of the shortage of financial support and effective leadership participation. ''President Edison,'' Willoughby wrote, ''cheerfully accepted fund raising as a major presidential responsibility.''

In retrospect, it can reasonably be said that the bright and broad spectrum of Edison's postwar accomplishments as a whole outshone those portions of his activities dimmed by occasional failure.

17

Florida's Fascination

INTRIGUED BY FLORIDA since childhood, Charles became increasingly fond of visiting there as he grew older. As a teenager he frequently accompanied his parents on their almost annual trips to Fort Myers, located on the Caloosahatchee River, not far inland from the Gulf of Mexico. Earlier, he had made a trip or two with them to Fort Myers, where Thomas maintained a winter home called Seminole Lodge,* a laboratory to keep his avid mind active, and an extensive tropical arboretum, beautifully exotic but also related to his researches.

"For a number of years when I was a child," Charles recalled in his taped memoirs, "Mother and Father didn't go to Florida at all during the winter. One year they did. I must have been about eight or ten, because I was still wearing short pants and sailor suits.

"After a gap of several years, we started going to Fort Myers again practically every winter for a number of years. A great deal of the excitement of my youth was centered in and around Fort Myers.

"At that time, the railroad ended at Punta Gorda; so we had to take an old stern-wheeler and go eighty miles through Charlotte Harbor and up the Caloosahatchee River to Fort Myers."

For Thomas, however, Florida was not all work and no play.

"Father," Charles recalled, "spent a great deal of time importing

---

*Seminole Lodge, the laboratory, and the botanical gardens were willed to the city of Fort Myers by Mrs. Thomas A. Edison at her death in 1947. Along with a modern museum building replete with rare items of Edisonia, the property is operated by the city as a museum and annually attracts in the neighborhood of a quarter of a million visitors. One section of the museum building is devoted to the furnishings, books, and curios, including an elaborate collection of owls, from Charles' office suite in his Waldorf Towers apartment.

exotic plants and trees from tropical climes all over the world. He also kept pretty busy in the laboratory he had had built. But mostly it was relaxation. He enjoyed life down there, as did the family. We had a good many visitors; people like John Burroughs, the naturalist, Henry Ford and his family,* the Firestones, and many others.''

Charles once told the author of an incident involving himself and Henry's son Edsel, a contemporary. They had ventured forth one morning for a day's outing in a Model T. Roads of any description were few and far between in that part of Florida in those days, around 1909. With the brashness of youth, they steered the car off into the hinterland, flat and sandy but passable despite growths of Spanish bayonets and a wide variety of cacti.

Because of Florida's heat and the vagaries of the Model T, the car ran out of water, overheated and refused to budge. With no water available, Charles and Edsel waited for the motor to cool and then used the contents of a coffee jug they were carrying to replenish the thirsty radiator. That got Tin Lizzie moving again, but not for long enough to get back to a road and civilization.

The poor little car stalled again. After again waiting for the engine to cool, Charles and Edsel resorted to improvisation worthy of the mental machinations of their respective sires.

''We did what seemed to be the obvious,'' Charles explained. ''Edsel and I urinated in the radiator—and it proved just enough to get us back to a road where a friendly farmer gave us some water.''

Memories of youth are among the most poignant. Small wonder then that Charles' early association with Fort Myers established his enduring fondness for it and the rest of Florida.

Seminole Lodge was unique in many respects. It was built by Thomas as a tropical hideaway for his second wife, Charles' mother. Even before Thomas had asked the beauteous Mina Miller for her heart in marriage, he was planning what their Florida home would be like.

Shortly after Thomas met Mina in the winter of 1885, he and a close business associate, Bostonian Ezra T. Gilliland, vacationed together in Florida. Their original travel plans were amended to include the out-of-the-way hamlet of Fort Myers after Edison learned that the area was lush with tropical flora, including bamboo standing sixty feet tall. Fort

---

*Because of his great admiration for Thomas Edison, Ford, who was 16 years younger than his idol, bought a home next door to Seminole Lodge so the two could spend more time together.

Myers he had to see, even though it was miles off their planned itinerary and approachable only by water. The stands of bamboo fascinated Thomas because that was the material, after carbonization, he was using for filaments in his newfangled light bulbs, barely six years after he had invented incandescent lighting by electricity. The bamboo he was using had to be imported from Japan.

Although Fort Myers was hardly more than a flyspeck on a map at the time, Thomas was so impressed that he immediately started laying plans for a home for him and Mina—if and when Mina consented to be his wife. He had not yet asked her, but his hopes were high. His hopes were not in vain. Mina succumbed to his entreaties, and they were wed in a matter of months, in February of 1886.

Another unusual feature of Seminole Lodge was that not only was it designed by Edison personally, the lumber for it was cut to exact dimensions in Maine and shipped to Fort Myers by boat for assembling. Thus, the Lodge became one of the earliest examples of prefabricated homes. A matching home* was built a few hundred feet away for Gilliland and his family. After all, it had been the Gillilands who introduced Thomas to Mina in Boston.

Charles' deep affection for Florida also stemmed from the fact that in the relaxed atmosphere of Fort Myers he shared a greater companionship with his father than was possible up north, where Thomas' energies were devoted in the main to working long hours, frequently seven days a week, in his laboratory and factories.

Camaraderie between father and son was never closer than during their days together in Fort Myers, when southwestern Florida was virtually unpopulated and unspoiled. Charles recalled seeing proud and stately Seminole Indians, dressed in native costumes, in and around Immokalee, then an Indian trading post about forty miles southeast of Fort Myers on the edge of the Everglades. In his taped memoirs, he said:

> The Seminoles were a fine-looking people—big, tall men. It was a wild country. The Seminoles were about the only people who were there, and they only lived around Immokalee when they weren't in the Everglades. Immokalee was a real frontier outpost with a sort of Buffalo Bill flavor. But time's passage, tourism, and the discovery of oil nearby changed all that.

---

*A few years later, there was a falling out between the Edisons and the Gillilands. The Gillilands left, and the Edisons acquired their property. It became the Edisons' guest house and, today, is a part of the Edison Winter Home Museum.

Our property had a dock that ran out to deep water in the channel of the Caloosahatchee. The dock was just under a quarter mile long. There was a big summer house at the end. We also had a swimming pool. So it was a wonderful spot to be. I thoroughly enjoyed it, and Father truly loved the place.

He'd go fishing off the dock or in a boat. He always used to say that fishing was the greatest relaxation he knew of, because "There's something about that line down in the water that forbids anything to enter your mind except the nibble you might get." He used to fish for complete mental relaxation.

We'd go out in a small boat together and troll a great deal. There was a world of fish in those days. Then as now the greatest catch was a tarpon. That was the king of all fish down there. The first tarpon caught in a season was always a great event in the town.

The day that Thomas Edison caught his first tarpon put a minor strain on the relationship between father and son. Charles related the incident in these words:

One day he wanted to go up the river in our electric launch. We only had about four mullet for bait, just about enough for one person. So, accompanied by a friend, I volunteered to stay behind in a small boat, try to catch more mullet in a cast net, and then fish there until the electric launch returned in the afternoon to pick us up.

The wind was blowing and the water was rough; not a good day for tarpon fishing. Not only that, our bait catch proved to be a lone mullet.

I threw mullet bait out on my line and settled down to read a book with the line across the gunnel and then going through my fingers. Pretty soon the line started going out slowly—very slowly. I thought I had a crab. Suddenly the line started out fast, then faster and faster. When I braked the line, a big tarpon jumped and tail-walked across the water. After a struggle, we gaffed the tarpon alongside our little cedar rowboat, its head out of the water. I settled down to read again and to wait for the electric launch to pick us up.

Suddenly the fish gave a mighty final gasp. The gaff and my pole went into the water. The boat almost upset, but fortunately the line was under my arm and, after a brief scare, the tarpon was subdued, half-dead by that time.

About then the launch appeared coming down the river, her flags flying, and with Father standing on the bow and laughing at me as he shouted, "I got a tarpon! I got a tarpon!"

His was a little one, only about ten pounds, whereas mine weighed 110 pounds.

Charles turned to his father and said, "Don't laugh. Wait till you see what I caught."

257

Thomas then turned to Fred Ott, who was operating the launch, and said disgustedly, "Throw mine overboard."

But Ott, for once, wouldn't obey orders. After all, it was his boss's first tarpon.

Said Charles, "We had them both mounted and hung them on a wall facing one of the wide verandas at Seminole Lodge. Father—in a friendly way—was always chagrined that I had beaten him. It was a family joke for years."

Fishing with his father was fun, but Charles' piscatorial prowess peaked a few years later when he was fishing without him in the Caloosahatchee River, not far from the family dock. His prize of prizes turned out to be a "mammoth sawfish over fifteen feet long with a 'saw' nearly four feet in length," to quote from the *Fort Myers Press* of May 22, 1922. The paper's account added that yesterday's catch was "probably the largest sawfish ever captured in this vicinity."

Charles, with his guide Captain Hugh Cooper, was fishing in the dinghy from their power launch at anchor some distance away. Charles spotted a large fish almost under their small craft. He plunged a harpoon into the fish. The newspaper account follows:

Suddenly it seemed as though an underwater cyclone had broken loose.

Mr. Edison realized he had "something." What it was he did not know. The sea monster was apparently bent on showing his displeasure at his treatment by turning the Caloosahatchee into a maelstrom. It churned the water into a foam, then darted at the boat. By careful seamanship, the boat was saved from capsizing. The fish made another dash toward the opposite shore of the river a couple of miles away. Again the line curbed it, and again the fish rushed the boat. This was repeated several times. Each time, by consummate skill, the boat was kept right side up, although the blows delivered by the big fish threatened its destruction. As the big fish made one more sortie, the launch was hurriedly brought alongside. While the small boat was being towed at a 20-mile clip by the fish a sensational transfer of the anglers was made, both boats being under full speed. Mr. Edison gained the launch with difficulty.

As soon as the larger boat entered the game, it was hoped that the additional weight would be sufficient to tire the fish and absorb some of his superabundant vitality. But the fishermen reckoned without their host. The fish seemed like some huge aquatic machine. He towed the big launch first in one direction and then in another, as easily as a big tug draws a single barge, and kept it up for two solid hours, with the harpoon in his back, interspersing the cross-country marathon with an occasional back charge at the boat, this, seemingly, with the idea of annihilation.

The fish evidently was under the impression that if it could ram the boat hard enough his troubles would be over. But it was doomed to disappointment. With Mr. Edison at the line, and Captain Cooper holding the key to the motive power of the boat, the fish was foredoomed to defeat. Both men were keenly alert, and although the fish did succeed several, yes, many times in ramming the boat, it was always a slanting blow, thanks to the clever manipulation of Captain Cooper, and it only resulted in a bad scar on the side and keel. Finally the fish showed signs of weakening. Slower and slower were his sorties, and less and less the violence of his charges. At last, by a dexterous stroke of the harpoon, Mr. Edison reached a vital part. The big fish was harmless.

As Charles matured and assumed active direction of the Edison industries, later serving the federal government in a variety of capacities nd New Jersey as governor, the pressures of these responsibilities narply curtailed the time he could spare for Florida vacations. But arting in the late 1940s and continuing almost to his death, his visits Fort Myers became virtually annual events.

By this time, Fort Myers was anything but the sleepy little village of ,000 of his youth. Its resident population in 1950 was still only about 3,000, exclusive of burgeoning environs, but hundreds of thousands of nurists and other escapees from colder climes overran the area during the season.'' To this day, the Edison Winter Home and Museum mains the focal point of Fort Myers' myriad natural and man-made tractions. By 1977, the city's population had reached 35,000.

In 1914 Thomas Edison made the comment, ''There is only one Fort Iyers and 90 million people are going to find it out.'' He was guilty of nderstatement.

Several years after Thomas' death in 1931, an energetic Junior Chamber of Commerce seized upon the fame of the Edison name to naugurate an annual Edison Pageant of Light, a week-long gala of ctivities overlapping February 11, Edison's birthday anniversary. The ageant of Light has become for Fort Myers what the Orange Festival is Miami, the Rose Bowl to Pasadena, and the Mardi Gras to New Orleans. It is replete with parades, athletic events, baby-judging ontests, fishing tournaments, turtle races, and all the ostentation ssociated with such extravaganzas. Unique to such celebrations, owever, are solemn memorial services dedicated to Thomas Edison. Highpoint of the Pageant of Light, long since outgrown junior chamber ponsorship into a community-wide undertaking, is a formal ball at *hich a king and queen of Edisonia are crowned each February. Forty ears after its relatively humble beginning, the Pageant of Light is igger and better than ever.

Starting around 1950 and with few exceptions until his death, th annual ceremony of crowning the new king and queen of Edisonia wa personally—and pleasurably—performed by Charles. He grew to cheris the Pageant of Light almost as much as he did Florida's natural won ders. Dearest of all, however, were his many old and new friends livin in Fort Myers. Many of his older friends also had known Thomas an Mina; and whether natives or transplants from north of the Mason Dixon, they were blessed with a hospitality worthy of the South o tradition. In their mellifluous drawls, they generally called him Mr Charles, honeyed words to one accustomed to such prosaisms as Mr Edison, Governor, Mr. Secretary, or Boss. Their hospitality was real, no just limited to Charles, his wife, Carolyn, and their friends or associate accompanying them; it was a way of life.

The Pageant of Light week was so crowded with events that littl leisure time was left to Charles. So, when possible, he tried to exten his stays for another week or ten days to permit relaxing with friends o touring other parts of Florida.

On one such occasion, he and Aurelius P. Hornor, an old M.I.T classmate and a vice-president of the Edison Industries, acompanied b the author, toured Florida south to north and west to east. The trip included a week of wonderful snook fishing in the headwaters of th Shark River, deep in the Everglades. As our rented auto tooled down central Florida highway lined on both sides by orange groves, Hornor familiarly known as Re (who, besides an ancient Roman, would want t be called Aurelius?), suddenly shouted, "Stop the car and pull over."

No sooner said than done, Re leaped from the car, ran into the grove and returned momentarily, his shirt bulging with ripe oranges.

"Re, what in the hell's the matter with you?" Edison inquired "You can buy them at any roadside stand."

"I know that," Hornor replied, "but when I was a kid in Arkansas used to swipe apples from the neighbor's orchard. I just had a yen to ea some stolen oranges. They tell me they're sweeter."

Hornor's bit of tomfoolery may have been prompted by shenanigan perpetuated a day or two earlier by Edison. Having fished the head waters of Shark River, Edison directed the crew of his hired cabin cruise to head downstream into the Gulf—no small journey. Once in the Gulf, "Captain" Edison ordered full steam ahead to East Cape, the southernmost point on the Florida mainland. Once there, he bade the anchor be dropped and he and his two guests be taken ashore in the dinghy.

Once ashore, he tried to ascertain the exact southernmost point on he cape, a difficult assignment without sextant or transit. Nonplussed, Hornor pointed to a sandy spot fifty yards away and assured Charles that, 'That's it.''

Charles strode to the spot and proceeded to wet down the waves with some of his own salt water. Now it was Hornor who yelled, "What the nell gives?''

With a broad grin, Edison replied:

"I've just satisfied a lifelong ambition. Having already performed his sacred rite at precise spots in Maine, in the State of Washington, and where California meets Baja California, I hereby lay claim to being the first to christen the four corners of the United States.''

He could be as frivolous as he could be serious.

Charles' final visit to Florida was anything but frivolous. In failing health, he was en route by train to the Republican National Convention in Miami Beach in August of 1968, accompanied by Alice Stevenson, a nurse and longtime friend and confidante of the Edison family. The Seaboard Coastline's southbound Silver Meteor, on which they were passengers, had halted on a siding to permit the passing of its counterpart, the northbound Silver Meteor. It never passed. For whatever reason, a switch did not work and a head-on collision occurred.

Numerous passengers were injured; two fatally. Miss Stevenson suffered a fractured hip that incapacitated her for months. Charles, who was lying down and resting at the time, was only shaken up.

Typical of his concern for friends, Charles personally paid the extensive hospital and doctor bills connected with Miss Stevenson's injury. During the weeks she was in the Winter Haven Hospital, followed by a protracted period of convalescence in Fort Myers, Charles remained in Florida to make certain she received the finest of care.

In February of 1969, he made his last visit to Fort Myers, one highlighted by his crowning of the king and queen at the annual Edison Pageant of Light.

A stand of giant goldenrod, developed by Thomas Edison as a source of rubber, forms a backdrop for Charles and old friend Robert Halgrim in the Edison botanical gardens in Fort Myers. Halgrim for many years managed the Edison winter home, laboratory, and museum.

Kay Holloway is crowned queen of the 1968 Pageant of Light in Fort Myers. The crown for King Frederick Morgan already is in place. Richard Powell, lord chamberlain of the Court of Edisonia, stands by.

At the coronation ball of the Edison Pageant of Light, Charles is surrounded by old friends. Standing (*from left*) are Mrs. Sidney Davis, a former queen of Edisonia; Charles; Carl Roberts; Miss Alice Stevenson, a trustee of the Charles Edison Fund; and Sidney Davis. Mrs. Clarence Zimmerman and Mrs. Roberts are seated.

Theodore Edison (*from left*), sister Madeleine Sloane, and brother Charles strike a happy pose (*circa* 1945).

onning one of the National Park Service's "Smokey the Bear" hats, Charles
miles for the camera on the lawn of Glenmont, the Edison family home in
'est Orange, now a National Historic Site. At left is a grandniece, Madeleine
dison Sloane, and Melvin J. Weig, a trustee of the Charles Edison Fund. At
e time (1967), Weig was superintendent of the Morristown-Edison National
istoric Site Group.

William F. Buckley, Jr., emcee of the testimonial dinner, listens to comments by Edison.

Remembering. Charles gazes down at the marker he had installed on the spot where he and his beloved Carolyn were married at the Edison winter home in Fort Myers, Florida.

Some of Charles' fondest memories were those of fishing with his father in Florida's Caloosahatchee River.

Admiral Ben Moreell puts over a point with his old friend Charles. Moreell was
the principal speaker at 1963 testimonial dinner honoring Edison.

Old friends, Edison and Max McGraw reminisce on the founding of McGraw-Edison Company.

Edison and Charles Franklin Kettering, head of General Motors Research and first president of the Thomas Alva Edison Foundation, discuss plans for the foundation at Thomas Edison's library in 1945.

Elder statesman. Charles as he appeared prior to his last illness.

18

The Final Years

ALTHOUGH NEVER really robust or athletically inclined, Charles enjoyed relatively good health for the first seventy years of his life. An inveterate smoker of cigarets, he generally eschewed overexertion* because of a chronic shortage of breath. Also, his years of being an insomniac cut down his stamina. His final nine years were ones of physical decline. Mentally, he remained alert to the end.

Early in December of 1960, Charles was stricken with agonizing pain in the abdomen and groin. He was in his Waldorf Towers apartment preparing to motor to New Jersey with Carolyn and Max McGraw. Instead, he was rushed in his own car to the Harkness Pavilion in the Columbia Presbyterian Medical Center. The date was December 9.

Surgery—drastic surgery—was necessary. Two days before Christmas his bladder was removed because of a cancerous condition. Using a revolutionary technique, the attending doctors (Dr. Hillary Holmes was the chief surgeon) grafted to his intestines the tubes that formerly drained the kidneys into the bladder. A cancerous prostate also was removed.

For days, it was uncertain whether or not Charles would survive. Then slowly, ever so slowly, recovery set it. He was permitted to leave the

---

*Carolyn Edison had her own method for holding down her husband during his occasional ventures into sports. She had a small, high-frequency whistle (such as some dog owners use), whose tone, inaudible to others, could be heard by Charles despite— or because of—his severe hearing loss. During a softball game between reporters and state officials at New Jersey's Summer White House in Sea Girt, Charles, fifty-one at the time, was trying desperately to beat out a hit. Suddenly, he slowed down, turned toward Carolyn on the sidelines, and waved. At inning's end, he retired in favor of a substitute. Carolyn had blown the whistle on him.

Harkness Pavilion on January 18, 1961, to begin a long period of convalescence in the familiar surroundings of his Waldorf apartment.

Charles was a meticulous man. Part of this trait may have been inherited, but much of it was acquired through painstaking practice. In the nine years of life left to him, this trait took on even greater dimensions.

For more than thirty years, whether his base of operations was Washington, D.C., Trenton, West Orange, or New York City, a secretary, usually Miss Mary E. Merritt, faithfully recorded daily entries in a diary—who telephoned and why; who visited and for what; where Charles went and at what hour he returned, alone or with whom. Another facet of his meticulousness was his handwriting. Its orderliness, patterned after his father's distinctive calligraphy, was almost half print, half script. No one ever had difficulty deciphering one of Charles' handwritten memos.

Also, he personally maintained what he referred to as his "slave sheets." These were sheaves of sheets of ruled yellow paper. Entered thereon were notations, brief but adequate, to remind him of a hundred and one things to be done—a stock to investigate before purchase, a possible acquisition by the company, letters to write, bases to be touched. No entry ever got dropped from his "slave sheets" until appropriate action had been taken.

Another area of his meticulousness was in planning. Already mentioned was his planning for the mausoleum for Carolyn and himself. After Carolyn died at age seventy-six on June 28, 1963 (that she was three years older than Charles was her zealously guarded secret throughout her lifetime), he began planning for his own demise. These plans went far beyond such customary things as the revising of a will or the reshuffling of financial matters; they included detailed instructions for his own funeral arrangements.

His instructions were set down on paper after consultation with Paul J. Christiansen, longtime business associate, friend, personal attorney, and president of the Charles Edison Fund:

Friends and family may pay last respects at the Frank E. Campbell Funeral Chapel, New York City. No flowers except from the immediate family. Closed casket. Casket to rest in front of the American flag, the flag of the secretary of the navy and the flag of New Jersey. Casket to be covered by the American flag.

Memorial services to be in the Madison Avenue Presbyterian Church, New York City. Two anthems to be sung by a choral group—"Battle Hymn of the Republic" and "Eternal Father, Strong to Save," also

273

known as the "Navy Hymn." Services to resemble as closely as possible those held for his dear old friend, William Francis Gibbs, the distinguished naval architect.

Casket to be transferred to West Orange, New Jersey, to the library in the Thomas A. Edison Laboratory, a part of the Edison National Historic Site museum. [This was to give opportunity to nearby McGraw-Edison Company employees to pay their last respects. It was in the same spot in the same building that his father's casket had rested thirty-eight years earlier.]

The casket then to be removed to nearby Glenmont, the home in which Charles was born, for a brief memorial service limited to a small number of close friends and relatives. Thence to the mausoleum he would share with his beloved Carolyn in Rosedale Cemetary.

Charles had left little to chance. Even his casket had been acquired at the time of Carolyn's death six years earlier, and it was an exact duplicate. When death claimed him, his instructions were followed almost to the letter.

It was during this nine-year period of failing health that Charles accomplished posthumous plans he had had for his father and mother. Overcoming the innumerable obstacles involved in such action, he obtained all necessary permissions for the exhumation of Thomas and Mina Edison from Rosedale Cemetery in Orange and removal of their remains to a private burial site on the grounds of their former home, Glenmont, by then a national shrine and property of the National Park Service. Their new graves are marked by modest monuments. Old friends and former employees or their descendants, known as Edison Old Timers, annually hold graveside memorial services on February 11, Thomas Edison's birthday anniversary.

Charles, however, did not let himself become preoccupied with death. He was never morbid, not even when things looked darkest for him; and he never lost his sense of humor.

"I'm just an old crock who has outlived most of his parts," he once commented to the author.

There were cracks in the "old crock," to be sure; but he still had the spirit and the zeal to speak out in support of his beliefs and against things he considered inimical to the nation's best interests. Many of his activities were in support of conservative causes.

As one of the principal speakers at a Conservative party rally in Madison Square Garden on October 22, 1962, Charles chided the U.S. Supreme Court for "daring to make laws which prohibit children from praying in our schools." In the same talk, he also made these points:

We see the federal government grow bigger and bigger, sapping the strength and dignity of each American. We see the rights of the states destroyed to appease the greed and thirst for power of big government.

We see the flag of the United States of America slowly being supplanted by the flag of the United Nations. Where will it all stop?

Concern over the outlook of and opportunities for youth, he played a key role in founding and financing Young Americans for Freedom, a conservative-oriented organization of political activists operating mainly on the nation's campuses.

Without Charles' knowledge, a group of old friends and admirers, many of them fellow marchers in the cause of conservatism, were laying plans for a testimonial dinner for their aging confederate. They wanted him to enjoy, in life, full knowledge of the respect and admiration in which he was held.

Two of his oldest and most revered friends headed the testimonial dinner committee. They were Herbert Hoover, as honorary chairman, and Ben Moreell, as chairman. Spruille Braden, William F. Buckley, Jr., Walker L. Cisler, William J. Grede, Max McGraw, Admiral Arthur W. Radford and Captain Eddie Rickenbacker were cochairmen.

In all, the committee numbered in excess of 200. It included such nationally known persons as U.S. Representative Bruce Alger; L. Brent Bozell; Louis F. Budenz; General Mark W. Clark; Admiral Charles M. Cooke; C. Suydam Cutting; Robert Donner; former New Jersey governor Alfred E. Driscoll; Max Eastman; General Bonner Fellers; Leonard K. Firestone; U.S. Representative Peter Frelinghuysen, Jr.; William Francis Gibbs; U.S. Senator Barry Goldwater; Joseph G. Grew; Frank Hanighen; J. Edgar Hoover; Robert S. Ingersoll; U.S. Representative Walter H. Judd; U.S. Senator William F. Knowland; Alfred Kohlberg; Clarence Manion; U.S. Representative Joseph W. Martin, Jr.; Jeremiah Milbank; U.S. Senator Karl E. Mundt; General W. Stewart Paul; Mary Pickford; Dr. Daniel A. Poling; Hobart Ramsey; General David Sarnoff; Igor L. Sikorsky; General George E. Stratemeyer; U.S. Representative Robert Taft, Jr.; Ralph de Toledano; General C.A. Willoughby; and General Robert E. Wood.

This extravaganza of a testimonial was held May 2, 1963, in the grand ballroom of New York City's Plaza Hotel. More than 500 attended. They came from the four corners of the nation. The inimitable and loquacious Bill Buckley was master of ceremonies.

For many reasons the event was a high point of Charles' declining years. It was, for instance, one of the last public functions in which

Carolyn was able to participate. She died slightly less than two months later. Also, Charles' response to the encomiums heaped upon him that night bore the stamp of a valedictory. He said in part:

I come from a long line of Edison ancestors who always were on the unpopular side of every argument or issue. Looking back over my own life, I think I have, on the whole, been faithful to the family tradition. I don't go looking for battles, but I always seem to be in one. If I have accomplished anything in life, it is because once in a while I win one of them. But battles usually make more enemies than friends; so I am a little dumbfounded at the number of friends assembled here tonight. I didn't know I had so many.

When I was governor of New Jersey, battling the Hague machine, one of the choicest little left-handed compliments I got was from the man [Louis Paladeau] who acted as go-between between Hague and the state legislature. He came to the statehouse in Trenton one day, and the reporters told him I wouldn't be in because of illness, to which Hague's man replied, ''I hope it's nothing trivial.''

Although you all do me great honor by taking the time to gather here tonight, I truly believe that it is not I who is honored. Rather, it is all of us—the gentlemen whom you have heard from tonight, all of those gracing the dais, all of you at the tables and the many thousands more around the country. We are in effect honoring all Americans who see fit to step forward and be counted on various problems which concern the future of our nation. And so I accept this honor for all of us. I am not just trying to be modest because heaven knows I have plenty to be modest about. I really mean it.

Now that you are all here and, in fact, a captive audience, I hope you will bear with me so that I might get some things off my chest.

I would like to speak about America—about how it was and how it is. America—our country—the culmination of the dreams of the Founding Fathers and the centuries-old aspirations for liberty of men throughout the world. Liberty—a word that seems almost archaic in these days—sort of old-fashioned and fondly remembered, but belonging to an *old* frontier somewhere back in the pleasant dead days when the United States was a power to be reckoned with. Liberty—a word and an ideal for which men pledged to each other their lives, their fortunes, and their sacred honor, for which farmers and merchants and artisans and iron-mongers and cobblers and writers and preachers, all of them together, withstood the bitter winter of Valley Forge to carve out a new nation and a new idea. The spark set by these men ignited a fire which swept the world and still—even in thse days of cynical hypocrisy—still has the power to inflame men to action—in Hungary, in China, in East Berlin, and, yes, even in Cuba. What did this word mean? What caused men to

276

leave their shops and their farms prepared to give their lives fighting against what must have seemed tremendous odds—against the mightiest colonial power of the day—against the might of England. Certainly, at that time, England must have seemed at least as powerful as Russia does today. Yet the thirst for freedom banished fear. These were men and women as you and I, with basically the same problems of bringing up children, of paying the bills, of trying to live their lives peacefully and well. What was it, then, that moved them so and brought forth every resource of courage and strength known to man? The word *liberty?* Yes! And the meaning behind the word.

Liberty meant the right to control one's own destiny and, above all, the God-given right of each individual man to pursue his life as he saw fit—without interference or control except as he was responsible to his neighbors and his community. This, above all, was the essence of the word and the dream—the rights of the individual above any right which may be seized from him by government, whether it be from a foreign shore or from within his own country.

And so the nation was founded—given strength by its individual citizens and given form by the Constitution drafted by the Founding Fathers.

And the nation flourished. Through the years, it became the new promised land to people from every section of the earth. And, for the most part, the promises were fulfilled. From every nation and every area they came—the immigrants, the new Americans—giving of their talents and the sweat of their brows to build America into a proud and free and fearless nation. From the famine-stricken farms of Ireland, from the peasant villages of Italy, from the snow-swept hills of Sweden, from the coal mines of Wales, from the ghettos of Russia—from the tyranny that was Europe they came. And, yes, many came involuntarily from the jungles of Africa and from the villages of China. And they, too, eventually found freedom and added their strength to America.

The American people marched on and settled the continent from the Atlantic to the Pacific. The true frontier moved forward. Our strength came from liberty and from the guaranteed right of each American to control his own destiny. The treasure of our country was brought forth from the earth and from the mountains to make the nation rich and give our people more of the good things of life than any other people on earth in any era of recorded history. And as we grew, we learned that liberty could not be held exclusively. With technological advances, the fate of other people's freedom became intertwined with our own. And our young men once again laid down their lives—in Cuba and the Philippines in the war with Spain, in World War I and World War II, in Korea, and today in Viet Nam—for liberty! For liberty and—the way things are going—perhaps for nothing!

This was our country and these were the American people—nurtured in the spirit of individual liberty and in their obligations to the nation through patriotic understanding of what America meant. Through those years, our nation produced heroes and villians—strong men and weak men. But, all in all, we produced a great and proud people. Unhappily, I speak in the past tense.

What has happened?

The spirit of the old frontier has been whittled away and eroded in the past thirty years until the American people now find themselves in the never-never land of the New Frontier. The eternal values of the nation have been labeled old-fashioned and not fit to survive along this new frontier. The strength of the American people has been sapped.

From a people who proudly held honor as among the basic tenets of individual and national life, we have become a people where more and more honesty and honor are looked on as being old-fashioned. A country where self-reliance, pride, hard work, and thrift are being replaced by ideas of dependency on government, pleasure before duty, higher pay for less work, and the right to government handouts.

And the honor of the nation—what has happened to that? An administration which permits a policy of news distortion or blackout of truth in apprising the American people of the state of affairs and excuses this by citing national security. A nation which has propagandized peoples throughout the world living in Communist slavery on the principles of liberation and on America's courageous dedication to freedom—this same nation cowers in fear when they are called upon to help the struggle for freedom carried out in other nations in the world. A bit of our nation's honor has been lost in the waters of the Caribbean along with the brave men who seek to liberate their Cuban island from slavery.

And what has happened to individual liberty—to the right of the American citizen to pursue his life and his destiny as he sees fit and within the limits of his capabilities? No longer can an American farmer grow what he wants. No longer can an American workingman be employed where he wants. No longer can an American businessman produce what he wants or employ whom he wants. No longer can an American exercise his full talents and his initiative in order to profit himself and his family. More and more everything is controlled, or else it is just not worth it to see the fruits of his labor be taxed away into the enormous federal bureaucracy.

The American citizen is today controlled by a bureaucrat Frankenstein which he created himself. More and more individualism is lost to the state. More and more the state does all—feeds, houses, clothes, cares for the aged, cares for the youth, cares for the lower income group, the middle income group—takes care of everyone and everything. Thus the empty philosophy of socialism is replacing the rich and free traditions of America.

There is a community of men today in the United States who live under this system. All their human needs are taken care of. They are fed reasonably well, they are housed in decent and air-conditioned quarters. When they are ill, there is medical care available. They are given work training and taught various trades and skills, and they have job security. Their recreation is assured. There are books and study programs available. They have no problems other than that of living. This is the perfect example of socialism. The place I speak of is in Leavenworth, Kansas. And this Leavenworth system—under different names and different slogans—is slowly being imposed on the American people. If this system is ever finally implemented throughout the U.S., it will be truly escapeproof.

We have already lost much of our individual liberty. Our people's initiative is being destroyed. The eternal values which have made us great have been relegated to the scrap heap. The New Frontier offers us culture and entertainment and security and welfare—and emptiness. The courage of our people—proved again and again from Valley Forge, through Gettysburg, through the trenches in France, through the islands of the Pacific, through the mud of Korea—has been squandered in fear and appeasement of tyranny and in international cowardice. Our leaders rush forward to embrace our enemies—knowing that each time this is done freedom is lost somewhere in the world. They seem unable to face up to the fact that the enemy *is* the enemy and meet it squarely.

The world has seen many dark times. One period of history was even called the Dark Ages. But even in those times, men carried on. In those years, there were monks who went from town to town, from country to country. Under their robes, they carried with them the manuscripts, the learning of the centuries gone before. They were hunted from place to place, and yet they carried with them the light of knowledge and the light of truth. Without them, all would have been lost.

Perhaps that is the function of Americans today—to keep on fighting and to carry with them the eternal truths laid down by our Founding Fathers. These truths are eternal, and they will survive.

I have lived a good many years. No one knows all the answers, but I do know this: in the time that is left me, I will continue fighting for America—for what it really is and what it really means. And so must we all—no matter what the obstacles and no matter how discouraged we may become. To give up would indeed be a sin against the memory of all those heroes of the past who have given us a nation.

Charles never let his head be turned by the honors that descended on him over his adult years. He was quick to remind himself that, at least to some extent, he lived in the reflected glory of his father. He never lost sight of the fact that he was born into and raised under advantageous circumstances such as enjoyed only by a relative few.

His response to the question, "Is it a help or a hindrance being the son of a great man?" was reported in the *New York Daily News* in these words:

> The question is one that cannot be answered with any measure of certainty.
>
> Being the son of a great man is, in a way, like being the nonprofessional husband of a motion picture actress. Such a man shares a reflected glory but also is relegated to being known as "the husband of Greta Greatstar." So it is with many sons of famous fathers. They are never able to step out of the shadow of their fathers' fame.
>
> On the other hand, having a great man for a father frequently opens doors to the son that otherwise might be closed to him.
>
> I would be less than honest with myself, however, if after balancing the pros and cons, I did not profess to believe that the advantages of having a famous father outweigh the disadvantages.

As the sands of time slowly ran out, Charles jokingly would predict that he would not reach his seventy-fifth birthday. He based his prediction (although it turned out to be erroneous) on the genealogy of his Edison forbears.

"My great grandfather died at one-hundred and four. My grandfather died at ninety-four. And Father passed on at eighty-four. Ergo, seventy-four should be par for the course for me," he would explain.

Although Charles' prediction missed by five years, he and those close to him realized that the road ahead of him was all downhill.

A dramatic change in Charles' condition occurred on Saturday, June 28, 1969. Having eaten well at dinner in his Waldorf Towers apartment, he seemed to be in great spirits. He settled down to watch a favorite television program. A few minutes later—around 9 p.m.—he walked slowly and unsteadily to the living room, looking bewildered and confused. Friend and nurse, Alice Stevenson, helped him to a chair, checked his vital signs, gave him nitroglycerine, and put him to bed. He had suffered a mild stroke, the examining doctor said. Residual effects were mild confusion and slightly impaired vision. Both conditions improved somewhat within a few days.

On July 14, he suffered a second attack, also deemed mild.

On Wednesday, July 30, at 7:30 in the morning, he had another seizure, this one much more severe.

He was taken to the Harkness Pavilion by ambulance late in the afternoon of the same day and placed under intensive care. He died the following afternoon. Had he lived three days longer he would have been eighty.

The funeral plans painstakingly worked out previously by Charles went immediately into effect under the joint supervision of his sister, Mrs. John Eyre Sloane, and his trusted friend and counselor, Paul J. Christiansen.

Admiral Moreell, whose friendship and close association with Charles extended over thirty-two years, delivered the memorial address at the Madison Avenue Presbyterian Church. After recounting the high points of Charles' career as civilian head of the Navy Department, as governor of New Jersey, as a business executive, and as a stalwart exponent of decency, Moreell used these words:

I have given here a skeletonized account of the career of a great American, illustrious son of an illustrious father. It falls far short of defining the true measure of the man. From my close association with him over many years, I offer these thoughts:

Based on the time-honored premise that what we *do* is far more important than what we *say* and what we *are* is most important of all, Charles Edison easily passes all of the requirements for immortality as a great American patriot.

Foremost amongst his many admirable traits were his profound reverence for his father, the greatest benefactor of humanity in the history of our country, and his devotion to his charming wife, Carolyn, his working partner for forty-six active years.

Charles Edison was a man of principle. He knew what he believed in, and he had the courage to stand up and be counted when the chips were down and the weather was rough. He never sacrificed principle on the altar of expediency. He adhered steadfastly to his own high standards of personal honor and official conduct.

He was a friendly man who inspired friendship in others.

He was an understanding man. Being fully aware of the frailties of human nature, he did not expect perfection in others just as he renounced any claims to perfection in himself. Thus, he was overly generous in his appraisals of his fellow man.

He was a humble man, who knew that without humility one cannot have an open mind which is receptive to the truth.

He was a generous man, who believed in and practiced the biblical admonition: "Give, and it shall be given unto you; good measure, pressed down, shaken together, and running over." Thus, he gave freely of his time, his energies and his material means to countless patriotic, charitable, and civic causes and to many worthy individuals who needed a helping hand over the rough spots of life's journey.

He was without the slightest taint of bigotry, intolerance, or prejudice, appraising every man on his own merits, respecting his personal dignity and his individual rights as a child of God.

He was a self-disciplined man. He knew that the optimum in personal conduct flows from voluntary obedience to the laws which govern a good life, which are enforceable only by the power of one's own conscience.

And, finally, he was a dedicated American patriot who loved his country, its ideals, its traditions, and its fundamental principles, which, together, have enabled ours to become the greatest nation in recorded history, in terms of human dignity, spiritual strength, and material prosperity.

Charles Edison was a leader of men who, by the power of his personal example, inspired countless others to emulate his devotion to righteous causes, even those causes whose futures looked very bleak. He was always ready to fight for what was right and what was good, even when the fight appeared to be for a lost cause. For he knew that fighting for a lost cause can give meaning and savor to life; that men are tempered in the fires of adversity; and that rough seas make good sailors!

The several services over, and after Charles' casket was placed within the mausoleum he had helped design, there remained one final assignment to be carried out to complete the instructions he had set down during his lifetime. This assignment was handled by two trusted associates—Edward G. Orbann and David O. Schantz, at the time executive director and curator, respectively, of The Brook Foundation. They entered the mausoleum and personally saw to it that the casket of Charles physically touched that of his beloved Carolyn. Thus Charles' final wish was fulfilled.

Postscript

Although the story of Charles Edison is completed, the author remembers him as such a warm and friendly man, one so outgoing in his contacts with others, that to end it on a note of sadness would be out of character.

Charles was reared in the Methodism of his mother's family and exposed to the gentle agnosticism of his father. Personally, he believed in a universal God, but without the trappings of religiosity.

The following comment was made by Charles, late in his life, to the author:

> Over the years I've managed to help worthy causes and charities backed by Protestants, Catholics, and Jews. Maybe I've just been hedging my bets on getting into Heaven.

Requiescat in pace (May he rest in peace).

Atque vale (And farewell).

Bila hamoves l'netzach (God will destroy death forever).

Index

285

286

287